ENCYCLOPAEDIA OF INDIAN WOMEN THROUGH THE AGES

ENCYCLOPAEDIA OF INDIAN WOMEN THROUGH THE AGES

Volume—I
Ancient India

Simmi Jain

KALPAZ PUBLICATIONS
DELHI–110052

ENCYCLOPAEDIA OF INDIAN WOMEN THROUGH THE AGES
(*Sociology, Women Studies*)

Rs. 3600 (Set)
Rs. 900 (each volume)

ISBN: 81-7835-116-1 (Set)
ISBN: 81-7835-172-2 (Vol. 1)

Published in 2011 in India by
Kalpaz Publications
C-30, Satyawati Nagar,
Delhi-110052
E-mail: kalpaz@hotmail.com
Phone : 9212729499

Printed at: G. Print Process, Delhi

Contents

Preface

The status of women in our sub-continent passed through a most intricate and complex socio-economic terrain. The male-dominated society was indeed a glaring phenomenon and had always edged over their social and domestic environments. Being the earning member in the family, he considered himself fairly superior in terms of his status. But women could maintain their identity and emerged as useful partners and bread-earner for her household affairs. Undoubtedly she did not shirk to meet any economic challenge with dignity and respectable disposition. The volumes on *Encyclopaedia of Indian Women Through the Ages* have been diversified into four categories and cover the themes in a fairly comprehensive and analytical way which are as follows.

The volume on Ancient India deals with a detailed description on social status of women in the Vedic period and in the Mahabharata Era. Emphasis has been laid on their marital status, numerous duties of household affairs, basic rights enjoyed by them, sexual life in practice, social status of a widow and the way of life she had to lead, ideology of motherhood, divorce and remarriage, property rights, the sati ritual, the views of Swami Vivekananda, and foreign accounts of marital arrangements.

The second volume lays emphasis on Medieval India. It includes social position of women, female slaves, women in politics, religious education and practices, observance of purdah, and divorce, *mehr* practices, nikáh-marriage, valid marriage, irregular marriage, the sense of equality, women in administration, dissolution of marriage, dower, social customs like birth ceremony, naming ceremony, selection of marriage partners, women education including higher education, their academic contribution, particularly of Gulbadan Begum, Hamidah Bano Begum, Zeb-un-Nisa, Jahan Ara and others, fairs and festivals, games, mostly indoor games, playing cards or *Tash* or chess, pigeon flying, kite flying, female costumes including cotton, silken and golden clothes and a detailed study of Khanzada Begum, Ayisha-Sultan Begum, Zainab Sultan Begum, Maham Begum and Bibi Mubarika.

The third volume has deep thrust on women and freedom struggle. The role of eminent women has been a glaring phenomenon in this volume. In fact these women have become a significant part of our history. Commencing from the historic role of Begum Hazrat Mahal, Rani Lakshmi Bai of Jhansi, Rani of Ramgarh, the theme lands us comprehensively into various social Acts, viz., mobilisation of sati, 1829; Widow Remarriage Act, 1856; the role of Consent, 1891 and the prohibition of Child Marriage Act, 1929. The volume has also highlighted the role of foreign women in our freedom struggle, i.e., Sister Nivedita, The Mother, Mira Behn, and Annie Besant. Mrs. Besant was elected Congress President in 1917—during the crucial period of the first global war.

The emergence of Mahatma Gandhi on the political stage of India in 1915 generated a new spirit of sacrifice for the attainment of *swaraj.* Such women were Kasturba Gandhi, Bee Amman, Parvati Devi, Sarojini Naidu, Kamaladevi Chattopadhyaya, Durgabai Deshmukh, Margaret Cousins, Sucheta Kripalani, Hansa Mehta, Mridula Sarabhai, Usha Mehta, Rajkumari Amrit Kaur and several others. They courted arrests in the Gandhian movements along with numerous women satyagrahas. Even after the attainment of Independence, their role in several fields of development including education, medical, defence, politics and administration is quite laudable.

The last volume gives us a comprehensive analysis on historical perspective and legal review. It deals with the changing social status of women, Gandhi and his contribution for the emancipation of women in economic and political sphere, Dalit women in politics and their changing socio-economic status with new awakening, vision of Annie Besant for generating patriotic spirit among women, role of the regiment of Rani Jhansi as a significant part of the Indian National Army, women and family welfare having deep bearing on sincere initiatives shown by women rather than men to plan their families despite their law position and lesser sex ratio. Other significant aspects on women in this chapter deal with their pitiable plight as labourers in a factory, field or road work, life of working women, regional status of women, particularly in Punjab, Haryana, Madhya Pradesh, sensible findings of a survey based research on women in a slum in Mumbai. Last but not the least a chapter has been well-written on Kerala nuns and nurses in terms of their working status and social difficulties. A few significant case studies on the two categories have been well-analysed.

I feel much beholden to several eminent scholars whose writings have been used in these volumes in order to fill up necessary gaps. The consistent academic support and help of several institutions of higher learning including the members of prominent libraries deserve my respectful acknowledgement. But for sincere support from these categories of scholarly and institutional help, these volumes probably would not have seen light of the day.

With this comprehensive academic survey, it could be judged with the remark that these volumes would be certainly welcomed by eminent social scientists, researchers and students in India and abroad.

Simmi Jain

Introduction

Status of women in India has gone through enormous charges over the ages. She has been assigned a privileged status as mother, wife and sister. She has been a goddess to us. Her capacity to propagate generations by giving birth to babies is unique and makes her rank above man.

But this whole respect and status has been only symbolic in this patriarchal society. There has been periods of history when women's status role and fell but in general, the position of woman has been degrading and she mostly spread life according to whims and fancies of a man, be it father father, brother or husband. And this status is so deep-rooted that even woman don't want this to charge much and prefer to live with this arrangement Modern times have sensed some change in this attitude. But here we shall be conceived with only the ancient times.

Womanhood in the vedic age had two main ideals, viz., that of brahmavadini and that of a sadyovadu. A Sadyovadhu was of a domestic type dedicating herself to the welfare of her family and devoting herself to her domestic duties. Just as many brahmavadinis were married, many sadhyovadhus were of a spiritual nature and strove for spiritual realisation in the midst of their domestic duties.

The two epics, Ramayana and Mahabharata, have many examples of the two types of Indian women Gandhari, Kunti, Draupadi, Savitri, Damayanti, Shankuntala and Satyabhama in the Mahabharata were women who, though housewives were also reputed scholars and saintly characters. The highest epitome of domestic perfection is found in the character of Sita in the Ramayana. The Rig Veda accorded the highest social status to the women of those days.

We find the marriage age of girls is varying in different times on account of certain definite views and circumstances prevailing in them. Girls were married at a fairly advanced age in the Vedic period. The very term for marriage, vudvaha, carrying away (of the bride) after her marriage, the bride went to her husband's house to live as his wife. A perusal of the marriage hymn shows that the bride was fully mature and quite grown up at the time of the marriage, she is expressely described as blooming with youth and pining for a husband.

In Vedic literature, we find references to polygamy even though monogamy seems to have been the references to polygamy. Atharvaveda has a number of hymns which are meant as a charm for weaning the husband's affections from a co-wife. It was an accepted norm for a man to have more than one wife but the woman was not supposed to have more than one husband. Harishchandra is said to have had a hundred wives. It is not to be supposed that polygamy was confined only to kings and nobles. The great philosopher Yajnavalkya had two wives, Katyayani who was worldly-minded and maitreyi who thirsted for the knowledge of brahma and immortality.

In the times of the Sutras, some sages wanted to hold up a high ideal. It was declared that when a man has a wife who is endowed with dharma and progeny, he shall not marry another wife; but if any one of the two (dharma and progeny) is wanting (in the case of the wife), he may marry another before he has consecrated the sacred srauta fires. In another place it has been prescribed that one who abandons his (faultless) wife should be put on the skin of an ass with the hair outside and should beg for alms at seven houses for six months.

Indian mythology and cultural symbols glorify women's role as mother—she is benevolent mother—goddess, the food giver but without actual control over external factors which govern the food supply to the home. The concept of motherhood demonstrates dichotony that while on the one hand the mother is extolled in the Ancient Indian literature with every available adjectives, on the other, she is denied of basic right of determining even the fortune of her own children. Because motherhood being very much undermale control and it operates strictly within the concept of motherhood was often used to unify the diverse forces to fight for the liberation and protection of mother, since mother always looks at her son to protect her because she neither has the power nor strength of her own.

The Vedic literature supplies us with very little information about the dress of the women of the age. The vocabulary itself of the period has got no separate words to denote women's clothes. The same words are used to denote the different clothes worn both by men and women. An undergarmentt (Vasahantaram) and an upper garment (paridhanam) were in general use among the members of both the sexes. A waistband was used round the lower garment. Probably both the garments were usually coloured in case of women, for the vedic literature refers to the dyer. In addition to the two garments, mentioned above, kings used to wear a gorgeous mantle (drapi) on ceremonious occasions. Queens also probably had the counterpart of this mantle in the form of an embroidered shawl, though there is no definite evidence on the point. In one place goddess Indrani is described as wearing a headdress; it is probable that the well-to-do ladies of the Vedic age were also doing the same.

In ancient India, the nature of social values was such that at no time she was poor or unprotected. Moreover, with the passage of time she acquired formal and independent property rights. Concept of stridhana had emerged as early as the Sutra period and it went on expanding and thus increasing her assets including sometimes immovable property. Widow also acquired a share in husband's property. It may also be observed that mere acceptance of legal rights does not lead to change in women's status which largely depends on the social ethos. For instance, in the Rigvedic period women had no formal property rights but they enjoyed very high social status, while later on their property rights increased but their social status declined.

The position of women in India gradually deteriorated as the Vedic ideals of equality and unity faded with the passage of time. During the period of the Smritis, the period of codification of social laws, women were bracketed with the Sudras and were denied the right to study the Vedas to utter Vedic mantras and perform Vedic ceremonies. Unquestioning devotion to and self-effacing service of husbands became their only duty.

1

Status in the Vedic Era

Though twin usages of polygamy[1] and polyandry have both been known in India from time immemorial in varying degrees—monogamy has always been the ideal.

The first wife only is the *Patnī* in the fullest sense of the term. She is the *Dharmapatni* while even the second wife (and naturally all other wives) is meant for sexual satisfaction only; a second wife is entitled to no unseen (adrishta) religious merit.[2] A man having several wives observes his religious duties with the first wife only; preference is, however, sometimes given to the *savarṇā* wife so much so that even though she may be the youngest, he will observe religious duties with her and in case the *savarṇā*, be she the youngest, is not present or unable to attend, the claim would devolve upon one coming from the class immediately lower. A *Śūdrā* wife is always to be excluded by a Brāhmaṇa.[3] According to Manu[4] the first wife attends personally and helps the husband in his daily religious rites; he cannot show preference to other wives in these matters for fear of being a Chaṇḍāla Brāhmaṇa. The *Karmā-kāṇḍạ-pradīpa*[5] also says that only the first wife has the *adhikāra.* Disparagement of marriages other than the first is expressed in the fact that during the second and following marriages, the polygamist is to marry a pitcher (kumbha)[6] or some such thing. According to Yājñavalkya, too, the religious rites should be performed with the first wife of the same caste, not with others.[7] Rites for the highest religious merit or salvation are observed with the first wife.[8] Highest results (such as obtaining heaven, etc.) may be achieved only if the rite is performed along with the first wife.[9] The wife first married is to be considered as the eldest, not the one who is the eldest of the lot[10] the *Śat. Br.*[11] says she is the consecrated consort.

The first wife performs all the important rites. Even though other wives are allowed to join in sacrifice.[12] In the Darsa Purnamaśesti she trims the fire,[13] husks and pounds the rice.[14] After the Patnisannahara (girding with the Yoktrapāśa) and Gārhapatyopasthāna the wives are required to sit to the north of the Gārhapatya; *Mukhyapatni* occupies the seat exactly to the north, i.e., the best seat while other wives take their seats somewhere to the north of the Gārhapatya, no doubt, but at a distance from the first wife.[15] After the Patnisaṃyāja the chief is to eat the Iḍā.[16] If simultaneously God-speed is to be wished now for the husband and the wife, it should be desired for the chief wife only.[17] Towards the close of the sacrifice the Kusha grass is removed from the lap of the wife and the cord with which she was girded is loosened; according to the Sāṇkhāyana school,[18] only the first wife is to observe these rites. During the utterance of the Sampatniya it is the first wife who is to touch the husband as this act is meant for "Parārtha = Supreme Bliss."[19]

In the Agnyādhāna and the Agnihotra only the first wife, so long as she is living, is entitled to participate. The newly-married couple establish the sacred fires and observe the Agnihotra in the same fire till the end of the life of one of them. The widower may marry if the first wife is no more. But in no case, after the Agnyādhāna, should the first wife be deprived of her right of participating in the Agnihotra, even if she be deficient in religious performance or in procreation. In course of her assistance in the kindling of the fires she has been for her life associated with and given to the service of these fires.[20] The fires are inseparable from her; so long as she is in the house, they are there; when she goes with her husband to a foreign place, they move with her.[21] If the husband lives without his wife and consequently, without the fires, be it even in the next village, it is nothing but living in a foreign land but when the wife and her constant companions, the Fires, go with him, even the most distant land will not be considered as such (Pravāsa).[22] If in any case the wife does not go with him, he must go without the fires and when he comes back he offers oblations to them but in order that they may be thoroughly pleased, he is to please the wife with his look.[23]

If a co-wife is left at home, the wife may leave the fires in charge of her, but that would mean that the co-wife would be simply representative of the wife and nothing more than that. As much as possible the wife should take the fire with her.

If the fire goes out, it is the first wife who is to re-kindle it. She should on the preceding day take her food in the day time,[24] observe *brahmacharya* and silence, wear silken garments[25] and towards sunset enter the Gārhapatya house from the south and seat herself to the right of her husband, both facing the east. At the beginning of the sacrifice, when the Adhvaryu offers both the Aranis to the sacrificer, he places the upper one on his own lap and hands over the lower one to her which she similarly places on her own lap.[26]

The husband and wife keep awake to keep up the fire. Before the Agnihotra actually begins, the wife cleans the surrounding areas of the fires;[27] from the beginning to end of the sacrifice she remains sitting to the south or the south-east of the Gārhapatya fire.[28] There can be no substitute for the first wife in the Agnihotra; nevertheless, she must be present or be considered as virtually present in her shed.[29] Whenever the husband offers oblations he does so for the absent wife also. Towards the end of sacrifice water-libations are offered to the Sarpadevayana, Bhūta and Mahat with either three ladlefuls of water or in three portions from the same ladleful;[30] the sacrificer then takes another ladleful of water or offers with the remaining portion of the water. Of this water he pours half on Earth and the other half he pours into the hands of the wife. In case of her absence from the sacrifice on account of unavoidable circumstances the whole quantity of the fourth ladleful or of the fourth portion of the same ladleful according to Bharadvāja, is to be twice poured, upon the seat of the wife or the Earth. The water should never be poured into the hands of any other wife than the first one.[31] The object of this pouring is to pray for domestic bliss and triumph for and by the wife;[32] no other wife than the first is ever entitled to be the mistress of the house.

At the end of the evening oblation the wife together with her husband should observe silence and fast till darkness has set in.[33]

As in the Vaiśvadeva, so in the Varuṇapraghāsas, it is the first wife who should husk the barley, and deposit the husk for the Avabhaṛtha.[34] She should make the Karambhapātras out of the barley-powder which she should herself make of unfried barley.[35] According to some schools, the wife is empowered to husk, fry and pound into powder the previous day. As a rule, the Adhvaryu and the Pratiprasthātṛ make a ram and a ewe respectively with their sex marks made prominent. But according to the Vājasaneya Ritual[36] the wife should, after having made the Karambhapātras, make the ram and the ewe, too, of the barley similarly fried and powdered. These rites should be observed by the chief wife alone as these are by no means Strisaṃskāras; moreover, in making the ram and the ewe, she is really a substitute of the priests, which other wives cannot be supposed to be. These Parāthaka rites should be done by the chief wife only.

After the rite of the declaration of paramours, the wife invokes the Maruts[37] when she is led by the Pratiprasthātṛ. She is offered the Krambhapatrās[38] in a winnowing basket which she places on her head. Both the sacrificer and the wife[39] now pass between the altars and seat themselves in front of the Dakśiṇa fire with their faces towards the west. The sacrificer places the dishes on his head which are given by his wife. The husband utters the Anuvākyā.[40] Then both the husband and the wife offer oblations to the Maruts[41] to expiate their sins which they have incurred either in village or the wild, in company or corporeal sense, etc., the dedicatory formula[42] being pronounced by both. According to Kātyāyana[43] the mistress alone is entitled to observe this rite. The priests are offered thanks for performing the ritual by the wife and husband.

In the Avabhaṛata it is the chief wife who should wash the back of the sacrificer and he should, in his turn, wash her back, too.[44] They offer their drenched garments to whomsoever[45] they like. The chief wife joins the priests and the sacrificer in the Sun-worship, and in adding fresh fuel to the Ahavaniya fire.[46]

In the Sākamadha the sacrificial food is cooked by the chief wife and partaken by all.[47] In the Traimbaka oblation after the sacrificer and priests, etc., and the maidens have walked round the fires, she lays fuel on and worships the Gārhapatya.[48]

In the animal sacrifice the chief wife anoints the surface

of the sacrificial post while the sacrificer anoints only the top of it. She rubs all over the post in order to impart to it lustre without omitting to rub any part of it.[49]

The prime duty of the wife in this sacrifice is to wipe the organs of the animal so that its Soul (literally, the lives here) may rest in peace,[50] and this is done by the chief wife.[51] The chief wife worships the sun before the procedure.[52]

During her advance towards the cātvāla the Pratiprashātr prays for offspring and increase of wealth. Then she propitiates and takes waters from the cātvāla. She also recites mantras for propitiating the sacrifice and then wipes each organ of the animal with appropriate mantras.[53] According to some, she pours the water on the organs and the Adhvargy wipes them or he pours water and she wipes them. The chief wife cleanses herself with mantras later on.

After the Patnisaṃyāja she offers to the killer the front leg and to the Adhvaryu some front piece.[54] During the idā-bhakṣaṇa to her and she hands it over to the Adhvaryu or some other priest.[55] The sacrifice ending, while all others worship the Ahavaniya, she adds fresh fuel to and worships the Gārhapatya.[56]

The sacrificer has to step into the seven footprints made by the cow. The wife together with the other wives, the sacrificer and the priests sit round the seventh foot-print wherein a piece of gold is laid. After due offerings the Adhvaryu takes one-third portion of the dust from there and hands it over to the sacrificer with the blessings for the latter's wealth. The sacrificer gives it to the chief wife[57] so that she may have wealth; while it is being given to her she prays that she may not be deprived of wealth. The dust is preserved by the wife.[58]

It seems only the first wife should hold on to the cart from behind;[59] because this is no Patni-saṃskāra. By this rite the chief wife, as the mistress of the household gear and as the approver of her husband's gift[60] honours the king Soma as a very worthy guest when he is brought forward on a cart. While she does so, the Adhavaryu offers the water libations to guest Soma. The chief wife may make the offering with her own hands.[61]

It is the chief wife who anoints the axes of the Soma-carts;[62] the object is to have children with heroic deeds.[63] While the Adhvaryu walks out of the hall by the front door with clarified butter taken a second time in four ladlings, the sacrificer's wife is led by the South.[64] The Adhavaryu lays down a piece of gold in the right wheel of the southern cart and makes offerings; he pours the residue of clarified butter into her folded palms. According to Baudhāyana,[65] she mixes half of the dust of the third foot-print with it. Then she anoints the right axle of the southern cart with her right hand.[66] The axle of the cart is a anointed twice by the wife.[67] Now, in order that she may anoint the axle of the northern car, she is made to walk round by the back of the Gārhapatya fire to the wheel-tracks on the north side. This time, the assistant of the Adhavaryu observes the same rites as the Adhvaryu in the previous case, and pours the residue of clarified butter after his offerings, into her folded palms.[68] The wife mixes the butter with dust anoints and prays. According to Kātyāyana[69] she should anoint both the axles simultaneoulsy with both the hands.

During the second pressing she approves of the gifts given by husbands to the priests and others.[70] In the third pressing, after all the rites up to the filling of the pots have been performed, the chief wife[71] churns the Soma in the shed for Agnidhra; then she enters into the Soma-cart by the western door and stays there.[72] She sacrifice and his wife carry the purified soma.[73] According to the scoliast on Kātyāyana,[74] she, touched from behind by all other wives, looks at it and addresses Aditya for children, wealth and sinless living.

As the personal attendant of her husband in religious affairs, it is the chief wife who should wash the back of her husband during the final bath (Avabhrātha).[75] When she comes back to her own shed she worships the Gārhapatya by laying on the Udumbara fuel which she cleanses beforehand in front of the cow-shed.

The wife burns Kusha grass in the end.[76]

According to certain Sākhās of the W.YV., she puts a lot of wood on the Gārphapatya fire without the utterance of any mantra[77] in the the Pravargya sacrifice.

In the Agnicayana the first wife makes the Ukhā, the fire-pan to which she prays for offspring; increase of wealth, cattle, horses and also for making the fellows of the sacrificer subject to him.[78] She also makes from clay the Âśāḍhā, the invincible brick, and marks it with three lines.[79]

In the Vajāpeya, the chief wife wears the garland of gold. The fee would pave the way of the wife as well as of the sacrificer to Heaven.[80] After twelve Āpti and Kḷpti offsprings have been offered on the Āhavaniya fire for procuring for the sacrificer all that the twelve months of the year and the six seasons can bestow, the Nestṛ or the Pratiprashātṛ makes the chief wife wear garments of Darbha grass or Dṛhara[81] while the sacrificer wear silken garment.[82]

The Nestṛ then leads her to the post against which a ladder having seventeen stairs has been put. The sacrificer now gets ready to mount the post and enquires about her willingness to accompany him.[83] She replies in the affirmative. Thrice the sacrificer asks and thrice she replies.[84] The sacrificer now wishes that he should mount for both of them to which the readily consents. She may herself mount the post if she likes.[85] In this case she should pray similarly as the sacrificer for the success of life by sacrifice and such other things.[86] Most probably she should stretch her arms, too, to show that she has mounted the top just as the sacrificer does and express herself the joy of approaching the gods and of being capable of becoming immortal and the offspring of Prajāpati. She should also look down to the ground and pray for offspring and increase of wealth.[87] If she does not accompany her husband, she is looked at by him from above after he has reached the top.[88] if she accompanies him, he helps her in descending from the post.[89] It is the chief wife who should observe the above rites as it is she who is to propitiate the sacrifice;[90] it is she only who makes the sacrificer complete by addition of one-half of his own self;[91] and as he is to achieve heavenly bliss together with her only.[92] She and her husband are one Soul divided into two bodies, not only on this mortal land, but also in heaven—to participate in worldly affairs, in sacrificial matters, in earthly blessings as well as in divine joy.

In the Piṇḍapitṛyajṇa the eldest wife stands on the black deer-skin with her face towards the south-east and husks the paddy in a wooden mortar. She must not sit. She removes the husk by means of winnowing basket, but does not separate the husked from those which are still not done. She husks them only once.[93]

Now, to come to the chief queen. The Mahiśī is the consecrated consort; all other wives are meant for sexual pleasure only.[94] In the Politico-religious ceremonies, viz. the Aśvamedha, Rājasūya, Puruśamedha and Rāḍ-yajṇa, she, properly speaking, performs all the important rites while the "Bhogini" queens are allowed to participate therein to keep company with the chief queen as it were; the part that they play therein is insignificant.

At the beginning of the Horse-sacrifice which occurs on the eighth or ninth of the month of Phālguna, the chief queen and the king prepare themselves for ritual observance in the regular way as they do in other sacrifices. They cook for themselves food for breaking fast mixed with clarified butter as well as milk and eat it (in the afternoon) and wash their mouths in a golden bowl.[95] Then they keep silent and perform Agnihotra in due time. According to Baudhāyana all the queens are allowed to wear silver ornaments[96] for the occasion; but the chief queen wears several ornaments in addition which signifies her power over man in general.[97] According to Kātyāyana all the wives should wear golden ornaments.[98] But the distinctive position of the chief queen is seen in the fact that the one hundred maidens that accompany her must be either daughters[99] or wives[100] of kings; while the maidens of the Vāvātā are to be daughters or wives of subordinate Chiefs, or of the Ugras;[101] those of Parivrkti, daughters or wives of Charioteers, and those of Pārāgali, daughters or wives of Revenue Collectors. In the evening they all enter the hall of sacrificial fires by the southern door.[102] After tha Agnihotra the Vāvātā avails herself of the coveted fortune of getting the king on her lap with his head towards the north;[103] this simply signifies the justification of her name "Vāvātā : the favourite" and nothing important so far as the supermundane bliss is concerned. The queens together with the maidens most probably help the king in keeping awake throughout the night. In other sacrifices as well as in this it is the chief queen who needs to keep awake along with the sacrificer and not all.

On the return of the horses on the second Soma-pressing day they are all bathed. Now the first three queens are to anoint the sacrificial horse and entwine pearls or ·coins into its mane and tail.[104] The order of anointing and entwining does not seem to be strictly observed. The chief queen anoints the fore-parts, the favourite queen the middle and a discarded wife the hind-part. Again, the chief queen takes recourse to the Gāyatrī metre, the most important of all metres; the second, the Triśṭubh; Parivṛkti, the Jāgati. The stiff that the chief queen uses for anointing is clarified butter mixed with the sap of the sacred Pūtu-dru tree; that the Vāvātā uses is clarified butter mixed with the ordinary thing bdellium[105] and that the Parivṛkti uses is Ghee mixed with with the sap of the Mustāplant that grows anywhere and everywhere. The companions that they have are the same as before. The varied rank of these maidens at once brings out the respective position of the queens. Again, during the entwining of pearls the chief queen adorns the parts in front of the place where the yoke rests with golden pearls; the Vāvātā below that and the buttocks with silver ones; the Parivṛkti below the buttock with any and every pearl that may come from the sea.[106]

After the wild animals are released, the horse is killed, most probably, by stifling in robes. Then the Unnetṛ or Pratiprasthātr.[107] or Adhvaryu.[108] lead them up from their ordinary place near the Gārhapatya to the victim. They carry in their hands jars of water.[109] According to Satyāśāḍha only the chief queen should be led to by the Pratiprasthātṛ; so, other wives are to follow her.[110] In order to make amends for the slaughtering of the victim and to invoke the divine helpers to help the chief queen in the most important rite that follews.[111] They walk round the victim nine times while fanning him with the flutter of their garments; for the first three times they tie iṇ a knot the right locks of hair and let loose the left ones and walk from right to left, smiting their right thighs; then they follow the exactly reverse course in all matters.[112] The chief queen, now, shows anxiety to approach the slain horse, who represents Prajāpati, in order to have seed from him. Then the chief queen lies down by the side of the horse. She, along with the utterance of mantras, makes various attempts while the Adhvaryu cloaks them together with garments. While she does the obscene act, she feels reluctant and censures the horse.[113] Three times the chief queen censures, three times the others persuade her. All sorts of indecent acts and talks are the concomitant factors of fertility spells;[114] here too, for the sake of fertility, indecent colloquy between the priests, queen and maidens, etc, begain. According to several schools only the maidens reply.[115] According to *Sat. Br.,*[116] the Brahman, the most important priest of all, addresses the queen consort, while the Udgātṛ addresses the Vāvātā and the Chamberlain, the fourth wife. The different schools vary very much, but there is no doubt that all of these insertions and omissions are meant for the fertility of the chief queen. All other queens as well as their maidens join herein only as help-mates in the Fertility Rite which is the chief one in the *Horse-sacrifice.* At the end of the obscene *colloquy* the queen consort is raised up by her own maidens.[117] Now, the first three queens mark out with metal needles the lines for the dissection of the victim. Here, too, the chief queen has all the preferences. She marks the lines in the fore-part, down to the breast, while the Vāvātā does up to the navel and the Parivṛkti the rest. She, again, makes the knifepaths (Asipathas) with golden needles, while the second wife with silver ones and the Parivṛkti with iron or lead ones.[118] The scholiast on Satyāśāḍha[119] says in this connection that the chief queen, the Vāvātā and the Parivṛkti, holding as they do the supreme, intermediate and worst postition respectively, should, accordingly, mark out the knife-path in varying parts of varied importance—the chief queen in the fore-part, i.e., the most important part, the Vāvātā in the middle part and the Parivṛkti in the hind-part. She is the *uttamā patnī* and accordingly she has her own exclusive rights and in the remaining, too, she leads everywhere.

In the Rājasūya the chief queen is the permanent Ratnin in as much as authorities differ as to the reckoning of the Vāvātā and Parivṛkti as Ratnins, Jewels of the king.[120] The *Sat. Br.* reckons neither the Vāvātā nor as Ratnin.[121] The king offers a pep for Nirṛti in the house of the Parivṛkti, not because she is a Ratnin, but because he likes to get rid of Nirṛti, calamity, while he is consecorated. As the Parivṛkti has no son, she is seized with Nirṛti; in order to propitiate Nirṛti, the king prepares a pap of black rice broken by nails with which to offer. According to Kātyāna,[122] she is to betake herself to a Brāhmaṇa's houses where the king has no power. The offering to Nirrti, the use of black rice broken by nails and taking shelter in a Brāhmaṇa's house at once direct to the degraded position of the Parivṛkti : and it is only natural that a good many authorites, led by *Sat. Br.,* do not recognise her as a jewel. Several authorities of the Taittiriya school recognise the Vāvātā as a Ratnin and recommend the offering of a pap to Bhaga in her house.[123] but this recommendation in her favour loses importance as no other Vedic school gives her the position of a Ratinin. According to all the authorities a pap to Aditi or Āditya is to be offered in the houses of the chief queen. She offers a cow as the sacrificial fee of this rite.

It is the chief queen who is to sit touching the king in the offering of scrapings of the consecrated waters which is offered at the house of a favourite son.[124] While mounting the chariot for a symbolic conquest of the quarters (digvijaya) the king touches the chief queen and the horses with the tip of the bow so that by the quickening of the Maruts they might bring him victory and that he might be united with power.[125] This bow he hands over to the chief queen for safe preservation so that their (eldest?) son might be victorious by means of this (symbolic) bolt *(vajra).*[126]

While adoring the king, the *Brahman* hands over the sword to the king, which he again lets pass amongst the Ratnins from hand to hand. They touch the sword to assure the king of their faithfulness. The chief queen is the only wife who, in common consent of all the authorities, is entitled to touch the sword which is the symbol of unity among the jewels of the king as well as of loyalty of them all to him.[127]

In the Human sacrifice,[128] too, the chief queen lies down by the side of the victim[129] as she does in the Aśvamedha. They are cloaked together under garments and the sacriicer exhorts her to do the obscene act. A similar colloquy as in the Aśvamedha follows. When it is finished, the Hotṛ and others[130] (most probably, the Udgātṛ, Adhvaryu and Brahman.[131]) raise her up. According to the Vaitāna only the Brahman is to do so. Now, the Hotṛ consecrates her with prayers in which he invokes the spirit of the parted sites (of the sacrificer);[132] the Udgātṛ consecrates her with the formulas in which he prays that the manes may live in happiness and sojourn during the sacrifice to the sacrificial place;[133] and the Adhvaryu with the prayer that she may live long and secure.[134] The Brahman makes her utter the Mantra in which she prays for the long life of herself as well as for her husband.[135]

In the Rāḍ-yajña[136] which has been mentioned in the *Pañc Brā,* alone and is intended to restore a deposed king to his kingdom, the chief queen is one of the eight viras who surround and sprinkle the celebrant.

Now, we set out the duties of the chief wife in establishing and keeping up of the sacred domestic fire. If the newly-married couple desire to establish and keep up fire from their marriage time,[137] they carry the Marriage Fire to their new house—or if they like to live under the same roof as the father to that house, and establish it there. They constantly keep it up by offering morning and evening oblations. According to certain authorities,[138] it is only she, and not the husband, who should offer these oblations, because she is the House and this Fire is Domestic. Either of them seems, however, to be equally entitled to offer it;[139] it is only natural that in case of the absence or sickness of either, the other will offer. The presence of both or at least, either of them is necessary .[140] If she cannot be bodily present, the Adhvaryu acts as her substitute with her permission, which, of course, follows automatically in case of her pregnancy, madness,[141] etc.

If the fire goes out, she fasts;[142] according to Vaikhānasa,[143] performs a Kṛcchra.She also fasts if the time of kindiling up the fire elapses.[144]

If the existence of the fire is interrupted for twelve days, it is to be re-established. According to Vaikhānasa, the rite of establishing fire is to be observed again if the husband and the wife remain without fire three days, and in this case the wife is required to undergo the Prājāpatya or Pādakṛcchra penance while the husband fasts one day.[145]

Either the chief wife or the husband offers the Bali,[146] but Gobhila[147] makes a special rule that the wife should offer in the evening and the husband in the morning. Naturally the option ceases if the husband is absent.[148] According to Bhāradvāja, it is only she who should offer the Vaiśvadeva, three times along with the utterance of the Yajus text and once silently.[149]

The cooking[150] and other preliminary things such as

husking[151] are always done by her. Before beginning the cooking, she washes herself.[152] Having finished the cooking, she purifies herself by sipping water, etc., and in a sweet distinct voice reports to her husband that she has finished it.[153] The husband thanks her that it is well done, and prays that the food which is Virāṭ may not fall short. Then she removes the cooking vessel to a secure place, and cleanses the upper part with water and the lower with cow-dung. She now takes four fuels in her hand, sprinkles and offers them along with the utterance of the prescribed formulas.[154] She makes offerings in praise of everything that helps her cooking, all the quarters and innumerable gods. During the Nr-Yajna, either the husband pours water and she washes, or she pours water and he washes; they wash with mutual help simply the portion of the leg under the knee.[155] Daily she propitiates thus the Guests, the Gods, the Beings, Brahma, and the Manes.

According to Pārāskara, the husband and wife may either take their meals together or the husband may take them earlier, but in any case they must partake of the remnant of the food after all the above-mentioned offerings.[156]

In the rites concerning the House, the chief wife enters first the newly-built house with a full jar on her head or lap;[157] it seems that only the chief wife as the mistress of the house should carry the jar. That she should enter first is indicative of her authority over the house; her decided authority over household affairs is also found in the statement that the wife is the house, ocurring in various places.[158] Anyway, it is certain that while entering the new house she heads the host of wives after whom come the husband and all others. It is on her lap that the husband should lie down and it is she whom the husband looks at again and again along with the prayer that they may together, in the house, overcome all hostile powers.[159] On this ceremonial day all the disputations are shunned by her as well as by others.[160]

In a rite named Gṛhaśānti her apartments are swept clean by the husband with the leaves of Apāmārga or Palāśa or udumbara or of some other tree or plant mentioned in the list.[161] While sweeping, he prays to Rudra that none of them in the house might be harmed, that the mother, particularly, could not be harmed, and that no injury might be inflicted on the seed, progeny, cows or horses.[162]

After the animal has been killed in a domestic sacrifice, the chief wife bathes the apertures of the animal with water alongwith the utterance of the *mantras.*[163] With the water-jar in her hands she worships the Sun. The procedure is exactly the same as in the Srauta rites.[164] At the end of the sacrifice the wife adds a fuel to the fire.[165]

In the ŝūlagava sacrifice, too, after the animal has been killed, she washes the apertures in the above-mentioned manner.[166] According to Bhāradvāja[167] and Hiraṇyakeśin,[168] she should offer rice to the consort of Siva after the husband has offered to Siva. According to Paraskara,[169] she also offers the Patni-saṃyāja offerings to Indrāṇi and Rudrāṇi, Śarvāṇi, Bhavāni and Agni Gṛhapati.

In one rite named Bauḍhya-vihāra mentioned only in the *Hir. GS.,*[170] and elaborated in the *Sams. RM.,*[171] the chief wife observes all the rites beginning from spreading the black deer-skin down to husking as have been mentioned in connection with the Sthālipāka.

The chief wife performs the Caitra sacrifice on the full moon day in the month of Caitra.[172] She together with her husband begins the Sṛāvaṇa sacrifice on the full moon day under Sravisṭhā.[173] The sacrifice goes on daily until the Agrahāyaṇi sacrifice when the beds are placed on the ground with the advent of drier weather. The sacrifice is directed against any danger from snakes.[174] Every day the sacrificer makes offerings to serpents which she puts away silently.[175] On the full moon day of Bhādra, she observes the Prauṣṭhapada sacrifice.[176] On the full moon day of the Asviṇa she offers the Asvayuga sacrifice or the Pṛśātaka ceremony,[177] in which her principal duty lies in preparing a mess of boiled rice-grains. On the full moon day of the Agrahāyaṇa[178] she observes the Agrahāyaṇi sacrifice.[179] She cleanses the house thoroughly, which is followed by a smoking. At this time the danger from snakes being over, the beds of all the members of the house are lowered down. At the end of the sacrifice, all the members of the household sit on straws and unwashed garments. According to Gobhila,[180] she sits immediately next to the sacrificer with her children on her lap or by her side; according to Apastamba[181] she sits to his north. After this rite she descends together with her husband

and children alongwith the utterance of the words. "Life, fame, strength, enjoyment of food, offspring." Then she lies down, together with all others on her right side, with her head towards the cast along with the prayer to the Earth for propitiating her.[182] She and all others rise up, praying for the exuberance of life, for blessed life. For four months and even more she and all others sleep on the ground.[183]

In the ancestral rites the most important rite that the chief wife is to perform is the cooking of the *ŝrāddhapāka.*[184] food to be offered to the Manes with honour. As she is supreme in all matters concerning cooking and such other domestic affairs, it is she who is to do this.[185] Gobhila,[186] says she should, at the end of the cooking, say "finished", after which the actual ceremony begins. Vyāsa,[187] says the wife should, after cooking, take a bath. It is she who is to serve food to the manes. Kṛkala's manes incurred sins because Sukalā was deprived of her right to offer the cake; and *Dharma* calls both him as well as the manes thieves.[188] The manes as well as the sacrificer, instead of aquiring religious merit, incur sin if the (eldest) wife does not serve during the *Sraddha,* the food by herself.[189] At the end of the ceremony she partakes with her husband of the remnants of food.[190]

On the 2nd astaka day after the animal is killed, it is she who washes all the fourteen apertures of the cow's body.[191] On the Anvaśṭakya day she[192] places a stone in the Kuśa grass and pounds on that stone a fragrant substance called *Sthagara,*[193] grinds some collyrium[194] and anoints therewith three Darbha blades. These are placed underneath the seats of three Brāhmaṇas who are invited to the sacrifice.

In the Pitṛyajña she, accompanied by the sacrificer, pays reverence to the manes. She also prays to Agni Gārhapatya for releasing her from any sin she may have committed to atmosphere, earth, sky, mother or father.[195]

The true significance of the performance of rites lies in the eating of *Iḍā*. The eating of Iḍā leads to the end of the sacrifice, the sacrifice of life, the fullness of human life and ultimately to *Prājapati*, Lord of Sacrifices, the Self of Sacrifices. The successful completion of domestic and social life of man, of the material and spiritual life, of his earthly and divine life, in a word, of his whole life—lie in this. The Christians observe this rite under the name of the Eucharistic sacrifice. In this sacrifice they offer bread and wine to Christ and by means of the utterance of holy *mantras* these are transubstantiated into flesh and blood of Christ. The Christians form a Holy Communion with Christ by means of eating these flesh and blood of Christ.[196] The eating of the Iḍā in Vedic ritual is nothing but the observance of the Eucharistic sacrifice and forming a Holy Communion with *Prājapati*, Lord of Sacrifice. In the *Agnihotra* the remnant of the milk offered is to be taken. In the New and Full moon sacrifices, etc., the remnant of the Puroḍāśa offering is to be eaten. In the animal sacrifice a portion of the meat offfered is eaten. Soma sacrifice, the remnant of the Soma offered is to be drunk.[197] In the Baliharaṇa, the husband and wife take the remnant of the food remaining after the five daily sacrifices.[198] In all the Sṛāddha offerings, the remnant of the food offered is to be eaten.[199] In this eating of the Haviś-śeśa, the Iḍā, only the chief wife is to participate, as this devolves on the wife and the sacrificer, all that the Sacrifice may, and consequently, is a rite designed to help in the other world as well. In this rite all the priests and the sacrificer also participate and together with them, she forms a Holy Communion between *Prājapati*, the Supreme Soul, and the establishers of the sacrificer. In ancient Indian society women were regarded as equal to men with access to and capacity for the highest knowledge. The *Rig Veda* contains hymns by as many as twenty-seven women called Brahmavadinis or women seers. It was not obligatory for Brahmavadinis or women seers. It was not obligatory for Brahmavadinis to take the vow of celibacy, renounce the world and meditate in a secluded mountains cave. On the contrary quite a few Brahmavadinis were married women. In the Vedic age domestic life was not regarded as in any way inconsistent with spiritual life.

Womanhood in the Vedic age had two main ideals, viz., that of a Brahmavadini and that of a Sadyovadhu. A Sadyovadhu was of a domestic type dedicating herself to the welfare of her family and devoting herself to her domestic duties. Just as many Brahmavadinis were married, many Sadhyovadhus were of a spiritual nature and strove for spiritual realisation in the midst of their domestic duties.

The two epics, *Ramayana* and *Mahabharata,* have many examples of the two types of Indian women. Gandhari, Kunti,

Draupadi, Savitri, Damayanti, Shakuntala and Satyabhama in the *Mahabharata* were women who, though housewives, were also reputed scholars and saintly characters. The highest epitome of domestic perfection is found in the character of Sita in the *Ramayana.* The *Rig Veda* accorded the highest social status to the women of those days.

Buddhism kept up the traditions of Brahminical religion in according womanhood an honoured place in social life. Women were made eligible for admission to the Bikshuni Sangha, the Order of Nuns, which opened to them ample opportunities for social service and public life. The Order of Nuns was the nursery which produced many learned women. The Buddhist nuns were called *theris.*

Some Buddhist nuns achieved great distinction by the prominent part they took in the work of the early Buddhist Reformation. Some of these women leaders of the Buddhist Reformation are mentioned in the commentary of Dharmapala on the *Therigatha* (Songs of the Nuns). They are (i) Soma, whom the Buddha converted at Rajagriha (ii) Anupama, daughter of wealthy parents who "cutting off the glory of her hair, entered on the lonely paths of life and wandered forth to lose the sense of home" (iii) Queen Khema (iv) Sujatha, wife of a wealthy citizen, who in the quest for Truth renounced worldly happiness (v) Chapa, who by her conduct drove her husband to be a monk till she herself chastened, by their separation, followed her husband to the order (vi) Kisagautami, whom the Buddha found to be fit enough for appointment as Superintendent of the convent as Jatavana and (vii) Sundari, a beautiful heiress, who renounced the world on her brother's death.

Some of these women after obtaining enlightenment took to missionary work for their faith. The most renowned of these leaders was Patachara, the bereaved mother who gave solace to 500 other bereaved mothers.

The position of women in India gradually deteriorated as the Vedic ideals of equality and unity faded with the passage of time.

References

1. RV. X, 146., AV., III, 18 (a charm for having predominance over a rival co-wife); Ait. Br. VII. 13 (100 wives); *Sat. Br.* IV, I, 5. I ff.

and Jai. Br. III, 121 ff: Sapatnī in *St. Petersburg* Dict.; Pār. GS. I, 4. 6–10 and corresponding passages in other Gṛhya and Dharma Sūtras.

2. *Dakṣa-saṃhita*, IV, 14, *Smr. Sam.* p. 79, 1. 19 (*Ona. Sam.* IV, 15, p. 443. II 7–8).
3. Viṣṇu XXVI. r–4, *Ona. Śam.* p. 66, II 8 f.
4. Manu IX, pp. 85–86.
5. F. 149b, I. 9 f.
6. *Op. cit.*, p. 150 f.
7. Yājṇ. 1–88; cf. *Sāṇ. ŚS*, Vol. II, p. 54, II. 4–5.
8. *Sat. ŚS*. Vol. I, p. 160, 1, 21 "Parārthāni, etc."
9. *Op. cit.*, 1. 22, "Sakṛtkṛtam, etc."
10. *Sat. ŚS*. Vol. III, p. 695, I. 3. "Jyeṣṭhatvaṃ vivāha-kṛtaṃ na tu vayaskrtam"
11. VI, 5. 3, I; p. 541, 1. 6, Webet's Ed.
12. VI, 5, 3, I, p. 549, 1.6, Weber's Ed.
13. *Āp. ŚS*, I, 6, 12; Vol. I, p. 23.
14. Of course, there is provision here that she might be replaced by a Sūdrā in pounding. However, no strict regularity seems to be observed in husking or pounding. See *Sat. ŚS*., p. 132, II. 17 f.; *Āp. ŚS*, I, 21, 9. According to *Āp. ŚS*, *op. cit.;* a ŝūdrā is to pound if the rice is to be pounded again; "Anena puṇaḥpeśaṇe dāsyā niyamo varṇyate." If for some reason or other the wife could not be present, the Agnidhra or some other priest might do this for the wife; *Sat. ŚS*., p. 132, 1. 23; *Āp. ŚS*, I, 20, 13, 70.
15. *Sat. ŚS*., p. 161, 1. 7. "Yathāpradeśaṃ mukhya-patny-upaveśanam samipa itarāsām tām eva diśam avalambya vyavadhānena, etc."
16. *Baudh. ŚS*., p. 30, II. 16.
17. Cf. *Sat. Br.*, I, 9, 2, 14, Weber's Ed., p. 90, II. 14.
18. I, 15, 10; see Comm. on the same, Vol. II, p. 54. According to other authorities, however, all the wives are to observe these rites as they do not think these are meant for Parārtha; *Sat. ŚS*., p. 228, pratipatni "vedādānāditi gamyate.
19. *Sat. ŚS*., p. 223, II. 23–24 Parārthāny ekena iti, etc."
20. *Āp. ŚS*, II, 5, 11, 13f; see the Scholiast in particular; Manu V, 167–168; Yā. I, 89.
21. *Sat. ŚS*., Vol. I, p. 358.
22. Sat. SS., Vol. I. p. 358, 1. 2; op. cit., vol. II, p. 541, 1. 16.
23. *Op. cit.* Vol. II, p. 543, I. 27.
24. *Sat. ŚS*., Vol. I, p. 358, 1, II ff.
25. *Sat. Br.*, II, I. 4, I.

26. *Sat. ŚS.*, Vol. II, p. 528, 1, 27.
27. Kat. *ŚS.*, Chow. Ed., p. 298, Sūtras 307–308; *Sat. ŚS.*, Vol. II, p. 535, 1. 5.
28. *Āp. ŚS*, Vol. I, p. 322, 1. 20, Scholiast on 6.3.1.
29. *Āp. ŚS*, VI, 5, 2, Vol. 1, p. 328, II, 15–17; cf. *Sāṇ. ŚS*, 2.7. Behind the Gārhapatya".
30. Compare the remark of the Scholiast on *Āp. ŚS*, VI, 5, I, Vol. I, p. 328. II, 12–13.
31. *Sāṇ. ŚS*, 2, 10, 5 "Traidham kardti'; *Sat. ŚS.*, Vol. I, p. 354. Ap. SS., VI, 12. 4–5; Vol. I, pp. 343–44. The W.Y.V. ritual, however, does not refer to this rite; cf. p. 304, Chow. Ed. Sūtras 341–42.
32. Cf. the Mantra "Gṛhebhyas tvā gṛhān jinva", B. YV.; "Saṃ tvā sṛjāmi prajayā dhanena" iti, RV.
33. *Āp. ŚS*, III, 12, 9. Bib. Ind., p. 50 and 25a; *Āp. ŚS*, p. 143, 11, 18-22.
34. Scholiast on *Āp. ŚS*, VIII, 5; 40, Vol. II, p. 28.
35. According to several authorities the husband also participates in this; e.g. *Sat. ŚS.*, p. 463, 1. 16–21.
36. *Baudh. ŚS.*, p. 136, II. 1–16; *Sat. ŚS.*, p. 462, II. 28–31.
37. As quoted in *Āp. ŚS*, VIII, 6, 4; Vol. II, pp. 29–30; cf. *Baudh. ŚS.*, Vol. I, p. 133. I. 12, also quoted by the Scholiast on Āp., *op. cit.*
38. *Tait. Samb.*, I, 8, 3, 6; Vāj. Saṃh., III, 44. etc.; Mān. *ŚS.* I, 7, 4, 12, p. 55.
39. According to Baudhāyana these dishes should have been given round the fire; *Baudh, ŚS.*, p. 136, II. 19, "Abhiparyagnikṛtāni."
40. The wife goes but the south door, *Baudh. ŚS.*, p. 137, II. 1–2.
41. *Tait. Saṃh.*, I, 6, 53, cf. I, 8, 3(c); Vāj. Saṃh., III, 46;*Baudh. ŚS.*, p. 136 1. 8.
42. "Praghāsasya Marut devatā", *Sat. ŚS.*, Vol. II, p. 465, II. 24–25.
43. *Vāj. Saṃh.*, III, 47; *Kap. Saṃh.*; I, 7, p. 35, II. 21–22; etc., *Sat. ŚS.*, vol. II, p. 465, II, 2I f. The adhvaryu might perform this for them while they kept on touching him, II. 26–27 (Sat. SS.) *Baudh. ŚS.*, vol. I, p. 137, 1. 10; *Man. ŚS.*, I; 7, 4, 15, p. 55; *Āp. ŚS.*, VIII, 6, 24.
44. Y, 5, II.
45. *Āp. ŚS.*, VIII. 8. 16.
46. *Āp. ŚS.*, VIII. 8. 17.
47. Scholiast on *Āp. ŚS.*, VIII, 8, 18, "Sarvam etat samānam patyuḥ."

48. *Āp. ŚS.*, VIII, 10, 10, Vol. II, p. 53; *Sat. ŚS.*, Vol. II, p. 473, II. 5–6 Scholiast "Patnistrikumārā" iti Vaikhānasaḥ".
49. *Sat. ŚS.*, Vol. II, p. 469, I. 28.
50. Prāṇāpyāyana: "Āpyāyayati taststhānam abhilaksya apah praksipati; praksiptodakasthānābhimarśanam āpyāyanam", Scholiast on Satyāṣāḍha, Vol. II, p. 424, II. 21 f.
51. Scholiast on Satyāśāḍha, *op. cit.*, "Parārthāny ekena kriyerann iti mukhyā eva abhiśecanam āpyāyanaṃ karoti;" similarly, Scholiast on Āpastamba (I. 8. 17), Vol. I, p. 436, II. 18–19.
52. *Baudh. Saṃh.* Vol. I, p. 118, II. 7–8; Mān. *ŚS.*, I, 8, 4, I; *Sat. ŚS.*, Vol. II, p. 424, II. 6 f. "Pūrṇapātradhāraṇam ekasyā eva āpyāyanasthatvāt."
53. *Tait. Saṃh.* 1, 3, 9; *Kat. Saṃh.*, III. 6; *Kap. Saṃh.* II. 13 (pp. 21–22); *Mait. Saṃh.* 1, 2, 16; *Vaj Saṃh.* VI, 14-16; *Āp. ŚS.*, VII, 18, 17, Vol. I, p. 436, II. 21 f.; *Sat. ŚS.*, Vol. II, p. 424; *Man ŚS.*, 1, 8, 4, p. 68; *Baudh. ŚS.*, Vol. I, p. 118, II. 12 f. It remains doubtful who the sacrificer and the Adhvaryu or the sacrificer and the wife, should use, *Vaj Saṃh.* VI, 15–16. For the reasons why the wife should wipe the organs, see *Sat.* Brā., III, 6, 2, 5.
54. *Sat. ŚS.*, *op. cit.*, p. 443. II. 11.
55. *Āp. ŚS.*, VII, 27, 12, Vol. I, p. 463.
56. *Sat. ŚS.*, *op. cit.*, p. 444. II. 11–12; cf. *Āp. ŚS.*, VII, 27, 16, vol. I, p. 464, according to which she is to have a wash, worship the Sun and the Ābavaniya.
57. Scholiast on *Āp. ŚS.*, X, 23, 4 "Patnyanckatve api mahisyāh prayacchati nīdhanārthatvāt;" similarly, Scholiast on *Sat. ŚS.*, vol. III, p. 629, II. 11–12 "Nidha narthatvād asaṃskārakarmatvāc ca;" *Baudh. ŚS.*, p. 170, 1. 5. According to the Scholiast on *Kāt ŚS.*, sūtras 176–177, p. 449, Chow. ed., the adhvaryu gives her the dust and the Nesṭṛ makes her recite the Mantra; *Śat. Brā.*, III, 3, I, 12; *Tait. Saṃh.* VI, I, 8, 5; etc. etc.
58. *Sat. ŚS.*, vol. III, p. 630, II. to f., specially thue Scholiast; *Āp. ŚS.*, X, 23, 10.
59. *Āp. ŚS.*, X, 30, 5; *Sat. ŚS.*, p. 652, II. 8–11; *Baudh. ŚS.*, VI, 16, Vol. I, p. 174, II. 14–15. "Apah praniya ātithyam nirvapaty anvārabdhhāyāṃ patnyām," *Kāt ŚS.*, Chow. ed., sūtra 2, Vol. I, p. 463.
60. Cf. *Tait. Saṃh.* VI, 2, 1.
61. *Āp. ŚS.*, X, 30, 5–6, vol. II, p. 288, II, 9 f.; Scholiast "Yadi patnyā hastena nirvāpas tadā hasto 'gnihotrahavanadharmān

labhate." *Sat. ŚS.*, vol. III, p. 652. II. 23; 653, II. 11.

62. Scholiast on *Sat. ŚS.*, vol. III, p. 695, II. 28 f. "Mukhyā eva anakti; Scholiast on *Āp. ŚS.*, XI, 6, 4, vol. II, p. 309 "Patnyanckatve' pi mukhyā upānakti. Aksasams-kāratvāt," *Baudh. ŚS.*, VI, 24, Vol. I, p. 184. II. 12 f.; *Kāt. ŚS.*, VIII, 8z f.; p. 480, II. 5ff., Chow. ed.
63. Cf. the Mantra "No viro jāyatām, etc."
64. *Śat. Brā.*, III, 5, 3, 13 ff.; *Kāt ŚS.*, Chow. Ed. Vol. I, p. 840, II. 6f. "Dakśiṇayā dvārā, etc." According to *Baudh. ŚS.*, Vol. I, p. 164, I. 12: "Pūrvayā dvārā."
65. *Baudh. ŚS.*, Vol. I, p. 184. I. 16, "Atha ctesam padapāṃsūnām, etc." Cf. *Sat. ŚS.*, Vol. III, p. 695, 1. 8 "Dvidhavibhaktasya ekāṃśena."
66. Scholiast on *Sat. ŚS., op. cit.* 1. 21.
67. *ŚS.*, XI, 6, 5, Vol. II, p. 309; see also Sūtra 8 "Sakṛd vā;" cf. Scholiast.
68. *Vaj Saṃh.*, V, 17 "Parāg devasrutau, etc."
69. *ŚS.*, Vol. I, p. 480, II. 6–11 ".....Pāṇibhyām....yugapat...."
70. *Kāt ŚS.*, X, 2, 38, Weber's Ed., p. 802; Chow. Ed., p. 570, Sūtra 62; cf. Commentary in Weber.
71. Scholiast on *Sat. ŚS.*, Vol. IV, p. 919, II. 9–10 "Patnibahutve mukhyā eva mathanaṃ pūtabhṛtyavanayanaṇca karoti, na tu sarvāh." The Mantra used in this connection; "Asme devāso vapuse cikitsat iti."
72. *Kāt. ŚS.*, Chow. Ed., p. 574, II, 4–5; Weber's Ed., X, 4, 3, p. 807; *Sat. ŚS., op. cit.*
73. *Sat. ŚS., op. cit.*
74. *ŚS.*, X, 5, 4, Weber's Ed., p. 810, II. 3 f.; Chow. Ed., p. 577, Sūtra 105. *The Mantra: Vāj. Saṃh.*, VIII, 5.
75. *Sat. ŚS.*, Vol. IV, p. 947, II. 14 f. For the ūha, see Commentary.
76. *Sat. ŚS.*, Vol. IV, p. 954, II. 22 ff.
77. Scholiast Devayajvan on *Kāt. ŚS.*, XXVI, 7. 40, Weber's Ed., p. 1108; Chow. Ed., p. 1042.
78. *Vāj. Saṃh.*, 11. 58; *Mait. Saṃh.*, 2, 7, 6; *Kāt. Saṃh.*, 1, 6, 5: *Āp. ŚS.*, XVI, 4, 5: Vol. III, p. 5; *Sat. ŚS.*, Vol. 5, p. 14, II. 7 f., etc.
79. *Sat. ŚS.*, Vol. V, p. 15, II. 22–23; *Śat. Brā.*, IV, 5, 3, I, 4; p. 541, II. 4–6, Weber' Ed.
80. *Kāt. ŚS.*, XIV, 5, 36, Weber's Ed., p. 868.
81. *Kāt. ŚS.*, XIV, 5, 3, Weber's Ed., p. 866.
82. *Sat. ŚS.*, Vol. V, p. 144. 1 2; "Paridhate" has been explained by

the commentators as "Paridhapayati." For the *Mantra* she utters: *Vāj. Saṃh.*, 10, 8; *Tait. Saṃh.*, 1, 7, 9, 1, etc.

83. *Vāj. Saṃh.*, (Kānva rec.) 10, 4, 3: *Tait. Saṃh.*,1, 7, 9. 1 *Śat. Brā.*, 5, 2, 1, 10; *Tait. Brā.*, 1, 3, 7, 2; *Kāt. ŚS.*, XIV, 5, 6; *Āp. ŚS.*, XVIII, 5, 9. *Sat. ŚS.*, Vol. V, p. 144. II. 9 fa. *Baudh. ŚS.*, XI, Vol. II, p. 80, II. f., etc., cf. Hill, Rithit, p. 142, II. 31 f.
84. *Sat. ŚS., op. cit.* 1. 11 "Evam tri."
85. *Op. cit.* 1. 17 "Ubhau vā."
86. For the Mantras, see *Tait. Saṃh.*, 1, 7, 9, 1; *Vāj. Saṃh.*, IX, 21 (cf. XXII, 32); *Kāt. Saṃh.*, XIV, 1; *Mait. Saṃh.*, 1, 11, 3: *Śat. Brā.*, V, 2, 1, 4: *Āp. ŚS.*, XVIII. 5, 13.
87. *Tait. Saṃh.*, 1, 7, 9 f.
88. *Sat. ŚS.*, Vol. V, p. 145, 1. 9 "Patnim iti bhāsyakṛt"
89. *Baudh. ŚS.*, Vol. II, p. 8, 1. 9.
90. *Sat. ŚS.*, p. 285, II 5 f.;
91. *Op. cit.* V, 2, 1, 10.
92. *Op. cit.*
93. ***Sat.*** *ŚS.*, p. 285, 1. 5f.; *Āp. ŚS.*, 1, 8, 10–11, Vol. I, pp. 26–27; śāṇ. śS., IV, 3, 7, Vol. I, p. 35; Scholiast, *op. cit.*, Vol. II, p. 170, I. II; Āsv. śS., (AśS) II, 6, 7, p. 68, II. 13–15.
94. *Amarakosa,* p. 124, 1. 10 "Kṛtābhīśekā mahisibhoginyo'nyā nrpastriyaḥ."
95. *Baudh. ŚS.*, XV, 2, p. 206, II. 7 f.; note particularly "Ubhau" in line 9. Cf. *Āp. ŚS.*, XX, I, 10 f., Vol. III, p. 142.
96. *Op. cit.* XV, 3, p. 206, II 13–14.
97. *Op. cit.* 1. 9.
98. XX, 1, 12, Weber p. 961.
99. *Kāt. ŚS.*, XX, I, 13, Weber, p. 961.
100. According to *Baudh. ŚS.*, cf. p. 228, II. 14 f.; cf. *Āp. ŚS.*, XX, 15, Vol. III, p. 159, 1. 8.
101. ***Sat.*** *ŚS.*, Vol. 5. p. 237. 1. 24 "Ugrāṇām rājadāsabhūtānām śataṃ Vavatayaḥ."
102. Commentary on *Kāt. ŚS.*, Ed. p. 829. Sūtra 17 .
103. *Op. cit.*, Sūtra 18.
104. Pālāgalī, a Sūdrā by birth, cannot observe these rites, cf. *Śat. Brā.*, XIII, 2. 6, 7. Anointing and entwining: *Kāth. Saṃh.*, IV, 9; *Mait. Saṃh.*, III, 12, 18. 19; *Vāj. Saṃ*, XIII, 5–8; *Tait. Brā.*, III, 9, 4, 1–8; *Śat. Brā.*, XIII, 2, 6, 1–6; *Āp. ŚS.*, XX, 15, 6, f.; *Kāt. ŚS.*, XX, 5. 10f.; *Baudh. ŚS.*, XV, 24. Vol. II.
105. Cf. Baudhāyana and Āpastamba.
106. Gaulgulava, known in Bengal as Guggul.

107. According to B.Y.V. ritual, each of them uses 1000 pearls; *Āp. ŚS.*, Vol. V, p. 237, ll. 17 f. According to W.Y.V. only a hundred; *Kāt. ŚS.*, Weber, p. 971: according to the Scholiast, one hundred and one.
108. *Kāt. ŚS.*, XX, 6, 12; *Āp. ŚS.*, XX, I17, 12.
109. *Baudh. ŚS.*, XV, 29.
110. Scholiast on *Kāt. ŚS.*, XX, 6, 14, Weber. p. 973, ll. 1–2.
111. *ŚS.*, Vol. V, p. 242. ll. 6f.
112. *Tait. Saṃh.*, VII, 4, 12, 1; *Tait. Brā.*, 3, 9, 6, 1; *Āp. ŚS.*, XX, 17, 13; *Kāt. ŚS.*, XX, 6, 14. Weber. p. 973, l. 1.
113. *Āp. ŚS.*, *op. cit.* Sūtras 13–16.
114. *Kāt. ŚS.*, XX, 6, 16–17, p. 973, ll. 6–10; *Āp. ŚS.*, XX, 18, 4, Vol. III, p. 163, II, 77 f.; *Vait.* S., XXXVI, 30, p. 52.
115. Cf. the Dialogue between the Brahmacārin and the Hetarai in the Mahāvrata.
116. *Kāt. ŚS.*, XX, 6, 20; *Āp. ŚS.*, XX, 18, 6; Āsv. śS., X, 8, 13; *Vait.* S., XXXVI, 32.
117. XIII, 2, 9, 1–8. It will be seen in this connection that from the very beginning the chief queen is, from the ritualistic point of view, dedicated to the Brahman. Most probably there is no other reason here than this that the chief queen holding the highest position can be dedicated to Brahman only who is the most important of all priests; *Āp. ŚS.*, XX, 10. 2. Vol. III, p. 153.
118. *Kāt. ŚS.*, XX. 6, 21, Weber, p. 973.
119. *Āp. ŚS.*, XX, 18, 7, Vol. III, p. 163, II, 2 f.; *Baudh. ŚS.*, XV, 30, Vol. II, p. 235. ll. 9 f.; *Kāt. ŚS.*, XX, 7, 1, Weber, p. 973, ll. 18 f.; cf. *Kāth. Saṃ*, X, 5; *Mait. Saṃ*, III, 12, 21; *Vāj. Saṃ.*, XXIII, 33–38; *ŚS.*, Vol. V, p. 244, ll. 3–5; "Rājṇah patnyas trividhā uttamā madhyamā'dhama ca iti tās ca Mahisī Vāvātā parivrkti ity etannāmadheyāḥ. Tāś ca mṛtasya aśvasya asinā chedanāya tattatsthānesu rekhāḥ sūcibhi kuryuḥ."
120. ***Sat.*** *ŚS.*
121. The Rājasāya practically ends with the Sunāsiriya offering; on the fourth to the fifteenth day after the Sunāsiriya, offerings called Ratnināṃ Havīṃsī are offered in the house of the Jewels of the King, his wives and high officers. For the order of Ratnins, cf. *Śat. Brā.*, V, 3, 1; *Tait. Brā.*, 1, 7, 3; *Baudh. ŚS.*, XII, 5, 6; *Āp. ŚS.*, XVIII, 10, 12–II, 23; *Kāt. ŚS.*, XV. 3, 1–46; *Kāt. Saṃ*, XV, 4, 5; *Mait. Saṃ.*, II, 6, 5, 6; etc.
122. For its eleven Ratnins cf. *op. cit.* Sūtras 1–12.
123. XV, 3, 36, p. 974, Weber's Ed.

124. E.g. *Āp. ŚS.*, XVIII, 10-14, Vol. III, p. 88, 1. 1.
125. *Baudha. ŚS.*, XII, 11; Vol. II, p. 102, 1 4; *Tait. Saṃ*, I, 8, 14, 1. etc.
126. *Āp. ŚS.*, XVIII, 17, 10, Vol. III. p. 97; cf. *Vāj. Saṃ.*, X, 21.
127. *Āp. ŚS.*, *op. cit.* Sūtra II; *Sat. ŚS.*, XIII, 6, 10, Vol. V, p. 179.
128. *Āp. ŚS.*, XVIII, 18, 9 and 14. Vol. III, p. 99; *Sat. ŚS.*, Vol. V, p. 181, II. 271–p. 182, 1. 2.
129. This sacrifice is prescribed in two texts only, viz. the *Saṇ. ŚS.*, XVI, 10 f., and *Vait. ŚS.*, XXVII, 10 f. In the Puruśamedha dealt with by the *Śat. Brā.*, (XIII. 6) only symbolical human victims are offered.
130. *Saṇ. ŚS.*, XVI. 13. 7; *Vait.* S., XXXVIII, 3, cf. *Kau. ŚS.*, 80, 15.
131. Scholiast on śāṇ. śS., XVI, 13. 13. Vol. III, p. 375, 1. 4.
132. Compare the following Sūtra and the Scholiast thereon.
133. The *Mantras:* RV., X. 57, 3–5.
134. The *Mantras:* RV., X. 58, 1–3.
135. *Mantras* X, 60, 8–10.
136. *Mantras,* RV., X. 59; 5–7; cf. Scholiast on śāṇ. śS., XVI, 13. 15. Vol. III, p. 375 and also, the foot-note.
137. XIX, 7, 1–4.
138. This fire could also be established at the time of the division of the property of the family, return of a student from his studentship, and on the death of the head of the family.
139. *Khā.* GS., I. 5. 17–18, p. 40; Gobh. GS., I, 3. 13.
140. *Pār.* GS., p. 113. Bomb. Ed., "Tyāgam tu sarvathā kuryāt tatrāpy anyataras tayoh, etc."
141. Saṃskāratnamālā, Vol. I, p. 613, II, I ff.
142. *Pār.* GS., *op. cit.* Saṃskāraratnamālā, *op. cit.*, II. 9f.
143. According to a good many authorities, only she should fast; according to some, the husband also may; Nārāyaṇa in Saṃskāramayūkha; Āśv.GS., I, 9. I, etc. Husband: *Āp.* GS., V., 17; *Hir.* GS., I, 22, 5.
144. She does so also if it comes into contact with some other fire, too.
145. Āśv. GS., I, 9, 3; cf. Nārāyaṇa and Gṛhyakārikā.
146. *Vaikh,* GS., VI, 15, p. 98, 11, 7-10, Nārāyaṇa and Gṛhyakārikā.
147. *Vaikh.* GS., III, 7, p. 41, II. 14–15; cf. VI, 17, p. 101, II. 3–4.
148. *Gobh.* GS., I, 4, 17, p. 153; particularly Sūtra 19, p. 154.
149. *Sāṇ.* GS., II, 14.
150. *Bhār.* GS., III, 12, p. 78, II, 4f. "Stri Vaiśvadevaṃ nirvapet, etc." The husband is to offer only if she appoints him to offer the Bali. "Yukto vā svayaṃ nirvapet."
151. *Bhār.* GS., *op. cit.* commentator on *Gobh.,* "She is supreme in

matters concerning food" and so on (cf. Manu IX, II). *Saṃskāraratnamālā*, p. 938.

152. *Bhār.* GS., *op. cit.*, I, 6.
153. *Bhār.* GS., *op. cit.*
154. *Gobh.* GS., I, 3, 15, pp. 116–117; *Khād.* GS., I, 5, 17.
155. *Bhār.* GS., *op. cit.*, I, 11. ff.
156. *Baudh.* GS., 1, 2, 22–23, p. 5.
157. *Pār.* GS., II, 9, 14–15, p. 262 of Bom. Ed.; *Karka,* p. 263, II. 3 f.; Paddhati. p. 266, 1. 2; Gadādhara, p. 267, II. 3 f. According to Viśvanātha, the wife and the husband should take together if no guest happens to be present. For the procedure of offering the five Mahāyajñas, see Padhārthakrama as given in Pār. GS., pp. 267 f.
158. III, 12, 8.
159. "Na gṛhaṃ gṛham ity āhur gṛhiṇi gṛham ucyate," commentary on *Gobh.* GS., I, 3, 13, p. 95; *Drāh.* GS., I, 5, 17; *Sāṇ.* GS., II, 16, 3.
160. *Hir.* GS., I, 29, 2, p. 57, II. 6–7.
161. *Op. cit.*
162. *Baudh.* GS., I, 18, 2, p. 220, II. 4–6.
163. For the *Mantras,* RV., I, 114, 7–8.
164. Ādityadarśana on *Kāth.* GS., I, 10, p. 223. I. 22; cf. *Brahmabala on op. cit.* 51.13, p. 228, 1. 3f.
165. See Pasuyaga, supra.
166. Brahmabala on *Kāth.* GS., 51, 13. p. 230, 1. 12.
167. Ādityadarśana on *Kāth.* GS., 52, 6, p. 232, II. 19 f. cf. *Baudha.* GS., II, 7, 10, p. 51, I. 17.
168. II, 9. p. 40, I. 14.
169. II, 8, 7, p. 70. 1. 19.
170. III, 8, 10, p. 342, Bom. Ed.
171. II, 9, p. 71.
172. Vol. II, p. 914 f.
173. *Sāṇ.*, GS., IV, 19.
174. *Gobh.*GS., III, 7, 3; Āśv. GS., II, I. 15; *Saṃ.* GS., IV, 15;11, 14, 9; Āp. GS., XVIII, 5 f.; *Hir.* GS., II, 16; Man.GS., II, 16, *Bhār.* GS., II, 1; etc.
175. The modern Manasā-pujā of Bengal seems to be a prototype of this rite.
176. According to Śāṇkhāyana. IV, 15, 19–20.
177. Recorded by Pāraskara alone, II, 15.
178. Āśv. GS., II, 2, 1; *Sāṇ.*, GS., IV, 16; *Pār.* GS., II, 16; *Gobh.* GS., III, 8, 1–8; *Khād.* GS., III. 3, 1. This rite seems to be the older form of the Aśmikumāra Vrata in which the mothers wait so

expectantly for the return of the sons away from home.

179. Āśvalāyana prescribes the 14th day as an alternative.
180. *Gobh.* GS., III, 9; Āśv. GS., II, 3; *Sāṇ.*, GS, IV, 17; *Pār.* GS., III, 2; Āp. GS., XIX, 3; *Bhār.* GS.. II, 2; Mān. GS. II, 7, 1–5, *Hir.* GS., II, 17. This is as the name denotes, the festival of the beginning of the New Year.
181. III, 9. 17; cf. *Drah.* GS., III, 3. 22. See the commentary on *Gobh.* for the arrangement of all others.
182. XIX, 8.
183. *Mantra, Vāj. Saṃ.*, XXXV, 21.
184. *Pār.* G.S., III, 6, 6f., p. 318. Bom. Ed.; cf. the various commentaries; Karka, p. 320, 1.4 f.; *Harihara,* p. 320. I. 32 f.; etc.
185. *Srāddha-kriyā*-kaumudi, p. 96; *Srāddha-maṇjari.* p. 6. II. 23-24; according to the Maṇjarikāra she is to cook if her husband is unable to do so; *Pār.* GS., p. 464, 17.
186. *Srāddha-kriyā-kaumudi, op. cit.,* I.
187. *Op. cit.,* I.
188. *Pār.* GS., 442, I. 4.
189. *Padmapurāna*, bhūmi-khaṇḍa, p. 222, II. I. f., particularly ślokas 20 ff., "Ami pitāmahās caura yaīś ca bhuktam taya vinā." etc.
190. Padmapurāna, bhumi-khanda, *op. cit.*, "Bhāryā pacati ced annam svahastenāmṛtopamam tad annam eva bhuṇjanti-pitaro hṛsṭamānasāḥ. Tenaiva tṛptim āyānti santuśṭāś ca bhavanti te," etc. Also *Pār.* GS., p. 470, I. 37; 71, I.r.
191. Drah. G.S., III 4, 8; Khā. GS., p. 109. 1.7–9; Gobh. GS., III, 10. 27, p. 177 (2nd part). For the fourteen apertures, see *Gobh.* GS., p. 177, 1.7.
192. Cf. Commentary, 'Ca-śabdat prakrta patni,' p. 207 of Gobh. GS., Vol. II, II. 2–3.
193. But see Gobh. GS., IV, 2, 29. Comm., Vol. II, p. 206 "Sthagaraṃ candanā-digandhadravyam."
194. According to the commentator this kind of collyrium is known as Sauvirāñjana.
195. *Tait. Saṃh.,* 1, 8, 5 (K).
196. Groten, *Christian Eucharist,* pp. 30 f. and 162 ff.
197. Baudh. *ŚS.*, VII, 15. p. 225; VIII, 4, p. 240; *Kāt. ŚS.*, Chow. Ed., p. 552 "Patni ca anyar, etc."
198. *Pār.* GS., II, 9. 14, p. 262, Bom. Ed, of the various commentaries.
199. "*Srāddha-tattava* of Raghunandana", Hṛṣikeśa Sāstrin's ed., Calcutta, 1909-10.

Abbreviations

Ait.Bra.	= *Āpastamba-brāhmaṇa*
Ap.GS.	= *Āpastamba-gṛhya-sūtra.*
Āp.ŝS.	= *Āpastamba-śrauta-sūtra.*
Āśv.GS.	= *Āśvalāyana-gṛhya-sūtra.*
ĀśŝS.	= *Āśvalāyana-śrauta-sūtra..*
AV.	= *Atharva-veda.*
*Baudh.*GS.	= *Baudhāyana-gṛhya-sūtra.*
*Baudh.*ŝS.	= *Bhāradvāja-gṛhya-sūtra.*
*Bhār.*GS.	= *Bhāradvāja-gṛhya-sūtra.*
Bib.Ind.	= *Bibliotheca Indica.*
*Drah.*GS.	= *Drāhyāyaṇa-gṛhya-sūtra.* [same as Khā.GS.].
*Gobh.*GS.	= *Gobhila-gṛhya-sūtra.*
Htr.GS.	= *Hiraṇyakeśi-gṛhya-sūtra.*
Hir.ŝS.	= *Hiraṇyakeśi-śrauta-sūtra.* [same as *Satyāśāḍha śrauta sūtra.*]
Jaim.GS.	= *Jaiminiya-gṛhya-sūtra.*
Jaim. Brā.	= *Jaiminiya-brāhmaṇa.*
Kap.Samh.	= *Kapiṣṭhala-saṃhitā.*
Kāṭh.GS.	= *Kāṭhaka-gṛhya-sūtra.*
Kāṭh.Saṃh.	= *Kāṭhaka-saṃhitā.*
Kāt.S.	= *Kātyāyana-śrauta-sūtra.*
Kbā.GS.	= *Khādira-gṛhya-sūtra.* [same as *Drah.*GS.].
Lāṭ.ŝS.	= *Lāṭyāyana-śrauta-sūtra.*
Mait.Saṃh.	= *Maitrāyaṇi-saṃhitā.*
Man.GS.	= *Mānava-gṛhya-sūtra.*
Mān.ŚS.	= *Mānava-śrauta-sūtra.*
Pār. GS.	= *Pāraskara-gṛhya-sūtra.*
RV.	= *Rigveda.*
Saṃs.RM.	= Samskara-ratna-*mālā.*
Sāṇ.GS.	= *Sāṇkhāyana-gṛhya-sūtra.*
Sāṇ.ŝS.	= *Sāṇkhāyana-śrauta-sūtra.*
Śat.Brā.	= *Śata-patha-brāhmaṇa.*
Sat.ŝS.	= *Satyāśāḍha-śrauta-sūtra.*
Smṛ.Sam.	= *Smṛtināṃ samuccayaḥ.*
Tait.Samh.	= *Taittiriya-saṃhitā.*
Ona.Saṃh.	= *Ona-viṃśati-saṃhitā.*
Vaik.GS.	= *Vaikhānasa-gṛhya-sūtra.*
Vait.S.	= *Vaitāna-sūtra.*
Vāj.Saṃh.	= *Vājasaneyi-saṃhitā.*
Var.GS.	= *Vārāha-gṛhya-sūtra.*
Yājñ.Sm.	= *Yājñavalkya-smṛti.*

2

The *Mahabharata* Women

The epic *Mahabharata* had three major female characters, namely, Gandhari, Kunti and Draupadi. All the three women were royal, extraordinarily beautiful and had very strong character.

Gandhari was the principal female character from the side of the *Kauravas.* Bhisma selected her to be married to Dhratarastra because she had obtained the boon to have hundred sons. When Gandhari came to know about Dhrtarastra's blindness she took a piece of silk, folded it a number of times and tied it around her eyes. Thereby abviating the possibility of her being superior to her handicapped husband. By her good conduct Gandhari pleased her husband's family for she completely identified herself with her role as a wife.

Gandhari was a farsighted and impartial woman and kept herself aloof from the selfish ways of her sons. She continually warned Dhratarastra not to plunge his family into misfortune by being unduly partial to his sons.

Dhratarastra did not listen to her warnings but when Duryodhana refused to give the kingdom back to *Pandavas* after the stipulated period of living in the forests was over, Dhratarastra tried to be persuade him to return to the *Pandavas* their rightful property. When he failed, he requested Gandhari to persuade him.

Gandhari highlighted the destructions and devastation created by wars and warned Duryodhana that one is never sure of victory in them.

Despite Gandhari's entreaties Duryodhana carried on his objective of robbing the *Pandavas* of their rightful share in the kingdom thus paving the way for the great war in which all the *Kauravas* were killed. Gandhari was a helpless witness of all the destruction. Gandhari emerges as a woman of wisdom, clarity of thought and righteousness. But all these qualities in her character did not stop her sons to take a more reasonable course of action or her own brother from giving vicious advice to her sons. Thereby demonstrating the insignificant position the women of that time had in decision making.

Despite her great sorrow Gandhari had enough detachment to understand that *Pandavas* could not be blamed for the death of her sons. However she did feel infuriated by the fact that Bhim killed Duryodhana unlawfully by hitting him on his thighs.

Despite this anger Gandhari was not a vindictive person with Yudhisthira's care and affection the old king and queen were finally freed of their rancour for the *Pandavas.*

Kunti was the daughter of Surasena and was the sister of Vasudeva but was adopted by his cousin Kuntibhoja when young. She was a girl of unparalleled beauty. Her father arranged a *svayamvara* for her in which she chose Pandu. Kunti was granted by the sage Durvasa which enabled her to have a son from whichever God she propitiated. While still a maiden she invoked the God simply out of an adolescent girl's curiosity but was overcome with fear when the God arrived and requested him to go back. But Kunti relented when he threatened to curse her if she did not accept to unite with him; as a result a son was born. Afraid of the social stigma of being an unwed mother she put the baby in a basket and floated it in a river. Shortly after her marriage Pandu was cursed by a sage that he would die if he had any sexual contact with a woman. Kunti invoked the Gods *Indra, Vayu* and *Dharma* and had three sons from them. On Pandu's request she gave the *mantra* to Madri who had two sons by invoking the twins Aswani Kumari. This practice of having pregnancy from another male when the husband was either dead or important is accepted in the *Dharmasastras*.

Kunti and the five princes were brought to Hastinapur after the death of Pandu and Madri. The princes got their education in Hastinapur. Kunti saw her illegitimate son Karna challenging Arjuna in a contest. The declaration of Kripacarya averted the duel but permanently injured and humiliated Karna by asking Karna to inform the assembly about his parentage. Kunti let Karna suffer humiliation for fear of the social disapproval but did not own him in public.

Kunti's conduct reveals both the prevalent values of the times as well as her own cowardice in owning her past. The guilt stayed with her almost till the end but she had a tremendous sense of practical attitude. This is evident when she proposed to Karna to join *Pandavas* before the war as he was their brother. Furthermore, we get a glimpse of her practical thinking when she invited a *Bhil* women with five sons to dinner at her house during *Varnavata*. The *Bhil* women with her five sons died in the fire while people thought the bodies to be of Kunti and five *Pandavas.* Kunti's matter of fact attitude was again manifested when she allowed Hidimba to marry Bhim and stay with him till a son was born.

Another instance of her grateful practicality is when Kunti's decided to send Bhima to confront the demon Baka when they were living with a *Brahman* family. She had seen the strength of Bhima and by sending him alongwith the food for the demon she felt she could both repay the debt of the *Brahman* family as well as free the people of the menace of the demon.

Despite being married to a king, on more than one occasion Kunti had to suffer the insecurity of being rendered homeless.

Kunti was overwhelmed with anguish when *Pandavas* alongwith Draupadi were banished to the woods for fourteen years. She felt envious of Madri who had not had the occasion of witnessing this misfortune of her sons. She felt disgusted with her attachment to life and wished that she were dead.

Kunti asked Krishna to tell Yudhisthira to follow his *dharma* as a *Kshatriya* and prepare for the war. She reminded him and his brothers of the great humiliation of Draupadi in the *Kaurava* court and held that as the major reason for them to fight back.

Kunti's entreaties to Yudhisthira to fight and get back his lost kingdom were not born of any selfish motive because after the war she retreated into the forest with Gandhari and Dhrtarastra. She wanted them to fight back and get their kingdom because they had become disheartened and passive by suffering so many pains and they had also fallen into ill repute. Once she had seen that Yudhisthira regained his lost glory she retreated into the forest to do penance in order to join her husband's realm. This was the essential goal of her earthly existence.

Draupadi, as the legend about her birth says came out from the sacrificial fire.

She had an irresistible charm and an extraordinary beauty.

In *Mahabharata* one finds interesting mythical justifications for Draupadi's polyandrous marriage to the *Pandavas.* These may have been to appease the dissenting voices towards polyandry. According to the story of her past life, Draupadi was given a boon by Lord Siva for five husbands. But she wanted only one husband to which Siva replied that since she had asked for a husband five times, so in her next life she will have five husbands. In her next birth Draupadi married all the *Pandavas* one by one.

Draupadi lived for one year with one *Pandava*. The second year with the second *Pandava* and so on. This rule was made by *Pandavas* to avoid discord and heartburning amongst them. Despite this Draupadi is said to have a greater love for Arjuna. This was never shown in her apparent behaviour but in their last heavenward journey she falls on the way and Yudhisthira associates her fall with her greater attachment towards Arjuna. She seemed to love each one of the *Pandavas* for different reasons. She said to *Satyabhama* that she neither sleeps nor eats before her husbands. She never does anything contrary to their wishes.

Draupadi stayed in the forest with her husbands and suffered all the misfortunes while all the other *Pandava* queens stayed with their parents. In the forest she was abducted by Jaidratha, and during the *Agyatvasa* she was harrassed and humiliated by *Kicaka*. All these men who humiliated her like Duryodhana, Karna, etc., had actually an overwhelming desire for her. Despite all these men hovering around her Draupadi had no interest in them because she was truly devoted to the *Pandavas.*

Besides being adept at household work Draupadi was well versed in many aspects of social life. In Vanaparva she talks of *Brahaspati's niti* in detail with Yudhisthira which she says she learnt from a learned *Brahmin* who taught it to her brothers.

In the *Vanaparva* Draupadi has long arguments with Yudhisthira urging him to fight back and win his kingdom. In one of these arguments the complex problem of desting and individual effort is discussed. Only an intellectually developed person can argue like this. Her acumen in logical thinking and presence of mind become obvious from the way she questions people in Dhratarastra's court about the justification of putting her to stake when Yudhisthira himself was lost. One is surprised to see that inspite of her intellectual equality to men there is a certain amount of helplessness and vulnerability in Draupadi's demeanour. This helplessness did not seem to come from her lack of self assurance but it appears to be due to the way women were treated in those times. That reveals clearly the low status of women in general during that time. There are a number of references of women servants being gifted alongwith wedding dowries. Women seemed to be easy prey to all kinds of sexual assault.

It is clearly shown by the lives of the three female characters the societal pressure on women to treat marriage and their marital identity as their sole characterization. The epitome of chastity lay in unquestioning fidelity. Gandhari willfully became a disabled equal to her husband. *Madri* expressed her fidelity by dying with her husband. Kunti by raising her children—the living momentous of her husband and finally retreating into the woods to do penance in order to join him. Draupadi achieved the same objective by her unflinching service of all her five husband and by giving up all royal comforts.

Manu's injunction that women ought to be protected first by this fathers, then husbands and finally by sons seems to be generally followed in the *Mahabharata.* Since women were not considered independent, their primary fulfilment was in marriage.

For women there is no *yajna,* no *sradha* and no provision of fasts. Their service of their husbands takes them to heaven.

There are many places where the miseries of widowhood are highlighted. One major reason looks to be widow's vulnerability to sexual assault. In the *Sambhavaparva* there is a *sloka* which epitomizes the plight of widows.

At the time of *Mahabharata* women were held to be fragile and vulnerable to male assaults and thus constantly in need of male protection either by their fathers, husbands, sons or disciples of their husbands. It was held that the need for them is even greater because of their built in licentiousness. They can easily be seduced because they have an inherent weakness for sex. And this licentiousness of women acts like a double-edged sword, it brings them to ruin by impelling them to have socially undesirable liasions and also destroys the austerity and spiritual merit of saints who get seduced by their enticing presence.

It is interesting to note that there is strong emphasis on the glory associated with motherhood.

The belief in the restorative quality of motherhood becomes obvious if we look at the female deities of India. The two goddesses that embody themselves in human form and become an indemic part of the drama the *Mahabharata* are Ganga and Durga. The story of Ganga's descent on earth is rendered in all its details in the *Vanaparva*. In her human form she is the bewitching female who entices Santanu to marry her but she is also the devouring female who submerges into her own waters her seven sons. The characterizataion of the destructive and rejuvenating mother is beautifully impersonated in the river-female character of Ganga.

The other feminine deity which gets embodied in a human form in the Mahabharata is Durga. Appearing in the form of Nanda's daughter who is exchanged for Krishna by Vasudeva she has a very brief appearance in the Mahabharata. She is killed immediately after Kansa is informed about her birth. She appears in her celestial form and informs Kansa about his impending death at the hands of Krishna.

Yudhisthira calls her the pure feminine form on this earth. Praying to Durga, Yudhisthira asks for her protection. There is a similar invocation of Durga by Arjuna in the beginning of war. He too addresses her as the sister of Krishna and the daughter of Nandagopal and wielder of sword, shield and spear. She is the killer of Mahisasura and is the rescuer of all living beings.

These two mutually opposed images of femininity emerge in the world of *Mahabharata.* On the one hand, we find the helpless female and on the other she is all powerful and destructive female. One may justify by saying that while the human female is helpless, the divine one is all powerful. But even that is not so. For the divine realm contains the same opposition. While *Parvati, Laksmi* and *Sarasvati* seem to be emulating the mundane paradigm of female docility and submission, Kali and Durga in their varied manifestations embody the destructive and domineering female. The only explanation seems to be in terms of the deep-seated fear and comfort the human infant feels in the hands of his mother. For she appears both comforting and capable of punishing. Thus the visualization of a feminine deity answers the primordial longing of human beings to be under the care of an all powerful mother.

The complex attitudes of love-hate and reverence that we find woven in the text of Mahabharata seem to embody the perennial paradoxes of human existence in the male-centric weltanschuung. Women are both revered and hated, they wield power over men by their seductive charm and are vulnerable because of their physical fragility. Perhaps it is because of these twin characteristics that the *Dharmasastras* enjoin them to be kept under male tutelage. One can hardly deny that this a typically male view of women. In a society where men and women be equals perhaps the *Dharmasastras* would be written in a new light.

3

The Marriage System

Everywhere in India (with the exception of matrilineal groups like the Nairs) marriage creates ties for a bride which are as blinding on her as the ties of blood. After getting married she becomes incorporated into the husband's group. The son-in-law has a special position in his wife's household where he is treated as a privileged guest. A girl in India is obliged to love and honour her husband's relatives in much the same way as she is obliged to love and honour her husband's relatives in much the same way as she is obliged to love and honour own parents.

We find the marriage age of girls is varying in different times on account of certain definite views and circumstances prevailing in them.

Girls were married at a fairly advanced age in the *Vedic* period. The very term for marriage, presupposes a post-puberty marriage, for it shows that immediately after her marriage, the bride went to her husband's house to live as his wife. A perusal of the marriage hymn shows that the bride was fully mature and quite grown up at the time of the marriage. She is expressely described as blooming with youth and pining for a husband.

The *Grihya Sūtra* literature composed at about 5 century B.C. lays down that the consummation of the marriage should take place on the fourth day. *Chaturthīkarma,* 'the event of the fourth day', long continued to be the technical name for the ritual prescribed at the consummation of the marriage. Some Grihya Sūtras also provide for contingency of the bride being in her monthly course during the marriage ceremony.

The evidence from the epics and the Buddhist literature also shows that down to about 400 B.C. brides in cultured families used to be about 16 at the time of their marriage. They are often described as eagerly pining for being united with a mate. Nuns like Visākhā and Kuṇḍalakesā, who had entered the nunnery before their marriage, are represented as being either of the age of 16 or of the age of discretion when their marriages were being contemplated. Brides in the Jātakas are also usually seen to be grown up. We often come across love affairs; thus in one place we find a maiden named Paṭāchārā eloping with her lover, because her parents would not sanction her contemplated marriage. Sītā, Kuntī and Draupadī were fully grown up at the time of their marriages, which were consummated immediately.

Marriages at a lower age began to be advocated from about the 4th century B.C. The writers of the *Dharamsūtras,* who flourished from c. 400 B.C. to c. 100 A.D., began to observe that marriages of girls should not be delayed long after their puberty.

It is necessary to point out that even those, who allowed a short period of three months after puberty, do not shower any curses upon the guardians, if they fail to perform the, marriages within the ninety days period of grace. Manu, who normally contemplates a pre-puberty marriage, goes to the extent of permitting the father to keep the daughter unmarried even to her life's end, if a suitable husband cannot be found.

We may therefore conclude that during the period 400 B.C. to 100 A.D. the marriageable age of girls was lowered and the tendency on the whole was to perform it at about the time of puberty. There was, however, no uniformity in practice in society. The Kāmasūtra, which belongs to the end of this period, presupposes the existence of both the post-puberty and pre-puberty marriages stories. The stories in the Kathāsaritsāgara, which depict the social life of about this time, refer both to child marriages arranged by parents and love marriages arranged by the parties themselves.

Soon after 100 A.D. society definitely veered round to pre-puberty marriages. An undue premium came to be placed upon absolute chastity; in order to prevent the theoretical possibility of unchastity even in 0.01 per cent of brides, it decreed that marriages should always be performed before puberty. Society was anxious that there should be no room whatsoever even for the possibility of any reports arising reflecting upon the character of maidens. At about this time *Upanayana* of girls came to an end and they had to follow no course of education worth the name. Parents must have felt that since girls were not preoccupied with completing any educational course, it would be desirable to get them married soon after, or at about the time of their puberty.

From about 200 A.D. pre-puberty marriages became the order of the day. Vājnavalkya, who wrote at about this time, insists that girls should be married before the age of puberty; otherwise every month guardians will be guilty of the destruction of an embryo. Yama, who came about 400 years later, states that even if a suitable match is impossible, the girl should be married before she comes of age even to an unsuitable husband. What a difference between the views of Manu and Yama! The former was willing to allow a girl to remain unmarried even to the end of her life, if a proper husband could not be secured. The latter did not mind a girl being chained to an unsuitable and undeserving husband for her whole life, if there was the least danger of fateful line of the age of puberty being crossed.

It was not always possible to celebrate a marriage in every case just at the time of puberty. If it was postponed to the last moment, there was the danger of crossing the puberty limit. No content therefore with prohibiting post-puberty marriages, *Smriti* writers of the period 500–1000 A.D. began to encourage marriages *much before* the time of puberty. They held that a girl should be regarded as having attained puberty at the age of 10, and therefore her marriage should not be postponed beyond that age. At this time the ritual of marriage of girls was regarded as corresponding to that of *upanayana* of boys; if the 8th year was the proper time for the latter it ought to be the ideal time for the former also. A girl of 8 was Gaurī and was therefore the most suitable one for marriage.

Vedic marriage mythology referred to Soma, Gandharva and Agni as the earlier divine husbands of the bride; her human husband was the fourth one. Writers of this period began to advocate the view that the different divine husbands get jurisdiction over the girl when different signs of impending puberty manifest themselves at different ages. They pointed out that one should forestall them all by marrying the girl at the age of 8.

Post-puberty marriages continued as local customs in areas that were under the influence of the old pre-Aryan culture. This, for example, is the case in Malabar even at the present day. A 15th century commentator observes that among the people of this province, the attainment of puberty before the marriage is not regarded as blemish. The influence of the matriarchate is responsible for Malbar's bold stand against child marriages.

In the course of time the advocates of pre-puberty marriages did not remain content with the girl's marriage at 8 or 9. There was an extreme section among them that clamoured for a still lower age. It is represented in *Brahma Purāna,* which recommends that a girl should be married at any time after the age of 4.

The anology of *upanayana* was also utilized for lowering the marriage age to this ridiculous extent. Parents anxious to ensure a rapid progress of their sons in education were advised to perform their *upanayana* rather at the age of 5 than at the age of 8. Marriage was the substitute for *upanayana* in the case of girls, and so it also could be performed the same age.

It may, however, be pointed out that the extreme views above referred to did not become popular for a long time. During the 11th century A.D. we learn from *Alberuni* that the normal age of a Brāhmana bride was 12 (II, p. 131). The ramification of the caste system into hundreds of sub-castes and the prohibition of intermarriages among them about the 8th or the 9th century A.D. further accentuated the evil of a child marriages. Parents did not like to take the risk of losing a good bridegroom by postponing the marriage to a later date. Paradoxical though it may appear, it seems that the popularity which the *Satī* custom acquired at this time helped the cause of early marriages. If the father died and the mother followed him on his funeral pyre, there would be a father-in-law at least to look after the young orphans if they were already married. The joint family system prevailing in society was also favourable for early marriages. Marriages could be performed long before the husband became an earning member because his parents, uncles or elder brothers used to take care of his wife and children till the time he began to earn. The economic conditions of the country were fairly satisfactory and they did not necessitate the postponement of marriages to the time when the husband became an earning member. Naturally, therefore society became more and more conscious of the advantages of early marriages and oblivious to their drawbacks. It further found that child marriages gave a good opportunity to the bride to know gradually the natures and idiosyncrasies of different members of her new household, to note almost imperceptibly the likes and dislikes of her husband, and to entertain an affection for him before the sex instinct had been aroused. There was further no chance of any scandals arising, as was admittedly the case in the earlier era of post-puberty marriages. Nor need the parents entertain any apprehensions of a daughter slipping into a nunnery against their wishes.

With the introduction of western ideas and civilisation, the advanced sections of society began to feel the necessity of deferring the marriages to a more advanced age. Social conferences began to advocate the cause of post-puberty marriages during the nineties of the last century, but their efforts did not bear much fruit till the beginning of the 20th century. The gradual disruption of the joint family system, the progressive realisation of the usefulness of female education, and, above all, the hard necessities of the economic struggle for existence have now induced the advanced sections to throw overboard the *Smriti* injunctions and to openly adopt post-puberty marriages. If, on account of economic factors, bridegrooms find it difficult to marry before the age of 24 or 25, naturally their partners in life have to be at least 16 or 17 at the time of the marriage.

In accepting and following the theory of post-puberty marriages, Hindu society is merely returning to the old custom of the Vedic and epic times. It need not therefore be regarded as anti-religious at all. The main reason that was responsible for popularizing post-puberty marriages in the early period of Hindu history was the great concern which society felt over the question of girls' education. Precisely the same is now helping the cause of post-puberty marriages. In the past a few ladies known as Brahmavādinīs used to remain forever unmarried as they were anxious to devote themselves entirely to the cause of education and social service. The Servants of Women Society of Poona has laid it down that its members shall remain unmarried, so that they should find it possible to devote themselves wholely and solely to the cause of their Society.

Sitting through the changes in the laws. Pertaining to marriage in India from time immemorial the arranged marriage forges ahead, with slight adjustments, not pretending to keep step with the developments in the world at large. The reputation of a child is not to be smirched by allowing her to be a free object in the matrimonial market, to provide her with a match most suited to her needs, and to leave her free from the embarrassment, inconvenience, and cost of unaided personal choice of a mate.

There are parts of India where the choice of mate for a daughter is left to her father, grandfather and/or uncles, and the boy or boys are 'viewed' by the male members of the family. The boy's family are barely allowed to see the favoured girl, and even after the betrothal is arranged the people do not communicate with each other. The size of the dowry or equivalent benefits, offered to their family and to the bridegroom, will be a principal consideration. The desire to marry off the daughter lies heavily on her family, and induces the father to promise much, especially when he aims to improve his social position by marrying this particular daughter into a higher grade of the same subcaste, and particularly when available sons in such grades are few in number. Apart from these uncomfortable considerations there are the unfortunate situations of girls who are deformed, very dark in complexion, of poor intelligence, or in bad health, girls who are ill-favoured, and who would, in any other civilization, be regarded as unmarriageable, or unfit for marriage. These can be married off by traditional methods, which resort, alas, to fraud and impersonation, if no other means can be avalied of.

Since the arranged marriage is traditional, what the great sages of India had to say on this subject has to be taken into account. The traditional ideas of the people are often enshrined in the old *Dharmasastra* texts.

Arranged Marriage in Dharamasastra

Most allegations of mismanagement of betrothals arise on the part of the bridegroom or his family and are directed against the bride, or rather, through her, at her parents or guardians. Therefore the natural place to look in that part is the *sāstra* which deals with faults in contracts. Since most marriages between *Brahmins,* and indeed many others, took the form of a gift, viz., the gift of a virgin *(Kanyādāna)* there were, and remain, some hesitations in inspecting the object of the gift very closely. In a period in which polygamy was legal an unsatisfactory girl could be superseded. Nevertheless marriage was (as in many quarters it still is) a means of securing the ritual and class standing of the two families, and the breakdown of a marriage, and its nullification, would damage the prestige of both parties severely.

It was because of this that the *dharmasāstra* approached our problem from two different but interlocking points of view. On the one hand the precepts relating to marriage set out in great detail the *qualities* requisite in a spouse, the qualities of the bride and the qualities of the groom. It is very noticeable that the list of qualities requisite in the groom, though every one is rational and could be accepted today without hesitation, is shorter than the list of qualities to be sought in the bride.

When one seeks for a bride for one's son, one tries, as best one can, to check off a long list of *laksanas,* the family background, reputation, looks, intelligence, age, etc. The *dharmasāstra,* with its acent on righteousness, protects the girl.

Two different types of fraud had to be considered : (i) impersonation, i.e., a faultless girl was shown to the groom's party at the betrothal negotiations, but a faulty one, or inadequate one, was substituted at the marriage-ceremony (ii) the deceit constituted by, (a) representation that the girl was free form fault, or (b) silence as to a fault in her which was known to the guardians.

Impersonation

Impersonation of the groom seems never to have concerned anyone. It was a question of playing off inferior (e.g. ugly. or older) bride on the groom and his family in place of a more presentable who was introduced at the stage of the betrothal.

In cases where the groom's family had delivered, or were due to deliver a fee or honorarium, the fraud was punished by depriving the bride's family of the fee they would expect for the girl originally presented for inspection. Annulment of the marriage was not considered. This is because the *samskara* of marriage has been undergone by the spouses and the deceit is discovered afterwards. Commentary is interesting. In Bhāruci's view this rule applies only where the girl actually given in the ceremony is defective. If she will 'do', as it were, the right to adjustment of the drastic type indicated did not arise.

Misrepresentation

The guardians of the girl clare to the groom's party the faults known to them, and a warranty of freedom from undisclosed faults was implied in the betrothal contract. A breach of this warranty would cause punishment. The deceived party therefore had the way paved for him to cause the bride's family to repent of their breach of the requirements of righteousness.

In the case of those whose hand-clasping ceremony is completed, revocation is legitimate on discovery of a fault relating to bed-worthiness. But this does not apply where they have produced a child. For giving a maiden in marriage without disclosing the maiden's fault relating to bed-worthiness the fine is there and the (compulsory) return of *shulka* (bride price) and/or *strīdhana* (bride-wealth). Or, for the suitor marrying without disclosing a fault on the groom's part, the fine is *double,* apart from the loss of (any) *sulka* (he may have paid) and/or *strīdhana* (he may have received).' The *dharmasāstra* amended this presentation by ignoring misrepresentation on the part of or relating to the groom, and by expanding the list of *dosas,* which are by no means confined to bedworthiness.

In all cases the gift is void *(dattā'pyadatta)* and the punishment depends upon whether the giver knowingly omitted to reveal the fault or not. If he did it knowingly he must suffer the penalty of theft, if not he is liable to the fine.

One who abandons a wife without fault is punishable; and one and who falsely imputes a fault is to be fined, 73. *Visvarúpa* is careful to imply that the guardian is liable to fine only when he fails to disclose an obvious fault, perhaps in order to obtain a better son-in-law that could obtained if one disclosed the fault. There is no suggestion in our sources that the guardian is absolutely liable, e.g., in respect of faults unknown to him.

The *dosas* of the maiden are those listed by Nārada, or by Sumantu, who says, plainly, that a girl should be abandoned if she is despised (or reviled), her behavior suggests the functions of a different caste, or overcome with disease, if she has been married but the female organ has not been penetrated. Aparāka correctly adds that if in fact she has lost her virginity consequent on marriage she must be maintained, and looked after. There is no question of nullity in such cases. In Aparāka's time girls who were found to be faulty, and whose faults had been disclosed, could be returned whence they came so long as their virginity was not lost (through the act of the husband). If the girl could be returned no fine was to be levied : the guardians had been sufficiently punished, the deterrent was adequate.

Bhāruci comments that the *dosa* must relate to a disease interfering with performance of *dharma* or the birth of children, or to her having had intercourse. He thus narrows down the grounds for the penalty severely.

If a man marries a girl without proclaiming his own defects, his suit must be lost (because of the basic principle that betrothals can be broken off by either side when a fault is discovered before the *samskāra* and he does not acquire that gift (of the maiden); similarly with a fault on the part of the maiden : the giver is punishable and the groom likewise' : this late text is strong in attacking fraud in betrothals, whether on the boy's side or the girl's, but it is obvious that it can hardly ever be in the girl's family's interest to have the marriage annulled and the groom fined.

The two *sāstras* leave us in no doubt that, whether or not nullity was available, in all stages of history for all cases of fraud, the latter was viewed solely from the angle of failure to perform the duty of disclosure. Betrothals were what we could call contracts and the duty of disclosure lay squarely on the guardians of the girl. Modern judges would be entitled to view contemporary fraud cases in this light. The guardians cannot be exonerated by silence concerning that which is specially within their own knowledge. No doubt they are not to be penalised in respect of what they could not know. Furthermore, the traditional learning regarded that silence is a criminal offence. A girl was to be protected against injury to her 'education, and likewise a boy was to be protected against the injury of have in a defective girl blamed off on him.

A severe deterrent is called for, especially since polygamors unions cannot be said to be practicable for the greater part of the population.

4

Marital Status

The wives other than the first had no right to participate in those rites which are meant for Supreme Bliss. They were, however, allowed to participate in those acts which are considered as Saṃskāras, and those which are meant only for earthly bliss *(ārād upakāraka)*.

On the New and Full Moon sacrifices[1] all the wives of the sacrificer are either girded by the Agnīdhra priest, or they gird themselves.[2] They sit either to the north of the Garhapatya[3] or to the south-west[4] with bent or raised knees. A triple cord of Munja is put round their waist, either outside or inside the garment.[5]

The Agnīdhra priest is to wind the cord round their waist from left to right and having fixed the southern end by twice twisting round the northern one, he draws the southern end to the encircling cord upwards so that it may hang down.

Then the wives worship *Agni Gṛhapati* and *Devānāṃ patniḥ*. They do so first silently and then again with the *mantra.*[6] They sit there till the unloosening of the girdle.

At the end of the sacrifice the grass cords of the wives are to be united. Then the wives themselves unite the gross-cords. The united cords[7] are placed on the hands of the wives and some Kusa grasses are placed on them. A pitcher full of water is placed in front of the wives. Now water is poured on the grasses and the cord after which they place the grasses within the thighs.[8] They wash their mouths with the water from the pitcher[9] and pray for cattle, children, etc.[10] Then they worship Agni Garhapatya which is the final rite.[11]

After the husband and the chief wife have offered oblations with the Karambha-patra, all the wives unite their grass-cords.[12] They all go now for the Avaghṛtha (final bath). They have baths, but do not put their heads under water; they simply pour water on their heads.[13] The spouces should repair to some quiet part of flowing water and take a bath in the above manner. The chief wife and the sacrificer should wash the backs of each other and most probably, the other co-wives might help one another in washing their backs.

During the consecration for a religious ceremony (Dīkṣā) they all wear on their heads nets made of thin silken thread or of wool collected from living rams or, at least, a net made of Kusha grass;[14] these should hang on both sides of their head.[15] They are consecrated on their own seats with upper silken garments that are slightly washed, new, white, with skirts and used by nobody else. The Pratiprasthātṛ anoints and decorates them with out mantras.[16] The sacrificer is made to wear a girdle; they tie ploughnooses.[17]

The nets are closely fitted in so that there may not be any chance of their loosening or failing down.[18] The *Pratiprasthātr* fastens pegs in the skirts of their clothes in order that they may scratch their skin, if required, with them.[19] They should not take meat and honey, nor do any impure act.[20]

The pegs that were fastened to their skirts during the Dīkśā should now be silently thrown to the Cātvāla when they all together with the sacrificer and the priests are about to go for the final bath called *Avabhṛtha.*[21]

During the Avabhṛtha they also participate with others in the concluding passage called Nidhana sung in chorus three times.[22] When the water comes to their sight, they pray to Varuṇa for overcoming the enmity and removing the sins they have committed.[23] After the bath they wear the Paryāṇahanas outer clothes tied round the Soma bundle.[24] While coming back to the sheds by the same way they went, they together with the sacrificer or the priests with Hotṛ at their head are led by the priest called Unnetṛ.[25]

Hot Milk Sacrifices, when the Mahāvīra pot is heated, they all cover their heads, according to the *Satapatha,*[26] for fear of being deprived of eyesight, because the Mahāvīra is the symbol of Aditya,[27] and according to the *Mānava-śrauta-sūtra,*[28] for having children.

Even though they may be very near, they should not look at the Pravargya; they should themselves cover their heads during the preparation. All the wives should observe this injuction, as otherwise it would be prejudicial to their own good; and as, according to the *Mānava-śrauta-sūtra*, this is really a *Strī-sanskāra*. After the Mahāvīra has been revered, their heads are uncovered. They keep on looking at the Mahāvīra pot and pray to Him for cattle and offspring and a safe happy life to themselves as well as to their husband.[29] According to the *Mānava-śrauta-sūtra*,[30] the sacrificer also looks at it alongwith them.

In the *Piṇḍa-pitṛ-yajṇa* the husband gives all the wives portions from the middle cake for having children. They all pray to the ancestors for children adorned with lotus-garlands.[31]

In the Domestic Ritual, the first *Sthālīpāka* is really a part of the marriage ceremony and as such each wife is entitled to perform this rite. Each one should cook at other times, too, in so far as the cooking happens to be a part of any of the strī-*Sanskāra*. The wife takes her meal in the day time together with her husband and avoids meat, etc. During the night she sleeps on the floor and refrains from any impure act. Next day she cleanses thrice the sacrificial place with a duster and thrice all around the fire with water.[32] The husband, after having the paddy washed, spreads the hide of a black deer, places mill-stones thereon and pours some paḍdy into them. She husks the paddy thrice and gets the rice perfectly in order. She washes it thrice and cooks it. While cooking she sprinkles clarified butter upon it by means of the purifying *Kuśa* grass.[33] The husband places this full cooking vessel on the strewn grass. Then she sits to the left of her husband and to the west of the *Gārhapatya* fire, and offers to *Agni* and *Agni Sviśtakṛt*. After the offering the husband does all the cleansing work during this particular occasion, but during the *Pumsavana,* etc., she is required to cleanse the sacrificial staff, etc.[34]

As *Garbhādhāna*[35] is a *Strī-sanskāra*., each wife observes this rite.

The wife on the night chosen for the rite, takes a bath and adorns herself with ornaments, clean clothes and wreaths.[36] The husband pounds the root of the Adhyāṇḍa[37] or the Phalini[38] plant or of the *Aśvagandha*[39] or the *Dūrvā* grass,[40] and drenches some portions of a piece of cloth with the juice of it. When the wife comes, specially decorated for the ceremony, the husband presses out the juice into the right[41] or both[42] the nostrils of the wife.

Agni and *Aditya* are worshipped and during the worship of the latter the wife joins her husband.

On the following day, the *Nāpita-karma*[43] is to be observed. The husband and the wife give the barber rice mixed with milk (rice pudding) and go towards the east or the north of the village. When they come across an Udumbara tree, they walk round it, sprinkle water on it and anoint it with scented things. Having covered it with flowers, they offer the Bali oblation. Then they go down into knee-deep water (in some pond), put fish in an unwashed cloth with the skirts streched towards the bank and ask a *Brahmacārin* to tell what he sees. He replies that he sees sons and cattle. Then they offer these fish as Bali to herons. Now they throw off the flowers, etc., cast off the remnant of food, put off their clothes and hang them on the Udumbara twigs. They take a bath, wash each other's back and swim towards the deep of the water. Having anointed each other and worn red or unwashed clothes, they go home in a carriage or on foot, have a wash, sip water and begin to sleep without a word. Next morning they talk again during the Vaiśvadeva.

It was necessary that the wives who had established śrauta fires to observe the domestic New and Full Moon sacrifices separately,[44] because they agree closely in the deity and other details with those of the śrauta; the only difference is that offerings of peps are substituted for cakes and no offerings to Indra or Mahendra are made.

On each New and Full Moon night they perform these sacrifices together with their husband. They are required to bathe and eat the fast-day food in the afternoon.[45] They prepare a Sthālī-pāka from which the husband offers oblations to the various deities. Then they should, according to Pāraskara,[46] offer the Bali outside the house to the wife, the Man, Age, and the black-toothed white one, the Lord of bad women and those who, dwelling in the village or the forest, allure their offsprings. They then pray for welfare and offspring. Then sleep that night on the ground. They are expected to pass that night with mutual entertainment recounting tales or other discourses. They commit nothing impure on that night. If the husband is on a journey, the chief wife acts as his substitute.[47]

In regard to the seasonal sacrifices, in the event of the absence of the chief wife and the sacrificer even a *Sūdrā* wife is entitled to offer the morning and evening oblations to Serpents in course of the daily observance of the *Srāvana* sacrifice uptill the *Agrahāyaneṣṭi*. So there is no doubt that all other wives are entitled to offer the same in the event of failure of the chief wife. As all the women of the household are allowed to participate in the rite of alighting from the bedstead,[48] there is no doubt that all the wives join in it; they should, with their children on their lap or by their side, sit in accordance with their seniority of the time of marriage one after another next to the chief wife.

If the pregnant wife dies, she should sprinkle with water mixed with cow's urine. When the dead body has been removed to the crematorium, the husband cuts open the child from the left side of her womb; if the child is still alive, he gives it the breast of its mother alongwith the prayer that the breast may be exhaustless, spring of pleasure, wealth-giver; etc.,[49] and puts it in front of the dead mother. He then tries to revert the opened womb to its normal position, at least, to make it as though no operation has been made; anoints it with curd mixed with sacrificial clarified butter; and bathes her with water mixed with mud, ashes, Kuśa and cow's urine. She is now wrapped up in new clothes and cremated.[50]

If the wife dies after child-birth, or during her courses, she should be bathed with water mixed with *Pañcagavya*, covered with a new cloth and cremated in accordance with the usual rites.[51] No sanskāras and such other rites should be performed for a menstruating woman; she should be bathed and cremated after three nights. If she dies in a foreign country and as a consequence, the above-mentioned rites are not performed, her bones are to be collected and purified with Pañcagavya bathing and ceremonially burnt again.[52]

If the wife of a Sāmavedin dies be she the eldest one or any other—she should be cremated with her face downwards.[53] During the collection of her bones, the sprinkling and such other rites should be done with water from an earthen water-vessel.[54]

On the *Śrāddha* days the wives should not have their hair dishevelled, should not cry, laugh or talk for nothing.[55]

As the eating of the cake is not meant for supermundane bliss, all the wives are entitled to partake of the cake or cakes; if there are six, they partake of the middle two.[56] The cake should be divided into as many portions as there are wives and each wife should be given a portion. A wife who is sick, afflicted (with some mishap) or otherwise incapable,[57] should not eat the cake. According to Apastamba, an ill-disposed or evil-hearted wife should also be avoided.[58] If the wives are not desirous of having children, they may not eat the cake.[59]

As the first wife and the husband raise up fires and are really the protectors of them, the husband is not entitled to give up the fires on the death of any other wife than that of the first. In case of the death of the latter, an *Ahitāgni* is to cremate her with fire kindled from a new fire-drill or produced from the either half of a jar heated or the *śrauta* fires.[60] The husband is to relinquish the fires as he offers these to her in her death. The second wife (and naturally the third wife and the following) must not be offered the sacred fires in death; the husband is not entitled to relinquish the *Agnihotra* out of fascination for her in which case he would be considered as the relinquisher of Brahman.[61]

The *Arya-Sūdrā* marriage seems to be a matter of accident.[62] The *Sūdrā* wife seems to have deserved nothing more than a few privileges from the Arya husband, she has no claims in religious matters.[63] It is definitely stated by Manu[64] that she can never be the first wife of an Aryan. Even though married, she simply serves to lead the family of the husband to degradation and the progeny to the status of *Sūdrās*; a Brāhmana is strictly forbidden either to cohabit with or have a child by her.[65] The sacrifice offered by her husband are not acceptable to gods.[66] If he enters her bed immediately after taking a funeral feast, his forefathers will suffer from lying in her Impurities for a month.[67] A *Sūdrā* wife of one belonging to one of higher castes is not entitled to churn the fire.[68] The only instance where a *Sūdrā* wife is allowed to act as a substitute in a rite is the *Srāvaṇa* sacrifice, where in the absence of the chief wife and the sacrificer and all other wives she may offer the daily oblation to snakes.

Despite all these religious incapabilities, the *Sūdrā* woman considers herself fortunate in having an *Aryan* husband.

Polygamy to a certain extent leads to the deterioration in the position of women. This was, however, counterbalanced by polyandry which has been known in ancient, and in a lesser form in modern India.

There are reasons to believe that polyandry existed in ancient India. The ancient Seers would never have mentioned of a common wife of the *Maruts* and of the *Aśvins* if polyandry were unknown or discarded in the society.[69] The case of *Draupadī* in the *Mahābhārata* is well-known.

As the polygamous husband observes religious rites with wife, the polyandrous wife observes them with the eldest husband. The same reasons we have seen in the case of a polygamous husband in connection with the first wife would apply here, too. Polyandry as well as Polygamy deprived a certain number of women as well as men of various religious rights. These twin usages seem to have counter-balanced the effects of each other on the society, and consequently, on the position of women as well as men and, at least, no emphasis can be laid on Polygamy as leading to deterioration in the position of women without any counteraction.

Just as the wife is enjoined to please the husband, the husband is also enjoined to please the wife.[70] Where the wife and the husband are whole heartedly pleased with each other, they acquire the three objects of life (Tri-varga). They must remain satisfied with mutual partnership in all matters; they must not even think of others; for the violation of these rules they incur the same sin and undergo the same punishment without any distinction whatsoever.[71] For grave offences[72] they separate from each other or they may marry again. She may remarry, if her first husband is impotent, outcast or dead or for other (similarly grave) reasons.[73] She or he is to remarry, however, on the fullest knowledge that her or his marriage for the second time cannot be considered as a sacred ceremony (saṃskāra). Even though they remarry another unmarried man or woman, still the marriage cannot be accredited as a saṃskāra as each saṃskāra is to be observed only once in life and her or his marriage ceremony has been completed for ever in the first marriage.

From time immemorial[74] the wife has doubly blest her husband, by procreation as well as by participation in sacrifices. She performs a religious duty by means of procreation. She as well as her husband have been born as owing debts to the gods, to the *Rishis,* to the fathers and to man.[75] In order to liberate themselves from the debt to fathers, they are to marry and have children: the fathers in the other world depend for their continuance on the offerings of their children.[76] The ardent desire for having children for religious purposes has given women an extremely high position.[77] So it is only natural that almost always prays to gods for children.[78] Owing to the urgent necessity of having children, productive unions are always to be effected in rituals so much so that even the vessels, spoons or other sacrificial implements are often imagined as males and females. Progeny is one of the primary objects of performing sacrifices. The wife as the bearer of this highest blessing on earth deserves respect from the husband as well as from the society. The husband is bound to respect her as in her, the Jāyā, he is born again, and as she, offered as great Brilliance to him by the gods and the seers, is his mother again.[79]

If the husband is a widower as well as sonless, the *Sapiṇḍana* may be performed for him by his brothers' sons; otherwise it is wholly omitted. In the same circumstances the *Sapiṇḍana* for the wife, too, may be performed by the sons of her co-wives, otherwise the omission is as inevitable as in the case of the husband. Moreover, the object of the *Sapiṇḍana* is to relieve the mane from the state of a mane, such a state of the wife in the above circumstances will cease because of the performance of other *Srāddhas*.

The woman is always pure.[80] Soma gives them Purity, *Gandharvas* sweet voice, Fire All Purity—as gifts for their enjoyment with her. The women can by no means be contaminated.[81] Whatever be the sin of a wife in the meantime, it is sure to be drained out of her body and she becomes absolutely pure.[82] Her temporary impurity is the cause of all purity.[83] The Brāhmaṇa is pure only in the feet, but the woman is pure in all her limbs.[84] Her mouth is never impure.[85]

The stress laid by the authorities on the ritualistic impurity of women during their monthly course, pregnancy and childbirth is due to their physical incapacity or some other unavoidable cause or causes. The injunctions are all very reasonable pieces of advice and cannot at all hint at their inferiority in position.

During her period she is not in her normal state of health.[86] There are positive rules which she should follow at that time[87] and declare that she must not be tempted to observe any rite as it is sure to make her undergo some painstaking observance at least. Even though she may not be bodily present therein, several rites, viz., the New and Full Moon Sacrifices, the Piṇḍa-pitṛ-yajṇa, the daily oblations, etc., are allowed to be performed. These are allowed, simply because they would otherwise cause some hindrance, necessitate some atonement owing to the lapse of the proper time. The performance of the optional sacrifices, the Paśuyāga, the Soma sacrifice, etc., is barred in her absence. Sacrifice continues, but inspite of her absence, she gets the benefit of its performance. Kātyāyana, however, mentions that if she becomes impure during the Soma sacrifice, she should continue wearing her Dikśā-garments, stay in sand during the emission, and should, finally, take her baths before the Altar during the morning and evening with water mixed with cow's urine.

If she is observing the impurity for childbirth, she should take her (purificatory) bath after a period of ten nights and participate in sacrifices. Some think a pregnant woman should not be initiated to the Soma sacrifice. According to the *Dharma-sūtras*, she may participate in the *Agnihotra* even within the period of impurity for childbirth. According to Budhāyana, she may participate in the New and Full Moon sacrifices, too.[88]

If the wife is herself to perform the *Srādha* for the husband, and in the meantime she cannot do so for some reason or other she does it later.[89] The wife has to cook the food to be served to the Manes. So, according to certain Authorities, if on the *Srāddha* day she is impure, the *Srāddha* should be performed with uncooked rice. If she has a co-wife, she might cook, but the Kalādārśa says it is improper (as cooking in the *Srāddhas* is the absolute Right of the Chief Wife) and the *Srāddha* should be performed on the expiry of the period of her menstruation. It is, however, sanctioned that only the Annual *Srāddha* should be performed with cooked rice (which, it seems, should be cooked by the sacrificer himself). The Samskāramayūkha quotes Vrddhagārgya to show that the Vṛddhiśrāddha may be performed during her monthly illness.[90] The above rules hold good if the wife is observing Garbhāśauca (impurity for pregnancy).[91]

The wife has been depicted throughout the Brāhmaṇic literature in the lovliest colour. Sachī boasts not a little to say that her husband must conform to her will and her frame is the most precious thing to her husband.[92] Her pride is quite justified as in prayers to gods and seers again and again refer to her as the ideal of love, sweet relationship, etc. Vāmadeva invokes Indra with tenderness which a husband has for his wife.[93] Atri invokes and prays to the Aśvins with the faith a wife has in her husband.[94] Viśvāmitra prays to Pūśan to accept his offerings, listen to his thought, and be to him what a husband is to his young wife.[95] Vāmadeva prays to Indra to love his voice as the husband loves the voice of her well-beloved wife.[96]

With so much influence over her husband it is only natural that she, the most blessed gift from the gods Aryaman, Bhaga, Savitr and Purandhi, would be the mistress of her household[97] having full sway over the father-in-law and others.[98] Careful and active,[99] benevolent,[100] untiring in endeavours to satisfy the husband[101] by any means whatsoever—the wife, best friend of her husband[102] in all her majestic glory, reserves the right of having her own favourite goddesses and gods to be worshipped towards the end of the sacrifice. He would not let the sacrifice be finished unless her Agni Gṛhapati has been satisfied with the oblation in the Patnī-saṃyāja. Of all gods her nearest connection with Agni is manifest. Agni enjoys her as her third God Husband.[103] He is her Lover, her God[104] and is the Aryaman between her and her husband and makes them one-minded.[105] He brings about sexual union and causes pregnancy.[106] In rituals she always sits by the side of her Fire.[107] We have seen her in connection with Fire-worship before:[108] beginning from her marriage when she offers the oblations for the first time down to the end of her life she worships the fire, but the worshipper is inseparable from the worshipped;[109] her Fire accompanies her in her death; if her husband dies before him, she gives him[110] (Fire) with him. Her fire saves her from having a co-wife.[111] She herself feeds with a log at the end of every sacrifice. So it is only natural that she would not allow the sacrifice to be finished without ceremoniously celebrating his worship. The priests, during the Patnīsamyāja, leave their respective places, come by her side, and offer various oblations to Him. She thus firmly establishes her connection with her Agni.

She also sees that the wives of gods are worshipped before the sacrifice is finished. The wives of the gods worshipped before are invoked herein to have equal share of oblations with their husbands. The sacrifice cannot be ended without the satisfaction of the wives and their human counterpart. After the Patni-Saṃyāja she once again partakes of the Iḍā; the samyu-vāc is recited and Saṃśrava oblation is offered. She concludes the sacrifice by having uttered the greetings to the priests and bidding them good-by.

Thus we see that in Vedic ritual the wife holds as important a position as the husband. As equal halves they perform the sacrifices with equal results. If the husband has many wives, the chief wife is, really speaking, the patnī in in the strict sense of the term; she has many rights, in fact; all the important rights in rituals in precedence over her co-wives. Other wives (excepting Sūdrās) also join in the sacrifices and perform certain rites; anyway, they are not nonentities in religicus matters so far as their personal earthly benefit is concerned. But the sūdrā wife of an Aryan has no right in rituals whatsoever. Polyandry and polygamy as existing side by side in the country in varying degrees have counterbalanced each other. Both of them are, however, abnormalities as monogamy is always the ideal of the society. The Vedic ritual imposes upon the widow as well as the widower equally formidable difficulties; the same are the problems for both; they are to decide which course would be the best for them. Even in the lifetime of both, they are allowed, in extreme cases, to remarry—however, on the full knowledge that such marriages cannot be recognised as sanskāras. The Vedic ritual nowhere gives any such evidence as to lead to the assumption that the wife is to be considered inferior in position to husband: ritualistic injunctions on her in connection with her impurities are reasonable pieces of advice and cannot suggest the least inferiority in her position. The ritual literature is full of praise for the wife, for her virtues, and it is no wonder that the concluding oblations are offered to satisfy her most revered and beloved God Agni and the Wives of gods, and that she concludes the sacrifice with final greetings. Every Vedic sacrifice begins with the worship of the mother (Mātṛkā-pūjā), culminates in the worship of the wife (Patnī-saṃyāja) and successfully ends with the worship of the Daughter (Kumārī-pūjā) just in the same way as the sacrifice of man's life (Jīvana-yajṇa) begins with the worship of the Mother, culminates in the worship of the Wife (Sakti-pūjā; Patnī-pūjā) and ends with the worship of the Daughter.[112]

References

1. As a rule, the wives take a bath and adorn themselves for their participation in sacrifices. According to Bhāradvāja, as quoted by the *Commentary* on Apastamba (II, 6, 12, p. 32) they should anoint themselves with cow-dung. Baudhāyana also recommends both adornment and anointment, and paiṭhinasi adds the smelling of scented flowers. Comm. on *Āp. ŚS.,* 1.6.12, p. 23, Vol. I.
2. *Sat. ŚS.,* Vol. I, p. 159, 1. 14f.
3. *Sat. ŚS.,* Vol. I, p. 161, 1. 5f; *Āp.ŚS.,* Vol. 1, p. 96.
4. The *Śat.Bra.* strictly forbids the wives to sit to the west of the sacrifice, with their faces towards the east, for in that case Aditi, who always sits like that, might be displeased with them. By sitting somewhat to the south (cf. I, 3.1.17) of the Gārhapatya fire they propitiate Aditi.
5. *Āp.ŚS.,* अभ्यतरं वा, Vol. I, p. 96, 1. 6; *Sat. ŚS.,* Vol. I, p. 160, II. 3f.
6. *Vāj. Saṃh.*, I. 30; cf. *Tait. Samh.* I. 1.10. k "Thou art the milk of great one's", etc.; *Āp. ŚS.,* 2.6.2, Vol. 2, p. 98; *Band. ŚS.,* Vol. I, p. 18, 1. 4f. For the rite to be observed by all the wives, cf. Rudradatta on *Āp.*, पत्न्यनेकत्वे चावृत्तिः बौधायने-नोक्ता, etc.
7. *Sat. ŚS.,* p. 229, 1. 4f.; *Baudh. SS.,* p. 31, 1. 9ff.; *ŚS.,* Vol. I, p. 10., 1.22; *Āśv. ŚS.,* p. 33, 1.10 f; etc. According to *Āśv.*, the cord is to be folded twice.
8. *Śan. ŚS.,* p. 11, 1. I ff.; also see immediately after the above references. See Varadattasuta Ānartiya on *Śan. ŚS.,* I, 15, 14; Vol. II, p. 11 "Anekā api kurryuḥ."
9. E.g., *Sat. ŚS.,* p. 229, 1. 21. मुख-मार्जनं पत्नी-संस्कारत्वात् प्रतिपत्न्यावर्तते ।। These rites are also accompanied with Mantras. Cf. Nārāyaṇa on *Āśv.* p. 34, 6f. अत्र पत्नी-द्वित्व-बहुत्वे सर्वासा वचनं कर्तव्यम्; aso प्रतिपत्नि योक्र्-विमोचनमावर्तते, etc.
10. Cf. *Sat. ŚS.,* p. 229, II. 26-28; *Āp. ŚS.,* comm. on III, 10, 8.
11. *Baudh SS.,* p. 32 अथ एनं ग्रहपतये, etc., *Sat. ŚS.,* p. 229, 1.29f.; etc.
12. *Āp. ŚS.,* VIII. 8. 14, इमं विष्यामीति, etc.
13. *Āp. ŚS.,* VIII, 8, 15; Rudradatta, सलिलोतृक्षेपरोन, सशिरस्कौ; *Baudh. ŚS.,* अनुपमज्जन्तौ ।
14. *Āp. ŚS.,* X, 9, 5, Vol. II, p. 232, I 4f.; *Sat. ŚS.,* Vol. III, p. 592, I 7 ff.
15. Mahādeva on *Sat. ŚS., op. cit.,* 1. 27.
16. *Kāt, ŚS.,* Vol. I, p. 433, Sūtras 77.

17. *Āp. ŚS.*, X, 9, II; Vol. II, p. 233, 1. I ff.; अत्र दर्श-पूर्णमासवत् पत्नी संनह्यति सं त्वा नह्यमीति विकारः। *Sat. ŚS.*, Vol. III, p. 592, 1. 22 f.
18. Gopinātha on *Sat. ŚS.*, Vol. III, p. 595, 1. 9 f.
19. *Baudh. ŚS.*, Vol. I, p. 161, 1. 8-9.
20. Rudradatta on *Āp. ŚS.*, X, 15, 13-14, Vol. II, p. 248, II. 17 ff. यावदुक्तं पत्न्या दीक्षित-व्यंजनानि (Sūtra 13); समानं ब्रह्मचर्यम् (Sūtra 14).
21. VIII, 18, vol. I, p. 259, I. 9-10.
22. *Sat. ŚS.*, vol. IV, p. 941, 1. 10f.
23. Mahādeva on *Sat. SS., op. cit.*, 1. 29; *Tait. Samb., Mait. Samh.*, I, 3, 39; etc.
24. *Man. ŚS.*, I, 4, 45, I; also quoted in *Kāt, ŚS.*, X, 9, 6; *Sat. ŚS.*, Vol. IV, p. 1092, 1. 24.
25. *Sat. ŚS.*, Vol. IV, p. 946, 1. 26-27.
26. XIV, I, 3, 16; Weber's Ed., p. 1029; S.B.E., Vol. XLIV, p. 463.
27. For the connection of the Pravargya sacrifice with the Sun-worship, cf. *Śat. Bra.*, XIV, 1. 2, 15; 3, 16; 3, I, 35.
28. IV, I, 33; p. 154.
29. *Bandh. ŚS.*, Vol. 1, p. 276, 1. 18-19; *Sat. ŚS.*, and Vāñchiśvarasudhi, Vol. IX, p. 872, I. 9 and II; *Āp. ŚS.*, Vol. II, p. 656, 1. 14-16; *Kāt, ŚS.*, XXVI, 4, 12, p. 1102, Weber's Ed. etc.
30. IV, 2, 37; p. 153.
31. *Śat. ŚS.*, Vol. I, p. 255; *Āp. ŚS.*, I, 10, 10-11, Vol. I, p. 36-37, Rudradatta : अत्र पत्नी-बहुत्वे विभज्य सर्वाभ्यः प्रयच्छति दान-मन्त्रश्वाऽऽवर्तते; *Āśv. ŚS., (Āś.S.,)* 2, 7, 13, p. 73, 1. 10-14.
32. *Āśv. GK.*, 1, 2, 13-14, p. 265.
33. *Op. cit.*, 1, 2, 30f., p. 266, for husking and cooking, cf. *Hir. GS.*, I, 23, 2-4; for cooking, cf. *Vaik. GS., III*, 5, p. 39, I. 13.
34. *Āśv. GS., op. cit.*, v. 57 f., p. 268.
35. *RV.*, Schools: *Śāṅ.* G. *Saṃgraha*, i. 19. (*I.S.*, pp. 35, 130; p. 9, Benares ed.). *Śāṅ.* G. *Saṃgraha*, p. 19. *Āsv. G. Pariśiṣṭa*, 125, p. 217. *Saunaka-Kārikā*, p. 23; Kumārila's *Kārikā*, I, 4; p. 269. *Prayogaratna* of Nārāyāṇa Bhaṭṭa, 37f. Āśvalāyana does not deal with the sacrifice, but refers to some upaniṣad. Saunaka in his *Kārikā*, (p. 30 of the MS.) refers to one *Yajñopaniṣad.* It seems from his statement that the ritual as is described in his *Kārikā*, differs from that of the *Yajñopaniṣad.*

    In the *Vaikhānasa-gṛhya-sūtra* III, 10, the Garbhādhāna is mentioned as distinguished from *Ṛtu-saṃgamana* does not find place in any other Gṛhya-sūtra except the *Vaikhānasa*. This rite has, however, been given importance in the Prayogas, Paddhatis and specially in the Compendia.

    Authorities differ whether the Garbhādhāna should be observed on each case of the wife's pregnancy, or it should be observed once for all. Thus, Bhaṭṭa Nārāyaṇa says "This sacrament purifying the womb named Garbhādhāna is in way of purifying the object itself. So, as the object, the wife, is once purified, any pregnancy that occurs in it (her), is purified. So this rite should be observed once only. So also in the case with "Pumsavana and Simantonnayana." But Karko-pādhyāya holds the opposite view: "These three sacraments are to be repeated in every pregnancy, otherwise no saṃskāra of the following pregnancies is to be considered as observed." Again, Vijñāeśvara says, "Garbhādhāna should be observed in case of the wife's pregnancy, but not Pumsavana and Simantonnayana." Sūlpāṇī says, "Simantonnayana is not to be repeated, but Garbhādhāna and Puṃsavana are to be observed again and again." Tarkālankāra in the Commentary on Gobhila thinks that Garbhādhāna and Pumsavana need to be repeated in each pregnancy, but not Simantakaraṇa.

The question remains to be solved, if the Garbhādhāna is to be repeated on each case of the wife's pregnancy, and if the Pumsavana rite should also be observed in that Ṛtu when the Garbhādhāna is also going to be performed. The Ṛtusaṃgamana really serves the same purpose as the Garbhādhāna does. Moreover, from the treatment by several authorities of the Garbhādhāna, it seems that according to them the Garbhādhāna is but a ceremonial observance of the Ṛtu-saṃgamana for the pregnancy of the wife, failing which first the Nārāyaṇa Bali, and still failing, the Nāga Bali are to be observed. So there does not seem to be any necessity of the separate observance of the rite Ṛtu-saṃgamana in that monthly period of the wife when the Garbhādhāna is held.

36. *Ā.G. Pariśiṣṭa, op. cit.,* Kumārila's *Kārikā, op. cit., Prayogaratna* of Nārāyana Bhaṭṭa, p. 38(2).
37. *Ś.G. Sutra, op. cit.,* p. 9. 1. I.
38. *Ś.G. Saṃgraha, op. cit.,* 1. 19.
39. *Ā.G. Pariśiṣṭa,* Śaunaka, Kumārila and *Prayoga-ratna, op. cit.*
40. *Ā.G.P., op. cit.*
41. *Ś.G.S; Ś.G. Saṃ;* Kumārila and Śaunaka; *Prayogaratna* of Bhaṭṭa Nărāyana, *op. cit.*
42. *Ā.G. Pariśiṣṭa, op. cit.*
43. The barbar comes, pares the nails, and gets some remuneration.
44. Cf. *Baudh. GS.,* IV, 9. I. p. 336.
45. *Drāh. GS.,* 1.4; *Gobh. GS.,* I, 5, 26, p. 219.
46. *Pār G.S.,* I, 12, 4, p. 130, Bom ed.; Karka, *op. cit.,* 1. 23; Jayarāma, p. 131, 1, 6f.; Harihara, *op. cit.,* 1. 37f.; Gadādhara, p. 134, 1. rof.
47. *Gobb. GS.,* I, 6, 9, p. 225.
48. Harihara on *Pār, GS.* III, 2, p. 321, 1.5, अत्र स्त्रीणामपि मन्त्र-पाठः.
49. For the Mantra; *AV.,* 7, 10, i; *Vāj. Saṃh.,* 38, 5; *Mait. Samb,* IV, 9, 4, etc.
50. For these facts: Saunaka as quoted in *Madana-ratna, Karma-kanda-pradipa,* f. 410a, 1. 4f. Also cf. *Gṛhya Kārikā,* (Reṇu) and Baudhāyana as quoted herein; Nārāyaṇa Bhaṭṭa's *Antyeṣṭikriya,* f. 213a,

1. 9f.

51. *Karma-kāṇḍa-pradipa,* f. 409a, 1. 14; 409b, 1. I. According to the *Baudhayana-paddhati* (f. 162) the water should be mixed with cow's urine.
52. According the Devayājñika, as quoted in *Karma, KP.,* f. 409b. 1. 2-3.
53. *Karma, K.P.,* f. 399c, छन्दोगानां स्त्री-मरणे विशेषः; etc.
54. *Jaim. GS., II, 5,* p. 30, 1. 20; p. 31, 1. i.
55. *Śrāddha-mañjarī*, p. I.
56. *Śrāddha-mañjarī*, p. 39. *Śrāddhatattva,* p. 200. *Śrāddha-sutra-kaṇḍikā,* Par. GS., Bom ed., p. 484, 1. 34; 485, 1. 4. *Manu.,* Nir. ed., p. 126, v. 262; according to *Kullūka,* however, only the eldest wife should eat it. *Kha. GS.,* III, 5, 30, p. 118 (Aṣṭaka). *Mantra-Brāhmaṇa,* II, 3, 14.
57. *Candrikā,* p. 402, *Sankhalikhita* quoted.
58. *A.p.,* as quoted in *Smṛti-candrikā,* p. 403.
59. Cf. the *Śrāddha-kāṇḍa* in *Smṛti-candrikā*, p. 402, where various authorities have been quoted with reference to this. Also see *Gobh.G. Pariśiṣṭa,* p. 125, पुत्र-कामा । *Jaim. GS.,* II, 3, p. 29, 1. 9-11 (in all the Śrāddhas).
60. *Jaim. GS.,* II, 5. p. 30 of *Caland's* ed.; for Comm., *op. cit.,* p. 66.
61. *kātyayana, Chandoga-Pariśiṣṭa,* Ch. XX, p. 334.
62. The custom of giving slaves as presents to princes (*RV.* VIII. 19, 36) and priests (as sacrificial fee), ritualistic recognition of Ārya Sūdrā Union *(Tait. Saṃh.,* VII, 4, 19, 2. *Vāj. Saṃh.*, XXIII, 50, 31), employment of Sūdrās as Anucaris and Pariveṣṭris *(Śat. Brā.,* XI, 2, 7, 4; *Kaus. Pan.,* ii, i, slave-concubinage, (cf. *AV.,* 22, 6; XII, 3, 13; 4, 9) etc. helped many Sūdrās to rise to the favour of Aryan Masters, so much so, that most probably—not infrequently, they married them. Several Sūtrakāras make provision for one Sūdra wife of one belonging to the higher castes (e.g. *Pār G.S.,* i, 4, 10). Cf. *Vaśiṣṭha*, I, 25, and for his own view, the following Sūtras.
63. *Manu.,* III, 18; *Viṣṇu* XXVI, 5; For the legal incapacity of her children: *Baudh. DhS.,* II, 2, 3, etc.
64. III, 14.
65. *Op. cit.,* 15-17; also 19. *Viṣṇu* XXVI, 6; *Vaś DhS.,* I, 27.
66. *Vāś. DhS.,* XIV, II.
67. *Gaut. Dhs.,* XV, 22.
68. *Karma-pradīpa,* 1, 8, p. 115.
69. Rodasi and Sūryā. *AV.* I, 167, 4-5; the express reading of *RV* with reference to Roadasī, is साधारणी पत्नी Common Wife.
70. *Manu,* III, 60-61.
71. Parāśara, 4, 12-13; similarly, Devala, Bṛhaspati, etc.
72. For those of the wife: *Yajnavalkya,* 3, 72-73.
73. *Vaś. DhS.,* XVII, 20; *Manu* IX, 175-176; *Yājñ.,* i, 67; cf. also

Kāma-sūtra, p. 248 (Nir. Ed.), *Sūtra* 31 (with Yasodhara's Commentary); Baudh. DhS., IV, 1. 16; II, 2, 3, 27; *Viṣṇu* XV, 7; *Nārada* XII, 45ff.

74. For the Indo-Iranian period: W. Geiger, *Ostiranische Kultur in Altertum*, p. 244.
75. *Śat. Brā.*, I, 7, 2, I; also IX, 4, I, 5; *Tait. Brā.*, VI, 3, 5; 10; III, 7, 9, 8; *AV.*, VI, 117, 3; Tait. *Āran.*, VII, II, 5; *Tait. Upan.*, I, 9; *Ait. Āran.*, I, 3, 5, 6; *Bṛh. Up.*, VI, 4; *Vaś. DhS.*, VIII, II; *Baudh. DhS.*, II, 3, 2, I, etc.
76. It will be seen in this connection that in the water-libations and Śrāddhas, water and cake are offered to the parents of both the mother as well as father.
77. *RV.*, I, 9, 20; III, I, 25; X. 85, 25, etc. AV., III, 23, 2; V, 25, II; VI, II, 2, etc. *Tait. Samh.* VI, 3, 89, 5; *Tait. Bra.* I, 5, 6; *Ait, Brā.*, VII, 13; *Ait. Āran.*, II, 3, 7, 3; 5, I, 1-7; Chand. Upaṇ., VI, 2, 13; etc.; etc.
78. Compare the references mentioned as "mantras", prayers, etc. in previous pages. Cook informs us in his *Zens*, Vol. II, p. 1114, that even at the present day women slide downrock in front of the church in order to propitiate Saint Marina for having children; cf. Miss M. Hamilton's *Greek Saints and their Festivals*, Edinburgh and London, 1910, p. 58f., as quoted by Cook.
79. *Ait. Brā.*, VII, 13.
80. मेध्या वै योषितः सदा; Yājñavalkya, I, 71.
81. *Vaś. DhS.*, XXVIII, 5-6; *Baudh. DhS.*, II, 2, 4, 5.
82. *Vaś. DhS.*, XXVIII, 2-3. In mind also: *Manu* V, 108, *Viṣṇu*, XXII, 91; cf. *Mahabharata*, XII, 165, 32.
83. *Vaś. DhS.*, XXVIII, 4; III, 58; V, 4. *Yajnavalkya*, I, 72; *Baudh. Dhs.*, II, 2, 4, 4.
84. *Vaś. DhS.*, XXVIII, 9. *Śat. Brā.*, V, 2, 1, 8 (some parts of her body to be covered with Kuśa grass) refers to the temporary Impurity and suggets an extra precaution.
85. *Yājñ.*, I, 193; *Baudh. Dhs.*, I, 9, 2; *Viṣṇu*, XXII, 49.
86. Anton Nemilov, *Biological Tragedy of Women*, ch. VI, p. 105f.; particularly the section on "Menstruation and its significance", p. 115f. For the legendary cause of menstruation, *Tait. Samh.*, II, 5, I; cf. Bṛh. *Up.*, 6, 4, 3; *Vāś. DhS.*, V, 5-9. Fear for unclean women in Rituals: *Sat Bra.*, III, 1, 2, 19. Impediment to Vedic Studies, San. GS., II, 12, 10; VI, 1, 3, 9, 13. For the various taboos on women during menstruation and childbirth among various peoples: Frazer, Taboo, Part II, pp. 145-156.
87. *Baudh. GS.*, I, 7, 22ff. For exhaustive treatment: *Saṃskāraratnamālā*, pp. 649-694 (various authorities have been quoted here). *Saṃskāra-paddhati*, p. 40: according to this Paddhati, during her first menstruation only, she may wear garlands of yellow and scented flowers and chew betels, not in others.
88. For the above informations: Commentary on *Āp.ŚS.*, IX, 2, I, Vol. II, p. 106; *Manu*, *Yājñavalkya*, *Jābāli*, *Bharadvaja*, and *Bhaudhayana*,

as quoted in the above (p. 107); *Sat. ŚS*., XV, I, 39-41, Vol. VI, pp. 269-71. For the Garbhini-prāyascitta: *Āp. ŚS*., IX, 20, 7, Vol. II, p. 200. For the Rajasvalā wife in the Soma Sacrifice, *Sat. ŚS*., Vol. IV, p. 993 ff.

89. *Śrāddha-sūtra-kaṇḍikā, Par. GS.,* p. 466, 1. 17; *Śrāddha-mañjarī*, pp. 97 and 181.
90. For the varying opinions on the subject: *Śrāddha-mañjarī*, p. 16.
91. Cf. *Śrāddha-mañjarī*, p. 97, एवं गर्भिण्याम् अपि । As the eating of the middle cake is meant for pregnancy, it is only natural that during her pregnancy she is not given the same again.
92. *RV.* X, 159, 2-3.
93. *RV.* IV, 20. 5.
94. *RV.* V, 78. 4.
95. *RV.* III, 62, 8.
96. *RV.* IV, 32, 16 (3rd *Aṣṭaka,* 6th Adh., *Sūkta* II).
97. *RV.* X, 85. 86.
98. *RV.* X, 85, 46; *AV.* XIV, 2, 18.
99. *RV.* 1, 66; 79.
100. *RV.* V, 61; particularly, Rc. 9.
101. *RV.* IV, 3, 2; X, 71.4. She has no grievance even against her guilty gambling husband. She suffers in silence, but has against him neither anger nor a hard word; her love for him and goodness towards his friends are constant. The guilty husband is sorely mortified—not so much for anything else, as for making her suffer, RV. X, 34.
102. She is so ever since she performs the Saptapadi (the rite of taking Seven steps) during the Wedding Ceremony. *San, GS.,* 1, 4, 5, seq.; *Gobb. GS.,* II, 2. II; *Kha. GS.,* I, 5, 26; *Hiran.* G.S., I, 20, 9 seq., *Ā.p.,* 4, 16, etc. Brb. Upan, 1, 4, 3; *Ait Brā.*, VII, 13.
103. *RV.* X, 85, 40-41; AV. XIV, 2, 3-4.
104. *RV.* I, 66, 8.
105. *RV.* V_2 3, 2.
106. *Śat. Brā.,* III, 4, 3, 4-5; *Sāṅ. GS.,* I, 17, 9.
107. E.g. Scholiast on *Āp.ŚS.,* VI, 5, 2; *Kāt. ŚS.,* Chow. ed, p. 274, Sūtra 193.
108. See *Indian Historical Quarterly,* March 1940, The wife in the Vedic Ritual. For particular stress laid on fire-worship by the wife, see Śaṅkha., IV, 15; *Una. Samh.,* p. 409; *Kātyāyana,* XIX, 3; *op. cit.,* p. 333.
109. *Gobh. GS.,* I, 3, 15; *Khā. GS.,* I, 5, 17; *Sān. GS.,* II, 16, 3; *Gaut. DhS.,* V, 40; *RV.,* III, 53, 4; *Śat. Brā.,* III, 3, I, rof.
110. *Karma-Kanda-pradipa,* f. 398a, I. 8ff.
111. *Ā.p. Dhs.,* II, 5, II, 13 f.
112. For Patni-pūja, cf. *Manu III,* 55, p. 88, Nir, ed.

5

Rights and Duties after Marriage

In Vedic literature, we find references to polygamy even though monogamy seems to have been the references to polygamy. *Atharvaveda* has a number of hymns which are meant as a charm for weaning the husband's affections from a co-wife. It was an accepted norm for a man to have more than one wife but the woman was not supposed to have more than one husband. Hariśchandra is said to have had a hundred wives. It is not to be supposed that polygamy was confined only to kings and nobles. The great philosopher Yājṇavalkya had two wives, Kātyāyani who was worldly-minded and Maitreyī who thirsted for the knowledge of brahma and immortality.

In the times of the *Sūtras*, some sages wanted to hold up a high ideal. It was declared that when a man has a wife who is endowed with *dharma* and progeny, he shall not marry another wife; but if any one of the two (*dharma* and progeny) is wanting (in the case of the wife), he may marry another before he has consecrated the sacred *srauta* fires. In another place it has been prescribed that one who abandons his (faultless) wife should be put on the skin of an ass with the hair outside and should beg for alms at seven houses for six months.

Narada recommended that the king should bring round the proper path by inflicting heavy fines on a husband who abandons a wife that is obedient, not harsh of tongue, vigilant (in household work), chaste and endowed with sons. Even Kaut prescribes that a husband should wait for eight years (before marrying another) if his wife gives birth to no child after one delivery or is sonless or is barren; he should wait for ten if she bears only still-born children, twelve years if she gives birth to daughters only. Then if he is anxious for a son he may marry another. If he violates these rules he must pay her gratuity, some wealth as strīdhana and money (prescribed to be given) on supersession and besides a fine (to the king). So far Kauṭilya appears to have only stated the ideal, because he follows up this remark by another statement which probably represented the commonly held popular view that a man may marry several wives after giving *shulka* and *stridhana* to those to whom nothing had been given at the time of marriage and money on supersession *(ādhivedanika)* and suitable provision for livelihood; for women are (married) for procreating sons. Though others held up the ideal of monogamy and Nārada and others prescribed a fine for marrying a second wife without sufficient cause, it is extremely doubtful whether a man was ever punished by the king for so doing. Manu (V. 80) and Yāj. (I. 80) both say that a husband may supersede a wife (and marry another) if she drinks wine, suffers from a disease (of long standing), is deceitful, is extravagant in expenditure, speaks harsh words, and gives birth to female children only. Manu (V. 81) and Baud. (Dh. S. II. 2. 65) allow a husband to marry another woman at once, if the first is harsh of tongue. Devala said that the Sūdra may have only one wife, a Vaiśya two, a Kśatriya three and a brāhmana four, but a king may have as many as he desires. This only reflected the prevailing practice of kings. The Ādiparva remarked that to have many wives is no *adharma* on the part of men, but to violate the duty owed to the first husband would be a great adharma in the case of women.' The *Mahābhārata* tells us that Vāsudeva (Krishna) had sixteen thousand wives. In Bengal the reasons for bad treatment of women were many, such as the great spiritual importance of sons, early marriages and consequent illiteracy of women, the spread of the idea of the ceremonial impurity of women and their being equated with sūdras and lastly the idea of the complete dependence of women on men. One must not be carried away, however, by the notion that marrying many wives was either very common or was not looked down upon. Modern opinion of educated people is most favourable to making marriages monogamous and efforts are being made to secure absolute monogamy by legislative action.

Polyandry

In ancient times polyandry was unheard of. Not a single Vedic passage can be cited which clearly refers to the practice of polyandry. The most glaring example of polyandry in *Sanskrit* literature is that of Draupadī as the wife of five Pāṇḍavas. Probably the tradition was too firmly rooted to allow the author to ignore it. The Mahābhārata shows that all were shocked by the resolve of Yudhiśṭhira to make Draupadī the wife of the five brothers. Dhṛsiṭadyumna tried vehemently to dissuade Yudhishṭhira, who tried to justify his action on the ground of ancient practice and the agreement of the brothers to share everything that any one of them may secure. But Yudhisṭhira could get only two instances in support of the practice viz. of Jaṭilā Gautamī (who had seven sages as husbands and of Vārkṣī who had ten Prācetasa brothers as husbands. There are two types of polyandry, one matriarchal where a woman forms simultaneous alliances with two or more men who are not necessarily relations of each other and therefore succession is traced through the female and the other fraternal, where a woman becomes the wife of several brothers. The practice once prevailed among the Nairs on the Malabar coast but it has now died out. The latter form of polyandry is still to some extent found in Kumaon, Garhwal and among people in Himalayan area up to Assam.

Mutual Rights and Duties of Husband and Wife

Manu remarked about the obligations of husband and wife and said that they should not prove false to each other till death (as regards *dharma, artha* and *kāma*) and that their constant endeavour should be not to be separate from each other and not to break faith with each other as to those three goals of human life.

Rights from the Ancient Times

The first duty of the husband and the privilege of the wife was to require and to give respectively her co-operation in all religious acts. It is required that from the time of marriage the husband and wife work together in religious acts, that they share the reward of such acts together and that they both have dominion over the wealth of the family and that the wife can make gifts in the absence of the husband if occasion necessitates. According to the commentator some said that the wife and the daughter could not perform the *homa* as they had no privilege to learn *mantras,* that they could only kindle the fire, while others said they could do so. In the *gṛhya* fire kindled at marriage one was to offer the daily *mahāyajṇas* and as regards *baliharana,* says that both husband and wife should offer Balis, or a Brāhmana may offer for them, or the wife may offer in the evening and the husband in the morning. Manu says that from food cooked in the evening the wife should offer Balis, but without *mantras.* This shows that though gradually women began to lose the right to repeat Vedic *mantras* (as shown by Manu), still she had a hand in the religious rites. She had to perform many acts in sacrifices, such as unhusking grain in Sthālīpāka washing the slaughtered animal looking at the *ājya* in srauta sacrifices. The Pūrvamīmāmsā establishes that both husband and wife own property and should join together in performing sacrifices, but that the male sacrificer alone is ordinarily to do every act in all religious ceremonies except such matters as are expressely declared to be performed by the wife also or alone. It is on account of the necessity of associating the wife in all religious acts that the hero Rāma was compelled to celebrate sacrifices with a golden image of Sitā by his side. Pāṇini derives the word *patnī* and says that it can be only applied to a wife who shares in the sacrifice (and its reward). It follows that wives who are not or cannot join with their husbands in *yajṇas* are only *jāyās* or *bhāryās* (but not *patnīs*). The Mahābhāśya says that the wife of a Sūdra is called *patnī* only by analogy (as a Sūdra himself has no *adhikāra* for *yajṇa,* his wife can much less have it). It is on account of this close association of the wife in all sacrifices (either *srauta* or *smārta*) that the wife if she dies before her husband is burnt with the sacred fire or fires and with the sacrificial vessels and implements.

But the wife is not authorised to do religious acts independently of her husband or without his consent. Manu ordains that there is no separate *yajṇa* for women (independently of the husband) nor *vrata* (vows) nor fasts (without his consent). Similarly Kātyāyana propounds a sweeping rule that whatever a woman does to secure spiritual benefit after death without the consent of her father (when she is unmarried), or her husband or her son, becomes fruitless for the purpose intended.

If a man married several women then there are detailed rules for precedence among wives. If all the wives are of the same caste, then the wife whose marriage took place first was to be associated with the husband in all religious acts; if a man had wives of different *varṇas* (when inter-caste marriages are allowed) the wife of the same *varṇa* with the husband had precedence, though her marriage might have been later in date. If there is no wife of the same *varṇa* as himself, the husband may associate with himself in religious rites even a wife of the *varṇa* immediately next to his own; but a dvijāli should never associate a Sūdra wife with himself in religious ceremonies. The Trikāṇḍamaṇḍana says that there were three views when a man had several wives viz. some said that all should be associated with him in religious rites, others held that only the eldest wife of the same *varṇa* should be associated and the third view was that the husband should never associate with himself a wife whom he married for pleasure after he kindled the sacred fires. Manu lays down that the wife of the same caste with the husband should always have precedence not only in the obligatory religious rites, but also in ministering to the physical comfort of the husband and if a *Brāhmaṇa* husband gets these done by a wife of another caste when the wife of the same caste is near, he becomes like a *chāṇḍāla*.

From very ancient times one of the articles of faith was that a man was born with debts, that he owned three debts to sages, gods and *pitṛs* and that by procreating sons he freed himself from those three debts respectively.

Manu stated that a man should not think of *mokṣa* (release from *saṃsāra*) before he has paid off the three debts and further says that by the very birth of the eldest son a man becomes free from the debt owed to ancestors. He declared that a *putra* is so called because he saves his father from the hell called *put*. Further the water and *piṇḍas* (balls of cooked rice) offered by the son to his father and other deceased ancestors were supposed to be of great efficacy for the peace of the souls of the departed. On account of these several benefits conferred by a son, the highest importance was attached to the birth of a son. The wife helped a man to discharge two of his debts, to the gods by associating with him in sacrifices and to the *pitṛs* by procreating a son or sons. Therefore the goal of the life of women was declared to be to get married and procreate sons. Manu says 'women are created for procreation and men have to propagate (the race); therefore in the *Veda* it is declared that the wife shares in common (with the husband) the performance of religious duties'. Nārada also declares that women are created for (procreating) children. It was on account of these ideas about the goal of woman's life and the supreme importance of a son that the *smṛtis* and Dharma-sūtra works recommended or allowed the husband to marry a second time even when the first wife was living.

All the *smṛitis, purāṇas* and the digests devote a great deal of space to the duties of a wife. All are agreed that the foremost duty of a wife is to obey her husband and to honour him as her god. Manu declared that a virtuous wife should serve her husband as if he were a god, whether he be of evil character, or lustful (loving another woman) or devoid of good qualities. This was the highest duty *(dharma)* of women that they should obey their husband's words; if he is guilty of some mortal sin, they should wait till he is purified. The Rāmāyaṇa remarks 'the husband is the god and the master of the wife, while she is alive and she obtains the highest heaven by serving her husband. This idea of the wife's entire submission to the husband is voiced even by poets like Kālidāsa, who makes one of the pupils of Kaṇva say about Sakuntalā 'this is your wife, abandon her or accept her, since all-round domination of the husband over the wife is proper.

According to Manu a wife should always present a smiling face, shuld be alert and clever in her domestic duties, should keep domestic vessels well burnished and clean and should not be extravagant in spending.' Manu asks the husband to set to his wife the task of conserving the wealth acquired and looking to its expenditure, of keeping things clean, of the performance of religious acts, of cooking food and of taking care of household paraphernalia. Manu adds that drinking wine, company of bad people, staying away from the husband, wandering about (to *tirthas* or elsewhere), sleep (by day), staying in the house of strangers—these six spoil married women. Adiparva gives expression to the popular notion that people do not like married women staying with their paternal relatives for a long time away from their husbands, since such a stay leads to loss of good name and character. Saṇkha lays down what is decent conduct for a wife 'she should not go out of the house unless she is asked (by her husband or elders) nor without putting on an upper garment; she should not walk fast; she should not speak with a male who is unrelated to her, except a trader, a *sanyāsin*, an old man or a physician; she should not allow her navel to be seen; she should wear her garment (or sari) in such a way that it may reach down to her ankles; she should not expose her breasts, she should not laugh loudly without covering her mouth (with her hand or her garment); she should not hate her husband or his relatives; she should not be in the company of dancing girls, gambling women, women who make assignments to meet lovers, female ascetics, female fortune-tellers, women who live by tricks, magical and secret rites and who are of bad character; since (the wise declare that) the character of women of good family is spoilt by the company (they keep).' They should perform the same *vratas* (observances and vows) which the husband undertakes; they should honour the mother-in-law, the father-in-law, other elders, gods, guests and keep the household utensils well arranged; they should not be extravagant in giving to others; should keep the gods well guarded; they should have no liking for magical practices (to win love) and should be devoted to auspicious conduct. Bṛhaspati says that a wife should get from bed before her husband and elders, should partake of food and condiments after they have eaten, should occupy a seat lower than that of the husband or elders. 'A wife can engage in *vratas,* fasts, observances and worship (of god & c.) with the permission of her husband. The Bhagavat says that the wife who looks upon her husband as the god *Hari* dwells in the world of Hari and revels with her husband. The *Skanda Purāṇa* has a long description of a *pativratā* 'she should not repeat the name of her husband, as such conduct leads to the increase of the husband's life and should never take the name of another male even when she is loudly blamed (by the husband) she does not cry loudly, even when beaten she is smiling. A pativratā should always use turmeric, *kumkuma, sindūra,* lamp black (for the eye), a bodice, *tambūla,* auspicious ornaments, and should braid her hair' (vv. 28-29). The *Padma-purāṇa* says that wife is *pativratā* who in doing work is like a mother in offering food and like a counsellor in adversity.

Special rules of conduct were laid down for a wife whose

husband was away from home on a journey. 'Women whose husbands are away from home should avoid amusements of swing and dance, seeing pictures, applying unguents to the body, walking in parks, sleeping in open places (or uncovered) partaking of sumptuous food and drink, playing with a ball, fragrant resins and perfumes, flowers, ornaments, ceremonial brushing of the teeth, collyrium (in the eyes).' Yāj puts these briefly 'a woman whose husband is gone to another country should give up play, the adornment of the body, visiting *samājas* and festivals, laughing, going to the house of stranger. Manu requires the husband when going abroad to make provision for the wife's maintenance, since a woman without some means of livelihood, though originally virtuous, may go astray and adds 'when the husband goes abroad after providing for maintenance, the wife should live thereby and abide by the restrictions (laid down for such wives); if he goes away without making provision for her maintenance she should maintain herself by crafts (such as spinning) which are unblamable.' The Veda-Vyāsa-smṛti enjoins upon a wife whose husband is gone abroad her face should look pale and distressed, she should not embellish her body, she should be devoted to her husband, should be without (full) meal and should emaciate her body.'

The rewards of the wife's single-minded devotion to her husband and her rigid observance of the rules of conduct prescribed for her are stated at great length in *smṛti* works. Manu says that woman who does not prove faithless to her husband in thought, word and deed secures the (heavenly) worlds together with her husband and is spoken of as a *sādhvi* (a virtuous woman, a *pativratā*); but by proving faithless to her husband a woman incurs censure in this world, is born as a female jackal (in the next life) and is afflicted with very bad diseases.' Yāj declares that the woman, who does not approach another while the husband is living or after his death and who is intent on doing what is agreeable and beneficial to her husband, who is of good conduct and has restrained her senses, attains glory in this world and plays with Umā (the wife of Siva) in heaven. Bṛhaspati defines a *pativratā* as one who is distressed when her husband is distressed, who is delighted when her husband is in delight, who is emaciated and wears dirty clothes when her husband has gone on a journey and who dies on the death of her husband.

In the *Mahābhārata* and the purāṇas hyperbolical descriptions of the power of the *pativratā* occur at every step. When Damayantī cursed the young hunter who had evil designs on her, he fell down a dead man. The story of Sāvitrī in the Vanaparva illustrates the power of a *pativratā* who wrung back even from Yama, and the dread god of Death, the life of her husband. Sāvitrī and Sitā have been held by the women of India for thousands of years as the highest ideals of womanly virtue, to which they have always endeavoured to approach and one may say that Indian women generally have most successfully lived up to that high and ennobling ideal that was set before them. Vanaparva tells the story of a learned Brāhmaṇa, who by his mere angry look made a female crane die when the latter voided its faces on to the head of the *Brāhmaṇa* and who was rebuked by a *pativratā* that the latter was not a crane, when the *Brāhmaṇa* tried to frighten the virtuous woman for her tardiness is welcoming him as a guest and for looking only after her husband. The *Salyaparva* narrates how awful the power of a *pativratā* like Gāndhāri is in that she can, if she choose, burn the world, she can stop even the motions of the sun and the moon.

Foremost Duty

As the foremost duty of the wife was to honour and serve the husband, she must always stay with him and she had a right of residence in the house. A wife was further entitled to be maintained in the house by the husband. Manu declares that one must maintain one's aged parents, a virtuous wife and a minor son by doing even a hundred bad acts'.

Manu prescribes that the man who abandons and does not maintain his parents, wife, and son, when they are not outcasted, should be fined by the king. Yāj. requires the husband to maintain a wife whom he has superseded in the same way as before, otherwise he would be guilty of great sin. It says that if a man abandoned a wife who was obedient, diligent, the mother of a son, and agreeable in speech, he was to be made to give one-third of his property to the wife, but if he had no property he had to maintain her. Nārada has a similar provision. The husband was required to be devoted to his wife, since women are to be guarded (against falling into error). The guarding of a wife from evil can be secured only by being devoted to her and not by beating her, as if the husband were to beat her, it might endanger her life. Manu also calls upon men to guard women, and says that they cannot be guarded by imprisonment or force, but by engaging them in looking to the income and expenditure, the furniture, beauty and purity of the house and the cooking and by inculcating on them the value of a virtuous life. In spite of this the husband possessed certain powers of physical correction over the wife which were the same as those possessed by a teacher over a pupil or a father over a son, viz. he could administer beating with a rope or a thin piece of bamboo on the back but never on the head.

As it was the husband's duty to provide residence and maintenance for the wife and as the wife was bound to stay with the husband, it follows that either party could after marriage enforce his or her rights in a court of law if the other party refused to perform her or his duties. In modern times a suit for restitution of conjugal rights can be brought and the decree can be executed against the wife by the attachment and sale of her property (if she has any), but not by detention in civil jail and against the husband by the court ordering the husband to make periodical payments of money for the maintenance of the wife and securing such payments by creating a charge on his property. To such a suit by the husband Indian Courts have recognised certain valid defences, such as desertion, cruelty or such conduct as endangers the health of the wife, change of religion, or keeping a concubine in the house or the husband's being afflicted with a loathsome disease (like leprosy).

Not only was the husband bound to maintain the wife, but he was called upon to cohabit with the wife and was supposed to incur the sin of embryo-murder if he refused without good cause to do so. On the other hand the husband had a right of consortium, i.e., the wife was not to refuse herself to the husband and if she did so her delinquency was to be proclaimed in the village and she was to be driven from the house.

The humane character of the legislation of the Indian sages is seen by the fact that even for adultery they do not allow the husband to drive the wife out of the house and to abandon her. A wife who violates her duty of chastity must undergo a penance, but she should be kept under guard and be given food. An adulterous woman should be deprived of her authority (over servants & c.), should be made to wear dirty clothes, should be given food just sufficient to enable her to live, should be treated with scorn and made to lie on the ground (not on a cot); a woman becomes pure from adultery when she has her monthly period after that, but if she conceives in adulterous intercourse she may be abandoned and also when she is guilty of the murder of her foetus or of her husband or of some sin that makes her an outcast'. The wives of Brāhmanas, Ksatriyas and Vaiśyas who commit adultery with a Śūdra may be purified by a penance in case no child is born (of the intercourse), but not otherwise' and remarks that the words of Yājņavalkya are to be understood in the same sense, i.e., a wife is to be abandoned only if she be in adultery with a Śūdra; and further that the abandonment consists in not allowing her to participate in religious rites and conjugal matters, but she is not to be cast on the streets; she is to be kept apart guarded in a room and to be given food and raiment. Vasiṣṭha says that only four (types of) wives are to be abandoned viz. one who has intercourse with the husband's pupil and with the husband's *guru,* and especially one who attempts to kill her husband and who commits adultery with a man of degraded caste (like a leather-worker). Nārada says 'when a woman commits adultery her hair shall be shaven, she shall have to die on a low bed shall receive bad food and clothing and her occupation will be the removal of sweepings of the husband's house'.

The following propositions can be deducted from the texts cited above:

(1) There is no absolute right of abandonment of wife in the husband on the ground of adultery;

(2) Adultery is ordinarily an *upapātaka* (a minor sin) and can be atoned for by appropriate penance undergone by the wife;

(3) the wife who has committed adultery but has undergone penance is to be restored to all the ordinary rights of wives as long as the adulteress has not undergone penance, she is to be given in the house itself starving maintenance and to be deprived of all her rights as wife;

(4) a wife, who commits adultery with a Śūdra or has had a child thereby, who is guilty of killing her foetus or of attempt

to kill the husband or guilty of one of the deadly sins *(mahā-pātakas),* is to be deprived of her right to participation in religious rites or conjugal matters and is to be kept confined in a room or in a hut near the house and to be given starving maintenance and poor apparel, even affer she undergoes penance;

(5) that wives who are not guilty of acts are to be given starving maintenance and residence near the house even if they do not perform penance

(6) wives who are guilty of the acts, if they refuse to perform penance, are to be refused even starving maintenance and residence near the husband's house. The propositions about maintenance set out here are accepted as the modern Hindu Law by the courts in India.

It has been shown above that Āp. postulated the identity of husband and wife in religious matters and Manu declares that the husband is one with his wife. But this identity of husband and wife was not accepted by the ancient sages for secular or legal purposes. The rights of husband and wife as to each other's property and the liability of each for the debts of the other will be dealt with later on in detail. It may suffice here to point out that the wife was not ordinarily liable for the debts contracted by the husband nor was the husband liable for the debts contracted by the wife alone, unless the debt was for family purposes. Similarly the husband could exercise no dominion over the wife's own property (her *stridhana* or peculium) except in a famine or for a necessary religious purpose, or in disease or when he was imprisoned.

Nārada does not allow the husband or wife to lodge a complaint against one another with their relations or with the king. Though a judicial proceeding between husband and wife as plaintiff and defendant before the king is forbidden, still, if the king comes to know personally or indirectly of wrong done by the one to the other, the king must bring round the husband or the wife to the path of duty by appropriate punishment, otherwise the king incurs sin. There were certain matters of which the king could take cognisance without the complaint of anybody: they were called *aparādhas* (they are ten) among which were included the murder of a woman, *varnasaṃkara*, adultery, pregnancy of a widow from some person other than the husband, abortion. We have seen that the husband is made to pay one-third of his estate or a fine for deserting a virtuous wife and there are many such provisions about the matters affecting the husband and wife in which the king interfered.

The wife was looked upon as half of the husband, in Vedic times women composed hymns and learnt the *Vedas* and they co-operated with their husbands in all religious acts. On the whole their social position was much better (except as to rights of property) than what it became in later times. But even in the Vedic times there was an under-current of opinion which was hostile to women, sneered at them and treated them with scorn.

Reading all that has been said in favour of and against women in ancient *Sanskrit* literature it may be said that the higher minds of Hindu Society were quite aware of the worth of women, that they insisted on chastity as the highest virtue for them, that there was no doubt an undercurrent among common people of poor opinion about women, that those who valued an ascetic life and wanted to wean people away from worldly ties and attachments looked down upon women and exaggerated their faults. It has to be borne in mind that many of the passages condemning women are put in the mouth of persons who were for some reason or other angry with women or wronged by them or dissatisfied with their conduct.

6

The Initiation

The *Gṛihya Sūtras* say that the *Brāhmaṇa* should be initiated in the 7th or 8th year after he was conceived or born; they make similar rules for the *Kśatriyas* and *Vaiśyas* too—only extending the age limit for them. Here by *Brāhmaṇa, Kśatriyas* and *Vaiśyas* too—only extending the age limit for them. Here by *Brāhmaṇa, Kśatriya* and *Vaiśya* the *Sūtra-kāras* mean that both the boy and the girl of these castes are to be initiated. As in the case of *Svargakāmah* in *Svarga-kāmo yajeta*, here also the gender is not intended to designate the masculine alone. By a rule like this *Brahmano na hantavya* (the *Brāhmaṇa* should not be murdered), it is meant that the *Brāhmaṇi* also should not be murdered. Similarly by saying *Maranadharma manavah* (man is mortal), we mean that the woman is also mortal.

Hārīta says women are of two types: those who speak about *Brāhmaṇ* and those who soon become wives (i.e. those who do not grow old in their parents' houses). Of them, the first type has (the right to) initiation, establishment of fire, the Vedic studies, and observance of begging alms in their own houses; the second is initiated and (soon after) married. Yama says that in ancient times the tying of the girdle is prescribed for girls; so also the teaching in the *Vedas,* and the utterance of the Sāvitrī. Nobody except her father, uncle or brother should teach her. The vow of begging alms is prescribed for her within (the limit of) her house. She should dispense with the deer-skin, the bark and the wearing of matted locks. Here Yama seems to refer to the existence of the custom not only in ancient times, but also in his own days. So he makes the rule for his own time that nobody other than the girl's father, uncle or brother should teach her, she should beg in her house only and she should not wear deer-skin, bark and matted locks.

Without being initiated ceremonially, nobody is entitled to utter holy *mantras.* But the woman is found to utter sacred mantras in various sacrifices, *gṛhya* as well as *śrauta*. In the Sākamedha, the third four-monthly sacrifice, the girl uses the *Tryambaka Mantra.* Mahīdhara in his commentary *Veda-dipa* says the unmarried girls of the sacrificer should walk round the fire three times alongwith the other males, the sons of the sacrificer and others while uttering the *Tryambaka Mantra* for Tryambaka's blessing. According to the Satapatha Brāhmana the priests and the sacrificer go round the altar thrice from right to left—smiting the left thigh; but the maidens go from left to right—smiting the right thigh.

While doing so, the maidens utter the formula, "We worship Tryambaka, the fragrant bestower of husbands. Even as a gourd is severed from its stem, so may I be severed from this world, not from thence." Katyayana[12] says, "Kumaryas ca uttarcna ubhayatra pati-kama bhaga-kama va: the unmarried girls (of the sacrificer) too (should go round the fire), the latter" while uttering part of the mantra, in both the directions (pitṛvad devavac ca parikramane: in gonig round both in the direction of the manes, i.e., the left, and in the direction of the gods, i.e., the right) either with the object of having husbands or fortune". Yajnikadeva in the *Paddbati* says, "Vacanat kumarya api mantra-pathah: the maiden too is to utter the sacred formula as it is so prescribed". Satyasadha also says that if the daughter of the sacrificer longs for marriage, she should take the reverse course (to that taken by the males) alongwith the utterance of the Tryambaka formula.

In the Varuna-praghasas, the second four-monthly sacrifice, after Havis is placed on the north and south altars, the Pratiprasthatr—while leading the wife to the fire for the Karambha-patra oblation—asks her if she has any lover or lovers. After her declaration she utters the formula "Praghasino havamahe marutah, etc.: we invoke the Maruts, the voracious consumers", etc. Then either the wife or the wife and husband both lift up the Karambha vessels on the winnowing baskets, place them on the head and offer oblations in the Daksinagni with the formula "Yad grame, etc; which in the village, etc.". On her way back, the wife recites the formula "Akram karma, etc.: having performed the work".

In the Agnistoma too, the wife, entering by the south door, anoints the axles of the Soma-cart with the remnant of the clarified butter left after the Savitri-homa with the utterance of the formula, "Deva srutau, etc.

There are several such instances where the wife or wives use sacred formulas. The Purāṇas and the Smritis as well furnish examples as to the right of women to utter the holy mantras.

The *Skanda-purāṇa* says that the wife should sacrifice with the sacred formulas in the rituals in accordance with the regulations; so, in the funeral rite too, she, according to the sacred law, is entitled to utter the sacred mantras. The Kaladarsa as quoted in the *Sraddha-mayukha* of Nilkantha Mimamsaka Bhatta, quotes the following lines from the same source to show that women are not entitled to utter the sacred formulas in the funeral and sraddha rites "Sarvabhave striyah kuryuh sva-bhartrnam amantrakam: in the absence of all others, the striyah, i.e., the women should offer to the bhartrs, i.e., the maintainers without mantras."

The word "Striyah" does not mean "wife", but any and every woman maintained by the deceased. In the *Sraddha-viveka,* after enumerating the long list of the sraddhadhikarins, the author says "Tad abhave *yathakathancit* parigrhitah striyah: these failing, any and every woman taken hold of by any means would do." These are the women meant in line above and not the wife. So by "Striyah" in "Sarvabhave Striyah kuryuh", the wife can by no means be meant. The words "apy evam" in line in the order to be uttered and that the rites following should be the same as mentioned before. The Kalpa-taru says that "Strinam apy evam, etc." Here it is evident that the women also utter the mantra in the Sraddha. After having said that the Ekoddista and Sapindikarana should be offered with mantras, Yajnavalkya says "This *Sapindikarana* as well as Ekoddista should be offered to the woman also". Yajnavalkya has suggested no distinction whatsoever. The *Chandogaparisista* also says that the Sapindikarana of the mother is said to be observed with the grandmother (on the father's side) in accordance with the rites as mentioned. Here also no distinction whatsoever is suggested. Here he thinks the couplet "strinam sraddham amantrakam", etc. is baseless (an interpolation) and is not found in all the Samgrahas and so the view that the woman is not entitled to perform the Sraddha with mantra is not tenable. The *Brahmapurana*[29] also says distinctly that the women should offer the Sraddha with mantras.

The prohibition (of the use) of *mantra* applies to those cases only where the women offer the Srāddha. The claim of the wife (Patnī) to perform the funeral and Srāddha for her husband follows immediately after the son, i.e. the son failing, the wife is to do so.

Saṅkha says that the daughter too after her saṃskāra should, like the boy, observe the Aśauca, perform the funeral rite, offer Piṇḍas and celebrate the Ekoddiṣṭa for her father. Here too no distinction has been suggested and accordingly the *mantras* are to be uttered by the daughter too.

The reason why the "Striyah" in line *a* above who are really "Yathā-kathañcit parigrhitāh striyah" in the language of the Srāddha-viveka-kāra should not utter the mantras is therefore, not that the woman, because of her sex, is not entitled to utter the mantra in the Srāddha, but because these women somehow picked out in the absence of all others need not utter the mantras. Such women will perform the Srāddha somehow, and nobody would like them to perform the Srāddhas in all the details. If the mantras are cut out, the oblations are also necessarily cut out and the ceremonies too become reduced by almost two-thirds. This is the reason why these "Yathakathancit parigrhitāh striyah" should not utter the mantras.

The *Nṛisimha-tāpanīya Upanisad* says "Sāvitrim pranavam yajuṣ *stri-sudrayor necchanti:* (some) do not recommend (the utterance of) the savitri, pranava and yajus for the woman and the sudra." Baudhyana says, "Amantra hi striyo matah: some say, women are not entitled to utter the mantra." The words "Na icchanti" and "Matah" in the above texts shows that the authorities themselves do not think that women are not entitled to utter the mantras though there are a few schools who think otherwise. Moreover, the authority of the Smrti cannot be reckoned as valid against that of the Sruti. Thus, Vedvyāsa says that where *Sruti, Smṛti* and *Purāṇa* differ (in opinion), the *Sruti* should be considered as the authority; of the (latter two) *Smṛti* precedes (over the *Purāṇa*). So, the schools whom Baudhāyana mentions need not be taken into serious consideration.

Āśvalāyana says that from the time of marriage onwards the house-holder himself, the wife, the son, the unmarried girl, or a disciple, should offer regular oblations to the Gṛhya fire. Gārgya Nārāyaṇa and Haradatta also cite the opinion of some schools according to whom the wife and the unmarried daughter are entitled to offer the oblation without any reservation. According to the Prayogaratna too, the wife, the unmarried daughter, the son, or the disciple, should offer the sacrifice following the order as mentioned here. So the wife and the unmarried daughter are entitled to offer the oblation alongwith the utterance of *mantras* unquestionably, together with the *Oṃ* at the beginning and end of each *mantra.*

Tarkālankāra thinks that the wife should be given, on this account, so much education as would suffice for this, because "without studies she cannot sacrifice, nor does the *Sūtra* say that she should offer silently. This much confession is sufficient to show that the wife is entitled to the initiation ceremony so that she may be entitled to read at all nor to speak of uttering the Vedic *mantras.*

Paraskara says that the wife should, if she is desirous of conception, offer the first oblation in the evening as well as in the morning along with the utterance of the prescribed mantra wherein she should utter the "Svaha" again. All the commentators Karka, Jayarama, Harihara, Gadadhara and Visvanatha agree to say that the wife should worship the fire with the first oblation in the morning as well as in the evening with the above mantra. The mantra prescribed for her is a Homa-mantra ending with "Svaha: Hail"; as she is to offer the first oblation with this, it is she who is to utter to Pranava also. Without the upanayana, the wife can never do so.

In the commentary upon the Sutra marked 5 by us, Haradatta says that because of the mention of "Eva" and "Tu" in the Sutra all this is said in the above Sutras (2-4) is not proper; and it follows that the names for males should consist of even syllables. The names of females should consist of an odd number of syllables. *Asulvalayana* thus finishes what he has to say about the *Samvyavaharika nama* and proceeds, without making any more distinction, to say about the abhivadaniya name of the child (male and female). (He) should find out a name to be used (by the child) at the time when the child bows down to her (during the upanayana); the parents should keep the name concealed (to themselves) till the child's Initiation. Kumarila Bhatta also holds the same view when he says "Nama abhivadaniyam tu pitror hrdya upanititah: But the name for the child's abhivadana the parents should keep secret till the *upanayana*." This name reserved for use during the initiation ceremony for the girl has no meaning if the girl is not allowed to bow down to the Guru at the proper time.

Sacred Thread

Gobhila says that the bride should wear the sacred thread when the bridegroom leads her to the altar. Leading her forward who is clothed in the proper way and wears the sacrificial cord (over the left shoulder), he should murmur the *mantra.* In the *Adhikara Sutra,* Gobhila himself as well as Katyayana say that one must always wear the sacred thread. So the repetition of yajnopavita here means that for ceremonial purpose the bride should change her former *Yajnopavita* and wear a new one.

Candrakanta Tarkalankara, however, thinks otherwise. He gives us two alternative explanations. Firstly, he says the word yajnopavitinim in the passage means "Yajnopavitinim iva, Yajnopavitavat-krtottariyam: The bride is pravrta krtottariya. How is she Pravrta?: Like a yajnopavitini, like one who has worn the upper garment in the form of a sacred thread." Secondly, *"Pravrtam"* means *"Prakarsena acchaditam smrty-ukta-ritya parihitadhariya-vasanam"* and *"yajnopavitinim"* means "Yajnopavitavat parihitottara-vasanam," i.e., the bride who has worn her lower garments in the manner prescribed in the Smrti Smriti and worn her upper garments in the fashion of a yajnopavita. The learned commentator also says the word yajnopavita may be used in the sense of the Uttariya for showing which way the uttariya is to be worn. These explanations are not tenable.

Tarkalankara quotes the Smrti to show how the bride should be properly dressed: "She should not show the navel, the virtuous wife should wear the clothes down to the heels and should not keep the breasts uncovered." According to his second explanation "Pravrta" means "she who has worn the lower garments" and "Yajnopavita" means "she who has worn the upper garments in the form of sacred thread." The explanation that he gives does not follow the direction he mentions. If "Pravrta" does not mean "One wearing both upper and lower garments" but "One wearing the lower garment" only, the breasts remain uncovered. The uttariya vasana used in the form of a sacred thread cannot cover her breasts.

This pair of sacred threads and the upper garment are here mentioned as a rule as requisite for every ritual; but the particular manner of wearing it—as of the upper garment so of the sacred thread—is to be known from those particular passages in those particular places." For this reason the word yajnopavita cannot be used in the sense of the uttariya. It is declared in the Smrti.

Again, three uttariyas to be made out of a cloth is an anomaly, for, in order to wear it properly, one is to wear the cloth wound round nine times on one's shoulder sideways. Two, and sometimes three of these, are to be worn. Nobody wants the sacrificer to carry a heap of clothes round about him. The real meaning of the passage is what is expressed in the couplet quoted above.

"Two sacred threads are to be worn in the Srauta and Smārta sacrifices; a third one also should be worn for an upper garment: this is prescribed if a cloth is not available." Here it is said that a third sacred thread is to be used if an *uttariya* is not available. If the *uttariya* is not wanting, the third thread is not to be used. Here the word Yajṇopavīta is not certainly used in the sense of *uttariya,* but it said that Yajṇopavita is to be substituted for the uttariya. A substitute for a thing can never be the thing itself. Nor is it reasonable to think that because two different things are worn in the same manner, Gobhila has used one word for the other.

The sacrificer is to wear three upper garments which is nowhere prescribed in the Ritual literature. The cloth, not a sacred thread but an accompaniment of the two threads normally used, is considered as making the number of threads three.

In a sacrifice to be performed even by the widow, she should wear the sacred cord on the right or left shoulder as prescribed and should herself offer the annual or other *srāddhas* to her husband, father-in-law, etc. When she performs an *ekoddista srāddha* for a son, daughter, etc. She should herself do all the initial ceremonial necessaries up to the initial resolution

(Saṃkalpa) and may then give permission to a priest to perform the srāddha on her behalf. In course of the cermony she wears the sacred cord on the right or left shoulder accordingly as the priest does. This is the case when she gives a priest permission to perform the rite for her; no wonder she will do the same in course of performing the rite herself. If she is not entitled to be initiated for the vedic studies and wear the sacred cord, she cannot wear the sacred thread during the sacrifice.

In the section on *Adhikāra-sūtra* prescribing general rules (to be observed in all the rites), Gobhila says that the ceremony should be performed by one wearing the sacrificial thread on one's left shoulder (as a rule) and having sipped water. In other places we have shown that the woman is entitled to perform the sacrifices. Without following the general rule, how can she perform the sacrifice properly.

Even in modern usage there is some relic of the woman's wearing the sacred thread. Now-a-days the bride is made to wear during the marriage the sacred thread of the bridegroom. This is a rite observed by women. Women, owing to their conservative nature, always stick to things of time immemorial.

Gobhila here means that the bride should be properly dressed with the lower garment *(adharīya)* as well as *(uttarīya)* and should wear a pair of new sacred threads; then the husband should lead her, hand in hand, to the marriage altar, while uttering the sacred formula. Though in the section on general rules (*Adhikāra-sūtras*) it has been made a general rule that the sacred thread should be always worn while sacrificing.

Kātyāyana says in the *Karma-pradipa* that in accordance with the seniority in caste and age, the honest wives should separately stir the fire. In stirring the fire the husband should not appoint a *śūdra* wife, an uncontrollable or a vicious one. The strongest of them who is the best of them as it were and certainly best of all those initiated, (i.e., the most learned) should stir the fire last of all with all her heart's content. This shows that Initiation for studies was a condition, not only necessary, but essential, for having preferential treatment in the religious, and consequently, in household affairs too.

In the *Rāmāyaṇa* queen Kauśalyā and in the *Mahābhārata* Sāvitrī and Ambā offer oblations alongwith sacred formulas.

Education

The brilliant record of their Vedic education also shows that women are entitled to be initiated for Vedic studies. The *Rig-veda* furnishes us with a long list of seers composing or discoursing on sacred texts *(Brahmavādinīs)*. According to *Bṛahad-devatā* they form three groups: (1) those that praised the deities; they are all, strictly speaking, vedic seers; (2) those who conversed with seers and deities; (3) those who sang of the evolutionary forms of self; these latter two groups may be called seers in that the hymns or the Rks were revealed through them.

Vājṇavalkya takes pride in teaching his wives Gārgi and Maitreyi the most abstruse philosophical doctrine of Soul. Gargi Vācaknavi is venerated as the champion of all the learned Brahmaṇas present in the court of Janaka to ask Yājṇavalkya, the most learned sage of his age, a series of questions in order to ascertain if they should debate with Yājṇavalkya or not. This time she asks him two questions which he manages to answer. On a subsequent occasion she takes up the question of the old water cosmology. Yājṇavalkya, is however, concerned—so much so that he begins to curse her. Umā Haimavatī tells Agni and Vāyu of the one Supreme Soul. The Vedic literature contains a long list of the names of female teachers of Philosophy and Ritual. The Sāṇkhāyana and *Aśvalāyana-gṛhya-sūtra* mention the names of Gārgī Vācaknavī, Vadava Prāthịitheyī and Sulabhā Maitreyi in the list of Rśis. The Aitareya and Kauśitaki Brāhmaṇas quote the authoritative opinion of a "Kumāri Gandharva-gṛhitā: maiden seized by a Gandharva" that the Agnihotra Ritual which was once performed on both days is now performed on alternate days only. The extensive use of matronymics also may partly be due to the wide reputation of the learning of the mothers, some of whom are most probably teachers. Kātyāyana recognises the established position and honour of women teachers in his Sūtras. Because of the honour shown to the learned women, the parents perform some special ceremony for having a learned daughter. They boil rice mixed with sesamum, eat iot with butter and make themselves worthy of giving birth to a learned daughter. Ātreyi goes from North India to the South to learn the Vedānta from Agastya and others.

Ubhaya Bhārati mediates in the controversy between her husband Maṇḍana Miśra and Saṇkarācārya who represent the Vedic learning in their age.

In the Vedic Ritual women have a recognised position for their songs and aptitude in music. Most probably, these were parts of their Sāma-vedic learning. Women are more willing to have singers rather than *Brahma-vādins*. Women love men who can sing. In the *Mahā-vrata*, wives sing and play various sorts of instruments. The *Satyasadha-srauta-sutra* mentions in this connection the name of the following instruments, viz., Apaghatalika, Talukavina, Kanda-vina, Pichora, and A a-kapisisna; the *Sankhayana-srauta-sutra,* Ghatakarkari, Avaghatarika. Kanda-vina, Pichora, etc.; the *Latyayana-srauta-sutra* also gives a similar list. The *Aitareya-Aranyaka* simply refers to the fact, but does not give any detail. According to Lāṭyāyana the wives should sit to the west of the Udgātṛ and each wife should alternately play two lutes. They must not play one particular instrument called Ghātarī slowly. As every part of the ritual must be perfectly performed, it may be fairly assumed that the wives were expected to be expert musicians and singers.

In one *Pravādana karma* mentioned in the *Vārāha-gṛhya-sūtra* in connection with the marriage ceremony the face of the bride is anointed with hands smeared with *ghee* for making her dear to her husband, brother-in-law and others and then she plays the various instruments and drums which have been consecrated beforehand for the purpose; she prays to the *Dundubhi* and *Gomukha* for excellent children and particularly for charming daughters who, growing up under the same roof and friendly with Indrānī, would play together, and also to Prajāpati for children and welfare.

No better honour could be shown to the learning of women than by depicting the deity of learning as a goddess. Vāc and Sarasvatī represent the highest recognition and respect the Hindu sages could ever show to women.

From our above arguments the conclusion follows that the girl is entitled to have the *Upanayana,* wear the sacrificial thread and utter the *mantras* together with the *praṇava.*

7

Costumes

The dress of women in the Indus Valley civilization consisted of a *sari* fastened by a girdle. A garment to cover the torso does not make its appearance.

The Vedic literature supplies us with very little information about the dress of the women of the age. The vocabulary itself of the period has got no separate words to denote women's clothes. The same words are used to denote the different clothes worn both by men and women. An under-garment and an upper garment were in general use among the members of both the sexes. A waistband was used round the lower garment. Probably both the garments were usually coloured in the case of women, for the Vedic literature refers to the dyer. In addition to the two garments, mentioned above, kings used to wear a gorgeous mantle *(drāpi)* on ceremonious occasions. Queens also probably had the counterpart of this mantle in the form of an embroidered shawl, though there is no definite evidence on the point. In one place goddess Indrānī is described as wearing a headdress; it is probable that the well-to-do ladies of the Vedic age were also doing the same.

The usual custom for the ladies was to arrange the hair in different artistic plaits, the grace of which could not be properly revealed, if the head was covered by a head dress or *oḍhṇi.*

We get no information or clue as to how the lower garment or *sari* was worn in these days. The art of weaving was well developed, and it is fairly certain that the *sari* was a long piece, about five or six yards in length. A portion of it was therefore very probably used to cover the upper part of the body as well, as is done in modern times all over the country. The additional upper garment was probably used only on ceremonious occasions. The same was probably the case with the head-dress.

The epics show that the dress of women continued to be more or less of the above type for a long time. Draupadī's remarks, when summoned to the gambling hall, make it clear that to go out without an upper garment properly covering the entire bust was regarded as indecorous[1]. Draupadi, when dragged out by her garment by Duśśāsana, is described as having the upper part of her *sari* falling down[2]. The additional upper garment was not absolutely necessary to cover the bust. It only formed part of the cermonial dress. Sita therefore could dispense with it when she wanted a piece of cloth to tie her ornaments in order to drop them down to Sugrīva, when she was very anxious to leave behind a clue about her abduction, as she was being carried away through the air by Rāvana.

The Headdress

The fashion of wearing a head-dress, which was sometimes followed in the Vedic age, became rarer in later times. Women are rarely seen wearing a *pagree* in Bharhut or Sanchi sculptures. Curiously enough, sometimes nuns appear with a head-dress at Sanchi. At Ajanta women's head-dress rarely makes its appearance.

Though a pre-fabricated head-dress or *pagree* went out of fashion, women used to cover their head by an odhni, or piece of cloth, which used to cover their head and fall gracefully over their shoulders and back. This fashion was popular in Central India and Mālwā, for ladies sculptured at Bharhut and Sanchi are invariably seen wearing graceful *oḍhṇis*. Apparently it was not popular in Eastern India, Sūrasena (Mathura area) and Deccan, for the Didarganj statue of Yakshini (*c.* 300 B.C.), the ladies sculptured at Mathura (*c.* 100 A.D.) and Nagarjunikonda (*c.* 200 A.D.) and paintings at Ajanta (c. 300-500 A.D.) are seen without any *oḍhṇis.* It would appear that opinion was divided; ladies of fashion wanted to fully exhibit their coiffure by discarding the *oḍhṇi*; others preferred to heighten their charms by costly *oḍhṇis* worn in graceful fashions, partly revealing and partly concealing the coiffure. Gradually both *oḍhṇis* and head-dresses became unpopular; we do not come across them in the medieval sculptures. Orthodox women found it more convenient to cover their head with a portion of their saris. Fashionable ladies did not like to conceal from view their elaborate and artistic coiffure.

Meagre Evidence

The classical *Sanskrit* literature supplies us with meagre

and disappointing data about the dress of women during the first millennium of the Christian era. It no doubt grows very eloquent in several places in describing in detail the beauty of young ladies and their attractive and numerous ornaments, but it rarely describes the constituents of their dress or the precise manner in which it was worn. The scanty available evidence shows that women normally required two garments during this period also. The upper garment or shawl was used only on ceremonial occasions. Goddess Lakshmi, who appears scated on numerous Gupta coins, is seen invariably wearing a shawl, which completely covers her bosom, bust and arms down to the wrist. When in standing posture, ladies used to wear the shawl in different ways. Sometimes it used to cover their entire person down to the ankles. At home the *sari* alone was sufficient, for part of it could decently cover the upper body as well. Women used to take part of their sari over their shoulders so as to completely cover the naval and the breasts. Their waistband, for instance, could become visible only if the upper part of the sari happened to slip down. This could usually occur either when a woman was beside herself, being confounded or overpowered with terror[3], or when she was anxious to disclose the charms of her person when bent upon winnng over a haughtly sage or an indifferent lover. Normally the upper part of the sari covered not only the bust, but it also reached down to the knees. Dharmśāstra writers also lay it down that women should be so dressed that their navel should never become visible and legs should be covered down to the ankles.[4]

The sculptural evidence, however, seems to be partly in conflict with the above observations, based mainly on the data of literature. In the early sculptures of the Punjab and the North-Western Frontier Province C. 100 B.C. to 300 A.D.) we undoubtedly come across several female statues, whose busts are covered with part of their *saris,* as described in the epics and classical *Sanskrit* literature. Such, for instance, is the case with the numerous statues of Hārīti[5]. Māyādevi, seated by her husband's side when listening to the prophesy about her newborn babe, and a beautiful standing Nāgī in human form are both shown covering their shoulders and breasts with a part of their *saris*[6]. The same is the case with several female statues at Mathurā[7].

But the sculptures in Central and Southern India and the paintings at Ajanta and Bagh caves have quite a different tale to tell. In the sculptures at Bharhut (c. 150 B.C.) the *sari* is generally seen covering the body below the naval; no part of it is taken round the bust so as to cover the breasts and shoulders. A separate upper garment is often worn by ladies, but it does not at all cover their bosom. The same is the case with the sculptures at Sanchi and Amaraoti[8] and paintings at Ajanta, which cover the first four or five centuries of the Christian era.

Cunningham did not make proper allowance for the circumstance that many of the carvings are not now left in the same condition in which they were, when finished by the artists. Havell has pointed out that the exaggerated thinness of the legs in the human figures at Amaraoti makes it clear that the sculptures had their finishing coat of plaster. Late Balasaheb Pantpratinidhi, Rajasaheb of Aundh, who was a distinguished artist and art critic, has adduced further evidence in support of the above theory. He has pointed out that in some bas-relies at Amaraoti ladies are to be seen having the *sari* at the waist and also at the feet rolling in folds. At their back also we see some folds hanging down. But the thighs and legs are bare (Plate VI). Now it is clearly impossible to so wear a *sari* that it should cover the waist and feet, but leave the legs and thighs bare in front. The only possible explanation is the one offered by the Rajasaheb, viz., in order to produce an effect of transparent garment the limbs of the body, such as the thighs etc., were first carved nude and then given the finishing touch of coating and colouring[9].

It is therefore clear that in Amaraoti sculptures at any rate nudity was not the order of the day; the *saris* were shown partly in carving and partly in plastering and colouring. The upper body therefore may have been covered by that portion of the *sari* which was to be shown in plastering and colouring. In one place in carving also we do actually get the example of a female taking a portion of her *sari* across her bust and over her shoulders, so as to completely cover her bosom.[10] This was the normal dress of the ladies of the age and province.

It must be, however, admitted that this explanation of the dress being shown partly in carving and partly in colouring does not hold good of many schools of sculpture in ancient India. Such is particularly the case with the sculptures at Bharhut and Sanchi in Central India. Here, unlike at Amaraoti, the whole of the *sari* covering the waist, the thighs and the legs is shown in carving; the method of its wearing also shows that no part of it was intended to be taken over the shoulders so as to cover the bust. It is therefore not possible to argue that the breasts of women in the sculpture at these places were intended to be subsequently covered by a garment that was to be shown partly in plastering and partly in colouring. This process would have been also a costly one for the sculptures at these places were intended to be exposed to the rain and sunshine throughout the year. Replastering and recolouring would have been frequently necessary, and the monks at these monasteries could not have found it always easy to get generous donors to defray the necessary expenditure. Are we then to conclude from the evidence of the plastic art that the women in central India used to move about with their breasts uncovered in the early centuries of the Christian era.

Nor can it be argued that the upper person of the women in these sculptures is bare, because the sculptors were not skilful enough to show the same *sari* as covering both the lower and the upper part of the body. They could have avoided this difficulty by using a separate upper garment to cover the bust. As a matter of fact at both these places ladies of position are often seen wearing an upper garment, but it does not cover the breasts[11]. In the case of the Ajanta paintings at any rate the excuse of inefficiency cannot be advanced. The artists were experts and they could easily have shown their women wearing the *sari* in such a way as to cover both the upper and the lower parts of the body. But they have not done so. It is true that most of the women at Ajanta, whose breasts appear uncovered, are in the privacy of their inner apartments where they may not perhaps be expected to wear their full dress. But in some Ajanta frescoes we find women moving about even in public streets, with the same insufficient dress. In one scene, for instance, we see a queen moving in a procession in the state carriage alongwith her husband; she is, however, shown as wearing neither a jacket nor a bodice, nor is her *sari* covering her breasts.

Shrimant Balasaheb Pantpratinidhi, the late Rajasaheb of Aundh, suggested that we can account for this insufficient dress of women at Elora and Ajanta on the assumption that the artists were Dravidian in culture.[12] He points out that even-to-day very few women in Kochin and Malbar wear any upper cloth. So Dravidian artists have shown their women folk as wearing just the dress that was current in Dravidian society. The Rajasaheb held that the artists at Bharhut and Sanchi, on the other hand, were following the Aryan tradition, and so have shown their women as wearing an upper garment which covers the breasts and falls over the left shoulder.[13]

This theory also is not free from difficulties. It may be at the outset pointed out that the distinction sought to be drawn between the so-called Dravidian artists at Ajanta and Elora and the so-called Aryan artists at Bharhut and Sanchi is not supported by actual data; for the artists of the latter places are as indifferent in covering the breasts of their women as those at the former.[14] Sometimes they show their ladies wearing an upper garment, but it is so worn as not to cover the breasts at all.[15]

It is further very doubtful whether all Dravidian women were actually accustomed to move about without covering their breasts. It is true that till quite recently women in Malabar used to regard a bodice or an upper garment as not very necessary. But the Malbar practice was probably a primitive one and cannot be regarded as typically Dravidian. At any rate the ladies in Tamil and Telugu provinces were not accustomed to move about without properly covering their upper portion. In this connection the *Saptasati* of Hala, which undoubtedly reflects the Dravidian life during the early centuries of Christian era, supplies conclusive evidence. Three verses in this anthology make it quite clear that Dravidian women used to cover their breasts with adequate clothing.[16] The first of these clearly refers to the breasts being covered by the upper garment. The anthology further shows that Dravidian women not only used to cover their upper person with a part of their *sari* or by a separate shawl, but that they also wore a bodice or *Kanchuki.* Its ends were tied together between the breasts,[17] and it was not entirely removed even in the privacy of the bed-room.[18] It is not therefore possible to argue that the women at Elora and Ajanta do not cover their breasts because they are the representatives of Dravidian culture. The *Saptasati* shows clearly that the Dravidian ladies in contemporary times used to cover their upper portion with a bodice and an upper garment; the so-called Aryan artists at Sanchi and Bharhut are as careless about covering the breasts of their women as are so-called Dravidian fellow workers at Elora and Ajanta.

The real explanation of women appearing without covering their busts properly in the sculptures and paintings of Southern and Central India seems to be the artistic convention of the age. Breasts are the most significant symbol of motherhood and the artists of these provinces probably felt that they may be shown uncovered in works of art, though they may be normally concealed in actual life under a bodice or a part of the *sari.* This convention facilitated the task of fully exhibiting the beauty of the female form without suggesting any indecency. It also gave the artists an opportunity to show the different beautiful ornaments worn on the chest, the neck and the shoulder. This would become quite clear from several statues like those of Indrani and Nārasimhī discovered at the Sutna residency, and now exhibited in the Indian Museum, Kolkata. In the case of these images the lower and upper rims of their shawls can be clearly seen at the elbow and shoulder respectively. But the intervening space as well as the entire bust are shown altogether uncovered by the shawl, obviously with a view to display the ornaments worn at the neck, the chest and the shoulder. There was nothing unusual in this procedure, for the art convention everywhere prescribes a much scantier dress for women than is actually used by them in normal life. This will be quite evident to all the students of ancient and modern sculptures and paintings of European countries. Just as we cannot conclude that women in modern Europe move about in a nude condition in society because they appear entirely uncovered in some wroks of art, so also we cannot maintain that women in ancient India moved about in public without covering their upper portion, because their breasts are shown uncovered in sculptures and paintings of Central and Southern India. The fact is that the dress in sculptures and paintings is not always a faithful copy of the dress actually in vogue in everyday life. The non-recognition of this truth will lead to strange deductions. We shall have to conclude that the Buddha allowed a much ampler dress to the nuns of his Orders than was ever worn by ladies of fashion. The former were allowed to have three pieces of cloth, while the latter in sculpture are seen to be wearing only one or two. We shall have to admit that maid-servants used to wear richer dresses than the princess they served; for at Ajanta the former are seen wearing gaudy and striped bodices which are never seen on the bodies of the latter. We cannot therefore ignore the conclusive evidence supplied by contemporary literature and conclude that women were not properly covering their breasts and busts in ancient India either by a bodice or by a portion of their *sari*. The standard of decorum universally accepted in Dharmasastra and in literature required a woman not only to wear a bodice, but also to cover her bust with an upper garment.

To conclude the artists of Central and Southern India held that the unfolding of the beauty of the female form by showing the bust uncovered in a work of art need not and should not give rise to any indecent thoughts, if the woman concerned were a lady of virtuous character. To the spectator she would strike as a mother. If, however, she was a dancing or singing girl there would not be this sacred atmosphere around her. The artist, therefore, felt that she should not be shown displaying the charms of her uncovered bust. As a consequence we usually find dancing girls appearing with a full dress covering their entire necks to ankles. They are seen covering their breast with jackets, blouses or frocks. This would become quite clear from the dancing scenes at Bharhut, Bagh caves and Sarnath.[19]

We may discuss here the controversial question as to whether stitched clothes were in vogue in the Vedic age. In the Indo-Iranian times the Aryans were undoubtedly living in a cold climate, where stitched clothes would have been welcome; but then they had not probably sufficiently advanced in civilisation to begin their use. The *Rig Veda* refers to Varuṇa as wearing a Drāpi while sitting in his heavenly court. But whether this was a mantle or an overcoat we do not know. In the marriage hymn the bride is described as wearing a Śāmulyam on her wedding night, which was discarded the next morning. This may have been the sari rather than a short. According to the Kātyāyana Srauta Sūtra the wife of the sacrificer was given a chaṇḍātaka or *dahara* to wear, when she had to ascend by a very high step to the top of the sacrificial pillar. While doing so, the thighs were likely to be exposed if there was no underwear, as the *sari* was very probably used in the *vikachchha* fashion. So a Chaṇḍātaka, which has been expressly described as a short would have been very desirable. The original Vedic passages where this ceremony is described, do not, however, refer to any Chaṇḍātaka being worn by the wife on the occasion; the word is also not known to Pāṇini, Pataṇjali and Amara. Kātyāyana is therefore probably referring to an innovation of this age, when he refers to the short or Chanḍataka, being worn by the wife on the occasion. In the Vedic age very probably only a *dahara* or *kaupina,* that is a strip of cloth to be worn on a girdle in between the legs, was used on the occasion. Though, therefore, sewing was known in the Vedic age, as is made clear by reference quoted above, there is no evidence of stitched clothes having come into general vogue at the time.

Sewn Clothes

The help of the art of sewing seems to have been first taken for preparing the bodice. This took place even before 600 B.C., for Buddhist and Jain nuns are enjoined to use it. Its traces can be seen below the breasts of the statue of Chaṇḍā Yakshiṇī at *Bharhut.* If the bodice is not shown on the other female statues of the peace, the desire to show off the ornaments on breast may have been the obvious reason. The bodice did not require much tailoring like the modern blouse. It had short sleeves but no buttons, and it was secured in its proper place by its ends being tied together in between the two breasts.[20] On one of the coins Samudragupta, Lakshmī can be seen wearing the bodice precisely in this way. We can see both the knot and the two ends hanging down in its continuation. From Kālidāsa, however, we learn that sometimes the ends of the bodice were tied in a knot on the shoulder;[21] what was the make up of this type of bodice and how it was tied on the shoulder is rather difficult to understand. The bodice required very little tailoring and women used to stitch it at home. It could be easily taken out, if necessary, to protect oneself against the lunar or solar rays. A narrow breast band was also used across the bosom in the Deccan and Ceylon. This fashion did not spread to northern India.[22]

Jackets, blouses and frocks seem to have come into vogue in the plains of northern India, when they were included in the dominions of the *Scythians,* the *Kushanas* and other Central Asian invaders. As these conquerors hailed from a very cold region, they were accustomed to wear shirts, trousers and overcoats. This is quite clear from the evidence of their coinage. Kushāṇa kings like Kanishka and Huvishka are invariably seen wearing a trouser and an overcoat on their coins.[23] In the Mathura and Gandhāra sculptures, which belong to the period of Kushāṇa supremacy (c. 50. A.D. to c. 300 A.D.), women begin to appear in blouses and frocks. In one bas-relief at Mathura even Sapta Mātṛikās are seen wearing frocks.[24] In Ganddhāra sculptures, which mostly hail from the N.W.F. Province, blouses and jackets are fairly common. In one place we find Hārīti wearing a blouse of long sleeves.[25] A Nagiṇi in human form is also seen doing the same. In another sculpture, Māyādevī is shown wearing a frock over her *sari.*[26] On one of the coins of the Scythian ruler Azilises even goddess Lakshmī standing on a lotus is represented as wearing a blouse and a trouser.[27]

Parts of India were under Scythian rule for different periods during the first four centuries of thue Christian era. This circumstance very probably facilitated the spread of the fashion of stitched clothes in Hindu society. The tendency to imitate the dress of the rulers is not peculiar to the modern times. It existed in the past as well.

Society, however, had a general prejudice against stitched clothes, and women were for a long time reluctant to take to jackets, blouses and frocks. We find only dancing girls adopting the new fashion in dress in the beginning. This would become quite clear from the fact that it is only women of this class, and not ladies of rank, who are seen wearing jacket and blouses at Bharhut, Bagh and Sarnath. At Ajanta we sometimes find maid-servants wearing shorts and jackets; ladies of position, however, are still seen avoiding their use. It is quite possible that greater stitching was introduced in the bodice (kaṇchuki) at this time, but the prejudice against full fledged jackets, blouses and frocks remained unabated. These became common among a section of ladies in the Muslim period. They continued to be regarded as a foreign innovation, and women in orthodox families engaged in religious duties used to remove them for the time being.

We may passingly refer here to the dress of the Buddhist

nuns. They were permitted the three pieces of cloth allowed to the monks, samghaṭi' (for the lower part), antarvāsaka (for the upper part), and uttarāsaṇga, (the covering garment). Kaṇchuki or bodice was also prescribed especially for the young nuns. Jainism permitted a larger number of clothes to its nuns, especially by way of shorts and underears.

The kind of cloth used by women for their dress differed with their status. Maidens and women in coverture used to wear gay and embroidered cloth. The ladies of the 4th and 5th centuries A.D. used to prefer dotted, striped gauzy and embroidered muslins for their bodices. This is quite clear from several paintings as Ajanta.[28]

Widows do not appear to have used any bodices. The colour of their *saris* was plain white in the early period. The widowed daughters-in-law of Dhṛitarāshṭra are described as wearing white garments, when they went to see their old father-in-law in the forest.[29] The orthodox practice of Deccan widows to wear reddish *saris* seems to be due to the influence of the colour of the garments of Buddhist nuns. The Gujarat practice of giving black garments to the widow seems also to be a post-epic development. Like the people in the west Gujaratis held that black was the proper colour for a person in mourning and therefore for the dress of the widow, who was to be in a perpetual mourning. In Bengal and northern India, however, the old custom continues and widows still wear white plain saris without any borders.

The *lahangā,* which is so common in Rajputana and northern India at present, was altogether unknown for a long time. We meet it for the first time in some rare Mathura sculptures of the 2nd century A.D., where only maid servants or milkwomen are seen using it.[30] It became popular in higher society only in medieval times after the establishment of the Mahomaden rule. It is not referred to in literature, nor seen in paintings and sculptures of the Hindu period. It however became quite common after a few centuries of Muslim rule. In northern India it even became an indispensable constituent of the traditional bridal dress. In south India the Muslim influence was less felt and so the *lahangā* or *parakara* became common only among small girls Grown up women did not take to it.

The paintings of the Moghul period give a fairly accurate

idea of the dress of women, who had come under the influence of the new fashions brought into vogue with the advent of the Muslim rule. These ladies used to wear a *lahangā* or *pyjamā* down from their waist. The former was sewn in different artistic designs, and nothing was usually worn over it. The *pyjamā*, however, was a simple one, and usually a short *sari* was worn over it. The bust was covered by a bodice or a jacket. An upper garment or *oḍhṇī* was also in vogue; it hung down from the head covering a portion of the back. In rural areas and orthodox circles the old dress continued to be current. Women are naturally more conservative than men, and so the British domination for 150 years did not effect any revolution in their dress. They continued to use their old dress consisting of a *sari*, a bodice and a shawl, even when their husbands have begun to don suits, neckties and collars. The bodice, however, is becoming more and more artistic and fashionable. Shorts and frocks have become common among girls in urban areas, but there are yet no indications that grown up ladies would take to them in large numbers. With increasing facilities in communications women are in a better position to observe the dress prevailing in neighbouring States, and there is a tendency among educated and fashionable ladies to borrow some fashions current in other parts of the country. Thus the *vikachchha* mode of wearing sari is now becoming common among the fashionable ladies in the urban areas of the Deccan. The dress of the average women, however, still continues to be the old traditional one of her province. The *lahangā* is the only exception. The main reason for this conservatism is that the fact that the traditional dress is on the whole well-suited for the climate of the country.

Ornaments

The reader must have seen that on the whole the dress of women was simple. Simplicity, however, did not characterise their tastes in the realm of ornaments. Since very early times they have been fond of wearing very brilliant and artistic ornaments in quantities that cannot be described as meagre. Men, however, are to a large extent responsible for the development of this taste among women; for a reader of the Vedic literature or a student of ancient sculptures and paintings will find it difficult to decide as to who was fonder of ornaments, men or women. Men used to vie with women in the number of ornaments to be worn on their person. They seem to have lagged behind them only in the the case of the ornaments on the forehead, which were generally used by women alone. This fondness for ornaments was to some extent a natural consequence of the general prosperous condition of our motherland in these days.

In the Vedic age bangles were worn both on hands and feet by men and women.[31] Their number was probably a large one; whether they reached right up to the elbow or the knee, as they did in the case of one figurine discovered at *Mohenjo Daro*[32] and in numerous images and sculptures of the ancient and medieval period, we do not know. Rings were used on fingers. Shoulders were not neglected; they had their own ornaments, which must obviously have been large in size.[33] Necklaces of gold and precious stones were used on the neck; they used to reach down to the chest.[34] Earnings (karṇaśobhana) are also referred to. An ornament called *kumbha* was worn on -the head; we do not know its precise size or nature.[35]

Gold, silver and precious stones were the chief material for these ornaments. Pearls are referred to in one passage in a very late *Brahmana* work.[36] The *Aryans* could have become familiar with them only when they reached the sea in course of time. It is interesting to note that glass bangles are not referred to in *Sanskrit* literature.

Sculptures, paintings and the Nāṭyaśāstra of Bharata throw a flood of light on the nature and number of different ornaments used by our women in the early centuries of the Christian era. It is not at all possible to describe them in detail in words. One can get an adequate idea of them only from their representations in sculptures and paintings. More than half a dozen different ornaments, partly made of gold and partly of pearls, were used to adorn the head and the forehead. One can get an adequate idea of their nature and gracefulness only by studying them in Ajanta paintings. The designs of earings were very graceful. The variety in the nature of necklaces of gold and pearls is indeed striking. Shoulders were adorned with Keyūras, of which there were several types. Nor was the portion just above the elbow neglected. The number of bangles worn on the hand was very large; in Bengal they were often joined together so as to form a composite ornament reaching almost to the elbow.[37] The fashion at Ajanta, however, prescribed only a few bangles for the hand. They were often set with pearls or diamonds. The number of bangles worn on the feet was a large one; some of them used to produce a gingling sound, when their wearers were in motion.

The fashions of dressing the hair were as numerous as graceful. An examination of the paintings at Ajanta will be an eye-opener even to the most fashionable ladies of the present generation. These fashion can be better seen in the original than described in words. It is customary at present to talk of Orissa as a backward province. The fashions of hair dressing were current there twelve hundred years ago were, so varied and graceful. The beauties of Orissa were not content with the quantity of hair, which nature had given to them; they used to add some padding or stuffing or false or borrowed hair to increase its mass, so as to render the different hair-arrangements possible. Some ladies used to arrange the hair in gradually receding tiers, some used to turn them up in a fantastic cone, curling and twisting upwards behind the head and kept in its position, probably by means of a wire concealed. Some used to arrange them in two artistic bundles hanging on either side of the head while others used to add a third one perched just at the top of their Crown. Pearl strings were liberally used to help the hair to retain its new shape and configuration. We find the hair arranged into six braids and then twisted up into six rays, kept into an erect position either by means of wax, or with the help of sticks or wires enclosed within. The Mathura fashions two thousands years ago were equally interesting. Some ladies arranged the hair in two tiers separated by flower gardens, others beautified them by tassels, hanging down beautifully shows a simple but artistic knot of the hair beautified by flower wreaths and gold plaques.

Ointments were used not only for the eyes but also for the lips and teeth.[38] Sandal paste and saffron powder were used for the face and the breasts. Different types of dyes and ointments were used for decorating hands, feet, fingres and toes. Ornamental linear figures were drawn on cheeks and breasts to heighten their charms. A streak of Sindhūra on the head or a circular mark of Kumkuma on the forehead was made by maidens and women in coverture. This was regarded as an indispensable sign of saubhāgya or married bliss. Inscriptions often describe how valorous kings used to kill their opponents and deprive their wives of the use of *Sindhura.*[39] Women were leading a simple ascetic life during their widowhood. The use of ornaments or embroidered clothes was therefore out of question for them. While describing the achievements of their heroes, the authors of inscriptions often state how the bracelets of the wives of their enemies dropped off alongwith their necklaces.

It is interesting to point out here that among the numerous ornaments described by poets and illustrated by sculptors and painters, the nose-ring and two-ring are conspicuous by their absence. This is rather surprising, because both of them are at present regarded as an indispensable for a women with her husband living. The omission of the two-ring may have been accidental, as it is otherwise not a very prominent or valuable ornament. But the case of nose-ring is quite different. It is a very important ornament. It is in use in all provinces at present. It is regarded as a sign of *saubhāgya* or married bliss. Till recently every bride used to get it at the time of her marriage. Women of the old fashion would never go out without wearing it. And yet we find that Bharata does not mention it in his exhaustive list of the ornaments of women given by him in the 23rd chapter of his Nātyaśāstra. Ornaments for almost every limb are to be found in this list, but there is no mention of the nose-ring for the nose. It is also true of the list of ornaments given in the Amarakosha also. Sanskrit poets and dramatists also show no acquaintance with the ornament. In fact there is no word in Sanskrit language to denote it. Words for the ornament in modern vernaculars cannot be derived from any Sanskrit original. The word *vesara* used for the ornament by a section of Hindi-speaking population is of unknown origin. The word *vāḷi* used by the Gujaratis is of a secondary origin; it originally denotes a *valaya* or circular ornament, and is secondarily used to denote the nose-ring because of its roundish shape. The words *natha, nathia, nathni, nathīhā, nathnag,* etc., which are used to denote the ornament in different vernaculars of India, are all derived from the *Prakrit* word *nattha,* which denotes the string passed through the nose of an animal in order to control it with ease. It does not denote any nose ornament at all in any *Prakrit* or *Apabhramśa* language. It has no prototype of its own in Sanskrit.

At Udayagiri and Bhuvanesvara in Orissa, at Bodhagaya and Patna in Bihar, at Bharhut and Sanchi in Central India, at Mathura in U.P., at Taxila in the Punjab, at Ajanta, Ellora, and Badami in the Deccan, at Amaravati in Madras presidency, we have found several sculptures and paintings of women who are over-loaded with a rich variety of ornaments all over their body. The nose-ring is, however, nowhere to be seen. These sculptures and paintings are spread over almost all the centuries of the first millenium of the Christian era. It is therefore clear that the nose-ring was unknown throughout the whole of India during the entire Hindu period. Hindu sculptures of Puri and Rajputana of post-Muslim period and mural paintings in the Padmanābhasvāmi temple at Trivendrum of the 14th century begin to show the nose-ring from the 13th century. Both the positive and the negative evidence thus shows that the nosering is not a Hindu ornament. It seems to have been clearly borrowed from the Mahomadens. It is indeed a mystery how this ornament of foreign origin should have come to be regarded as the most important insignia of *saubhāgya*.

The above conclusion, however, is not accepted by some scholars,[40] who point out how the nose-ring is clearly referred to in several poems (stotras) of the great Śaṇkarāchārya clearly refers to this ornament in the Saudarya-laharī.

It may be observed in reply that a very large number of poems *(stotras)* have been popularly ascribed to the great Śankarāchārya, but his authorship of all of them is by no means certain. The above poems may have been composed by a late medieval writer, and been later ascribed to Śaṇkarāchārya. *Arabs* probably borrowed the ornament from the *Hebrews,* as it is mentioned in the old Testament.[41]

The modern economist may perhaps regret that so much money should have been locked up in the unremunerative investment in ornaments. It is, however, to be noted that there were not many safe and productive sources of investment in the past. It may be further pointed out that from the purely woman's point of view, the habit of investing a large part of family savings was desirable development. For a long time women are denied the right to have a share in the immovable property of the family. As far as moveables like ornaments and jewelry were concerned, they were allowed to have a complete sway over them. Ornaments worn by a woman during coverture, and intended really for her alone, constituted her Strīdhana, and could not be taken away from her by coparceners. The more the amount invested in the ornaments, the stronger therefore became the economic position of the wife. The large amounts invested in them have enabled thousands of Hindu women to tide over difficult times.

References

1. एकं च वासो मम मन्दबुद्धे सभां नेतुं नार्हसि मामनार्य ।।
   II, 89, 44.
2. प्रकीर्णकेशी पतितार्धवस्त्रा दुःशासनेन व्यवधूयमाना ।।
   II, 89, 47.
3. Compare, for instance, the description of Gopīs given by Bhāsa when they were terrified by Krishna's fight with Kāliya serpent:—
   संभ्रान्ता गलितोत्तरीयवसनास्त्रस्ताकुलव्याहृताः ।
   Bālacarit, IV, I.
4. Compare, for instance, Aśvaghoṣa's description of one of the damsels sent to dissuade prince Siddartha from renuncing the world:—
   मुहुर्मुहुर्मदव्याजस्रस्तनीलांशुकापरा ।
   आलक्ष्यरशना रेजे स्फुरद्विधुरिव क्षपा ।।
   Buddhacarit, IV, 133.
5. न नाभि दशमदागुल्फाद्वासः परिवध्यात् । न स्तनी विवृति कुर्यात् ।।
   Sankhasmriti
6. Bachhoffer, *Early Indian Sculpture,* Pl. 150 B; Grundwedel, *Buddhist Art in India,* (Eng. Trans.), fig. 55, p. 104.
7. Hargreave, *The Buddha Story in Stone,* Pl. VIII; Bachhoffer, Pl 150.
8. Agrawal, *Mathurd ki Bauddhakald,* Pl. XIV.
9. Cunningham, *The Stupa of Bharhut,* Plates XIII an XXI.
10. *A.B.O.R.I.,* Vol. III, p. 19.
11. Cunningham, *Tree and Serpent Worship,* Pl. LIX.
12. Cunningham, *The Stupa of Bharut,* Pls XIII, XXI.
13. B.S. Pantpratinidhi, *Elora,* p. 100.
14. *Ibid.,* p. 97.
15. *The Stupa of Bharhut,* Pl. XXII. 3; XXIII. 3.
16. *Ibid.,* Pb IXIII & XX.
17. रक्तदुकूलान्तरितः स्तननखलेख इव नववध्वाः ।
   VI, 69

बलादाकृष्टवस्त्राधन्तिप्रस्थिते मंथरं त्वं व्रज ।

II, 62.

नीलपटप्रावृतांगीति मा खल्वेनां त्वं परिहर ।

VI, 20.

Sanskrit renderings of the Prakrit verses is being quoted here.

18. द्वयंगुलकक पाटपिनद्धसविशेषनीकलन्चुलिका ।
दर्शयति स्तनस्थलवर्णिकामिव तरुणीं युवजनेभ्यः ।।

VII, 20.

19. ग्रामतरुण्यो हृदयं हरन्ति विदग्यानां स्तनभारवत्यः ।
मदने कुसुम्भरागयुक्तकन्चुकाभरणभ्रान्ताः ।।

VI, 45.

20. Cf. Mahāvsnetā's descrition.
स्तनयुगुलनिवद्धग्रंथिना कल्परुलतावल्कलेन कृतोत्तरीयाम् ।

Kadambari, p. 248.

21. इदमुपहितसूक्ष्मग्रंथिना स्कन्धदेशे स्तनयुगपरिणाहाच्छादिना वल्कलेन ।

Sukuntala I, 19

21. Smith, *History of Fine Arts in India and Ceylon,* Pl. LVII, Gopinath Rao, Hindu Iconography, I, ii, Pl. 99.
22. In the early period of their coinage Gupta kings also are seen wearing this foreign dress; it took a few decades for them to discard it in favour of the national Hindu dress.
23. Agarwal, *Mathura ki Buddhakala,* Pl. 21.
24. Bachhoffer, Pl. 150, B.
25. Indian Museum, Calcutta; Gandhār gallery exhibit No. 13.
26. *Punjab Museum Coin Catalogue,* Vol. I, Pl. XIII, No. 332.
27. Smith, *A History of Fine Arts,* p. 288, fig. 207
28. शुक्लोत्तरीया नरराजपत्न्यः ।
Motichandra—*Bharatiya Veshabhursha*, p. 125.
29. *R.V., V.* 54, II; I, 1168, 3.
30. Kramrisch, *Indian Sculpture,* pl. I, 4.
31. अंसेष्वा वः पप्रथेषु खादयः ।

R.V.I., 166, 9.

32. *R.V.,* V, 54, II; I, 122, 14.
33. *Ibid.*
34. कुरीरमस्य शीर्षणि कुम्भ चाधिनिदध्मसि ।

A.V., VI, 138, 3.

35. *Shadrimla Brahmana,* V. 6.
36. Bhattasali, *Iconography,* Plates XIX, XX.
37. नेत्रयोरन्जनं कार्यमयरस्य च रन्जनम् ।

दन्तानां विविया रागाश्चतुर्णा शुक्लता तथा ।। *Naityaidstra,* 23, 20.

38. यस्यानने शरदखण्डशशिप्रसन्ने कोपं व्यनक्ति हृदयस्थमरिप्रियाणाम् ।
सिन्दूरभूषणविवर्जितमास्यपद्यमुत्सुष्टहारवलयं कुचमण्डलन्च ।।
Khajuraho Inscription, 953 A.D., *E.L.;* I., p. 129.

39. E.g. Dasgupta, *Calcutta Review,* May, 1937.

40. *New Indian Antiquary,* 1943-3, p. 25.

41. पत्यौ जीवति यः स्त्रीभिरलङ्कारो धृतो भवेत् ।
न तं भजेरन्दायादा भजमानाः पतन्ति ते ।।
Manu, IX, 200.

8

Sexual Life

In ancient India, the father gave his daughter to a man of good character, good knowledge and good business.

Bhīshma said: "The good must give the daughter to a wooer gifted with excellencies, having informed themselves of his character and way of life, his knowledge, his origin, and his business. That is the Brahma form of good *Brahmans*. Let him that gives her away of his free will[1] win thus as son-in-law a man fitted to wed his daughter. This is the unswerving duty of the learned (that is, of the *Brahmans*) and of warriors. If a man without regard to his own wish (the father's, etc.) shall have to give the maiden to gun whom she loves and who loves her, then the Veda-learned call this the Gandharva kind.[2] If a man buys the maiden for goods in one of the many ways and means, enticing her kinsfolk, then the wise call that the demon form. If a man by force robs the weeping girl from her home, slaying and cutting off the heads of the weeping (kindred), that is known as the *Rākshasa* form. Of five now there are lawful, and two unlawful: the *Paicaca* and the demon custom must never be practised. The Brahmanic form, the warrior form and the *Gandharva* form are lawful: either separately or mingled they are to be followed. Three kinds of wives are for the *Brahman,* two for the warrior, the Vaisya shall only wed in his own caste. The children of these (wives from different castes) are on an equality with one another (all take the father's caste). Let the Brahmanic wife be the first (of a Brahman), the *Kshtriyā* of a *Kshtriyā.* For pleasure a Sūdrā is also allowed. But other people say no. The begetting of offspring with a Sūdrā wife is not a thing praised by the good. But if a *Brahman* begets with a Sudrā wife, then he must atone for it.[3] Let the man of thirty years wed a ten-year-old wife, a nagnikā (one that has not yet menstruated), or let the man of twenty-one get one seven years old. A man shall never take for himself a woman that has no brother or no father, for she is under the duty whereby her son must be held to be the sons of her father. Three year shall a maiden wait after the first coming of her menses, but when the fourth has come, let her get a husband herself. She will then never have lost offspring and the pleasures or love. But if she do otherwise, then she offends against Prajāpati. One that on the mother's side is not akin trough the offering to the dead, and not on the father's side through having the same clan *(gotra)*—such a wife let a man seek; this is the law Manu proclaimed.

Yudhisthira spoke: "If one man has given the price and another has said: 'I will give it,' a third demands her win violence, a fourth shows money, and a fifth has taken hold of her hand, whose wife is the then, O grandfather? Be those for us, who would know the truth, the eye." Bhishma spoke "Whatever be the deed of a human being, It is seen to serve him in life when it is furnished with holy sayings (mantra) when it is discussed with them. False words, however, are a crime leading to the loss of caste. Even a wife, a husband, a high priest, a master, and the scholar's teacher are deserving of punishment, if they utter an untruth.

'No', other people say. But Manu does not praise a living together with reluctance. What is untrue is without glory and rightness, a harm done to virtue.[4] In no man is only perverseness to be found.[5] How should it come to be there, whether the kinsfolk give the daughter free according to the law, or whether she is bought?[6] When the kinsfolk have given their consent, holy words and sacrifices may be used, then these words have an effect; but none whatever in the case of a girl who is not (anyhow afterwards) given. Yet the mutual contract concluded with holy words by the wife and the husband is declared to be weightier than that concluded by kinsfolk.[7] The husband, according to the law's teaching,[8] acquires the wife given by the gods. So he[9] brings to nought the words of gods and men as untrue." Yudhishṭhira spoke: "If the maidens has already acquired (brought in) the purchase price, and a better wooer now comes, in whom virtue, love, and advantage are found in full strength, can we in that case speak of falsehood?[10] Here, where from both sides there is a threat of error, he that has to act yet would fain do what is best . . . ." Bishma spoke: "The father in no wise accepted it with the thought 'The price is what decides.' For the good never give their daughter because they are thinking of the price, but, it is from a wooer endowed with other advantages that the kinsfold demand the price when a man gives her away of his own free choice, decking her out and saying: 'Take her home.' And when he thus gives her away, it is no purchase price, no sale. If he has accepted it, he must then give it (to his daughter), that is a law never to be broken. I a man has earlier thus spoken: 'I will give thee my daughter,' then those are no words (that does not hold); if anyone has said this, of if he has said: 'No,' or: 'Of a truth' (none of that holds). Therefore they woo one another (they woo on both sidews) up to the taking by the hand. The wooer of the maidens is bestowed by the Maruts, so we have heard. To none that is not according to her wishes shall a daughter be given. That is demanded by the Rishis. That is the root of offspring which has its root in love. This is what I hold.[11] Pondering now, know that in this twofold business[12] there lie many mistakes, for here it is that we have to do with living together. Heat how the purchase price never decided the matter. I brought may two maidens for Vicitravirya, having therein overcome all the Magadhas, Kacis and Kocalas. Of one the hand had already been taken, the other had had the purchase price. "The girl that has been taken (already by the hand) must be as once sent away,' said my father. 'Bring the other girl here.' So spoke the Kuru scion. I asked many others, since I doubted my father's word; for my father's thirst for virtue and right seemed to me mightily exaggerated.[13] Thereupon, O king, I kept on speaking these words, for I was striving after the right way: 'I would fain come to know the right way to the truth.' When now I had uttered these words, my father Rulhika spoke as follows: 'If ye believe that it is the purchase price that decides, and not the taking by the hand, tradition declares: 'He that has received the purchase price, may take steps for another wedding. For the law-learned do not state that according to tradition a guiding thread is given by the words (the agreement in marriage affairs by word of south). Toward those who derive the decision from the price and not from the taking by the hand, the well-known expression, too, which speaks of *giving* the daughter, does not inspire any trust (that is, it makes them out to be wrong).[15] Those who see in the purchase price a sale are not law-learned men.[16] To such as these a man shall not give his daughter, no shall anyone bring home such a woman; for the wife ? in no wise be bought or sold. Therewith is judgement, too uttered on the greedy, the evil minded, that buy and so a woman as slave (concubine)."[17] On this matter folk asked Satyavant: "The payer of the purchase price for a girl, which latter has had the purchase price, has died, and suppose she had another man taking her hand; we are then in doubt as to what is right. Decide thou this for us . . ." Satyavati spoke: "If so ye wish, then give her away. In this a man need harbour no hesitation. A man so does, even when (the payer of the purchase price) still lives. If he is dead, then there is no doubt whatever. The maiden may in such a case unit herself to her brother-in-law, or once again, following his guidance only, practise mortification in her longing after the taking by the hand (after actual marriage). According to some they (the brother-in-law) lie with her at once, according to others gradually(?). Those that speak thus on this matter know the decision in this present question. The same is true where, before the taking by the hand, an interval goes by, filles with all the happiness-bringing usages and with holy sayings. A fraud, however, is a crime leading to the loss of the caste. The deciding and culminating point in the holy words of the hand-taking is in the seventh step (at the wedding ceremony). She is the wife of him to whom she is given with water.[18] That is (the daughter) to be given away. A pleasing obedient[19] wife, given away by her brother before the holy fire, her shall the twice-born one wed, walking round the holy fire.[20]

In the next chapter we read among other things: "I do not see that in the following case any ground is given through the Law of the daughter's son: the son of daughters sold belongs to his father. Those born of the marriage by purchase are curious, given up to unrighteousness, takers of other men's goods, filled with malice, of evil life. Here those with the knowledge of olden times bring up the following verses sung by Yama, they, the wise in the law, they, who are bound to the law books,[21] the bridges of virtue and rightfulness. He then seeks to earn money through selling his own son, or that for the sake of his life gives away his daughter for a price, such a blind one will feed on sweat, wine, and excrement in the dreading hell called Kala, the deepest of the seven. Some call that yoke of cattle in the *Rishi* form a purchase price; that is quite a mistake. Whether it were small or big there would be sale therewith. Even if some have had a custom, it is not therein a law for ever. We can see in the world, indeed, the practice of others too: those that carnally enjoy a maiden who is forced, such doers of evil will lie in thick darkness.[22] Indeed another human being must not be sold, how much less so one's own children! From such a possession rooted in wrong so good can come (or: nothing right can spring). They that know the times of old bring forward this saying of Pracetasa according to Nil. of Daksha): If the kinsfolk of a maiden take nothing for themselves, then it is no sale. This is an "honouring" (a gift of honour *arhana*) of a girl, and a thing that shows very goodwill. And all of it without leaving anything over must be given up to the girl. Women must be honoured and adorned by father and brother, father-in-law and brother-in-law, if they wish to have much happiness. True it is that, if the wife is not pleased, then the husband, too, is not rejoiced by her; and if the husband has no joy, then no offspring grows." The Brahman may take his wives only out of the three higher castes; if from love, greed, or baseness he weds a Sūdrā, then he must make atonement. In sharing an inheritance the son of his Brahmanic wife first gets a tenth of the whole estate, that is to say, the most valuable things, such as carts, bulls, etc. The rest is split up into ten shares. Of these the son of the Brahman woman gets four, that of the Kshatriyā three, the son of the Vaisya two, that of the Sūdrā wife one, although under the law nothing whatever falls to him; for while the Brahman's sons by the wives from the three higher castes are Brahmans, he is not one. He is given a little *(alpam)* or the tenth part because charity is the highest virtue, but only if the father grants it to him. Three thousand at the most is to be given to the wife as her share in the estate, and of this property given to her by the husband she shall have the usufruct, which is meet and fitting. This share in the inheritance given by the husband is for the wife, of this property of the husband nothing shall in any way be taken from the wife. But whatever property has been given the Brahmanic wife by her father, that her daughter is to have, for she is as the son.[23] Yudhishṭhira wonders at the property being shared so unequally among the sons of the wives from the three higher castes, for they are yet all Brahmanas. Bhīshma enlightens him: "Wife" is uttered in the world with one name only, but within the name thus uttered there is a very great distinction. If a man has first of all made three (non Brahmanic) women his wives, and then gets a Brahman woman, then she is the eldest, she is the honourable one, the head-wife. The bathing and adorning of the husband, the tooth-cleaning and the anointing, the sacrifices to gods and forbears, and at else that is done in the house on works of the holy law, all this no other may ever care for, so long as she is there, but the Brahman woman must attend to it for the Brahman man. Food and drink, wreath, clothing, and ornaments must be handed in the husband by the Brahman woman, for she is the most important. The Kshatriyā shall stand altogether beneath her, the wise man goes on, as the Vaisyā again under the Kshatriyā for the warrior caste, as being the royal one, has a very high and weighty position for the welfare of the world. If a Kshatriyā man, although he is really allowed only two kinds of wives, has three, then the sons inherit thus: the son of the Kshatriyā woman gets four-eights and the father's war booty, the Vaisyā's and three, the Sūdrā's son one, if the father so grants. Of the property of the Vaisya man the Vaisya woman's son receives four-fifths, the Sūdrā woman's one, but again only if the father gives at him. As the Sūdra man can only take a Sūdrā, his sons naturally all inherit quite equally.[24]

In the *Mahābhārata* also, purchase marriage is treated with such contempt, although not only elsewhere in the world but in India, too, it is an institution from olden times. The whole catechism of the ordinary Brahman had only the one word: "Give!" and the *Mahābhārata* itself shows us in Brahmanic parts one ever recurring variation on this one time; from the soft, wheedling words of the glib, sly rascal which, however, are those least often heard up to the shrill, may screaming of the dirt-begrimed, howling dervish, with matted shaggy hair, this all-conquering word of her faced beggardom runs right through the mighty Epic. How then should the *Brahmans* not have seen the highest god, and what at least for them was the only dignified course, at those forms of marriage which imply a giving away of the bride without, or essentially without, any price being paid. The warrior, on the other hand, found his pride in quite another direction. "Take!" was his shibboleth—first of all: "Take for thyself by main force! Thou art the strong and to the strongs belongs the earth." But then it gratifies the pride of and mighty man if he can say to others: "There, take it!" And always we are hearing in the *Mahābhārata*: The Kshatriya can only bestow, never can he let anything be bestowed on him; and often the contempt for the Brahman, ever begging and accepting, finds expression. In the tale of Devayānī and Sharmishthā we have already seen an example of this. This warrior, therefore, praised marriage by capture, and with the *Gandharva* marriage, in which latter, likewise, leave asked of no one on earth, but the more or less reluctant maiden was carried off as booty. Not only Kṛishṇa, the conscienceless fellow, who rose to the lofty dignity of highest god from being an obscure new-comer, is set before us as a bold woman-watcher (v, 48.74; 158.7 ff; cp. iii, 12.31, 115f.),[25] and not only the Arjuna so wrongly praised to the skies by later members of the Kuru saga, but also the truly noble Bhīshma. Among his heroic deeds we often find the abduction of maidens and when he is dead, his mother Gangā sings his praises for this. Twice the *Mahābhārata* tells the tale of how he carried off the daughter of the king of Kāci for his half-brother Vicitravīrya. In the first and very vivid passage we read: "When Bhishma, wisest of the wise, saw that his brother had reached manhood's years, he set his thoughts on finding him a wife. Then Bhīshma heard how the three daughters of the king of Kaci (like the fairies of heaven they were) were all holding their choice of a husband. Thereupon this best of the chariot-fighters, the overcomer of his foes, the mighty one, with the approval of his mother drove with one chariot to Viriṇasī. There Bhīshma, Cāntanu's son, now saw gathered together the kings that had come from all sides, and these maidens. But when the names of all the kings were called out, and the surpassingly glorious maidens saw the lonely, old Bhishma, they all, as though gripped by an unrest, ran away from him, with the thought: 'He is an old man.' 'On what ground has the Bharata steer shamelessly come hither, old, with a surpassingly virtuous soul, wearing wrinkles and white hair? What will he say, who stands there among the people a breaker of his vow? For false is the renown on earth of Bhishma as one thirsting after chastity.' So spoke the low-ended among the princes, and laughed. When now Bhīshma, the mighty one, heard the words of Kshatriya, he was fired with anger, himself he made these maidens choice, and spoke with voice of thunder to the wardens of the earth, as he, Bhīshma, that strikes in all directions, lifted the maidens onto his chariot: 'The bestowal of daughters on valiant men, when these have themselves been summoned, has been handed down in tradition by the wise. While they deck out the daughters to the best of their power and even pay money besides, others offer them for a yoke of cattle. Others gave consent for a fixed sum of money. Others approach men who are unaware of anything, and others wed on their own terms.[26] Others acquire a wife by following the ṛishi way. Then, as the eight kind, known yet that and chosen out by the poets.[27] The self choice by the maiden (*svayaṃvara*) again is praised and practised by the noble. The carrying away by main force of the maiden, however, declared by the law-learned to be the best thing. These maidens here, ye herders of the earth, I mean to take away hence by force. Make ready with all your strength, whether now it is for victory or for defeat. Here stand I, ye herdel of the earth, resolved to fight.' When he of the hero soul, the Kuru scion had thus spoken to the wardens of the earth and the king of Kaci, and had lifted all the maidens onto his chariot and taken leave of the gathering, he drew swiftly away with these maidens. Then sprang up in rage of those princes, feeling their arms and biting their lips. Great was the confusion among them, as in tearing haste they took off their ornaments, and girded on their armour. Like the meeting together of stars was this gathering of all the ornaments and the armour from every side,[28] owing to the ornaments being strewn about here and there with the armours. Their brows were drawn with anger and indignation, and their eyes reddened; thus did these heroes climb into their chariots, made ready by their drivers, shining, harnessed to noble steeds, and now set out, brandishing their weapons, after the Kuru soon as he drove off. Then between them and him, between the one and the many, there was fought a raging, fear-bringing fight . . . But when the best of all arm-bearers had overcome them in the fight, he went on his way, down to the Bharatas, the Bharata he. Bhisma, Cantanu's son, was attacked from behind by the Calva king, the great chariot-fighter, to the man of unfathomed mind, as the warden of the ward, the strongest of the strong, who is after the female, thrusts another elephant in the back with his two tusks. Yearning for the woman, the prince shouted to Bhishma: "Stop! Stop!" he the Calva king, the strong-armed graded by rage. Then this tiger among men, the tormentor in the foemen's armies, roused by his words, blazing up with anger like a smokeless fire, his stretched bow in hand and his forehead in furrows, faithfully followed the warrior custom and turned his chariot round to meet the Calva, without fear or confusion, he the great chariot-fighter. When all these kings saw he had turned about, they came up as onlookers to the meeting between Bhisma and the Calva. The two men endowed with strength and valour rushed on one another like two strong bellowing bulls fighting for the cow. Then the Çalva king, the best of men, overwhelmed Bhishma, Cantanu's son, with quick flying arrows in hundreds of thousands. When now these princes saw Bhishma at first thought into evil plight by Calva they were astonished and shouted: "Bravo, bravo!" . . . When now Bhishma, Cantanu's son, the taker of foemen's strongholds, heard the words of Kshtriyas, thee these clear open words, O slayer of foes.' To the Madra king made answer Bhishma, overlord of men: 'This law is the highest, O king, proclaimed by Brahma himself. There lies nothing of evil in it. The forefathers made this rule. And well-known, O Calya, is this prescription, approved by the good, and laid upon thee.'[29] After these words the very mighty one gave wrought and unwrought gold, and many kinds of jewels in thousands; elephants, horses and chariots, apparel and ornaments, precious stones, pearls and coral, that shone, did the son of Ganga bestow. All this did Calya take with joyous heart, and gave him his sister for it, having decked her out. Bhishma, the son of her that wanders unto the sea, took Madri,and went off with her to the Hastinapura. When then a fitting day and moment was come, approved by the excellent ones, King Pandu took hold of Madri's hand according to the holy prescript (i, 113, I ff.)."

iii, 115.20 ff. is quite the same, a passage with a rather ancient look about it. In Kanyakubja was a great and very mighty prince, famous under the name of Gandhi; he went off to live in the forest. But while he was living in the forest a daughter was born to him, like an Apsaras. Ricika, the offspring of Bhrigu, sought her in marriage. To him, the Brahman of unbending piety, Gadhi then spoke: "In our family a thing is customary which our forefathers brought in. A thousand fiery white steeds, each with one black ear[30] is the purchase price. Know this, O best of the Brahmans. And yet I may not say to thee, the holy one: 'Give,' O offspring of Bhrigu. Yet must I give my daughter to a noble-natured one like thee." Ricika promised him the steeds, and got them from Varuna, who made them to come up out of the water. The place where it happened is the famous horse-tirtha on the Ganga in Kanyakubja. The holy man delivered over the precious race-horses to the father, who gave him his daughter in marriage, and the gods themselves were groomsmen. All this was done dharmena (according to the law).[31] These thousand wonderful horses were then given by Gandhi to the priests, and six hundred of them play a great part in the tale of Galava and Madhavi, which also belongs here, and has already been given.

In xiii, 2.18 the ideal king Duryodhana of the race of Manu and Ikshvaku bestows his daughter in marraige on Agni, and demands instead of the purchase price (culka) the continual presence of the fire god. But it may be that rather we have here a turn of speech.[32] But it does not at all fall naturally under the conception of the culka, when the fisherman Daca gives his adopted daughter Satyavati as wife to the enamoured king Cantanu only under the condition that her son shall be definitely king (i, 100).

As we have now seen, it does indeed happen that a mythical king may marry a Brahman maiden, even if it is not without preliminary scruples because of his own unworthiness. But the Indian dislike which runs so strongly against dragging down the woman by marriage into a lower caste has here borne down almost everything before it,[33] and the Kshatriya wants a Kshatriya maiden, as Dushyanta shows. Cp. also xii, 320.59. It is true that in xii, 123.21 marriage into a holy family is prescribed as an atonement (cp. xii, 134.2) for the king who has done wrong. But whether by the mahakula a Brahmanic one is meant cannot be said for certain, but seems here to be necessary. On the other hand, in consonance with the orthodox teaching,

Brahmanas very often unite with daughters of Kshatriyas. But here also, as elsewhere in the Mahabh, we meet with the traces of a more primitive view, and one less flattering to the pride of the priest, among the ruling caste. To the king Duryodhana, just mentioned, Agni comes first in the figure of a Brahman, and seeks the Kshtriya child in marriage. But, "Poor he is and not of my caste," so said the king, and would not give his daughter to the Brahman. In xiii, 4 we find a variant of the tale of the thousand wonderful horses. There we learn that why Gadi had withdrawn into the forest was because he wished to win offspring by penance. There a daughter was born to him, the incomparably lovely Satyavati; she was desired by the Brahman Ricika of the greatly famous family of the Bhrigus. But Gadhi, crusher of foes, did not give her to the high-souled Ricika; for he thought within himself: "He is poor." When the wooer came back again after his rejection, the best among kings spoke to him: "Give me the purchase price, then thou wilt obtain (vatsyasi[34]) my daughter." Ricika spoke: "What shall I give thee as price for thy daughter, O prince of kings? Speak without hesitation. Let no reluctance be there." Then Gadhi demanded the thousand horses, gleaming like the moonbeam, swift as the wind, black in one ear; and the Brahman got them from Varuna, who brought them up from below the Ganga at the very place the suppliant wished. Gadhi was astonished unto death, for he had naturally by his demand only wanted to be rid of the unwished for man, but he was afraid of the holy one's curse, and gave him his daughter for this payment. "And when she had got such a husband, she was taken with the greatest joy."

But it is not only the caste which must be looked to in marriage, but the younger brother must not marry before the elder, nor the younger sister before one that is above her in years, an offence of which, indeed, the law books often speak. In the case of such an offence all three (the two brothers and the wife) must, since they have lost their caste through this wrongdoing, undertake the Cāndrāyaṇa or the Kṛicchra mortification to be freed from their sin. On the other hand, lays down an atonement only for the two brothers, and that only a twelve days' Kṛicchra vow; but the younger brother must marry a second time "re-marrying man" (*parivettar*) must respectfully offer the "re-married man" (*parivitti*) his wife as daughter-in-law *(snushā),*[35] if then the elder brother has given him leave, and if his offence has been atoned for, then he shall take her to himself by gripping her hand.[36] Thus the two men and the woman are freed of their fault. As opposed to this, xii, 35.28 declares: "natu striya bhaved dosho, na tu sa tena lipyate, but in the woman is no guilt, she is not thereby stained," which is in contradiction with the view also represented elsewhere in the Smriti. According to Manu, all three, together with the girl's guardian, and the sacrificial priest who officiated at the ceremony, go to hell. Ram., iv, 17.36 teaches: "The murderer of king or Brahman, the cow-slayer, the thief, he that rejoices in destroying living creatures, the atheist (nihilist), and the re-marrier—they all come into hell." According to xii, 34.4 the following stand on the same level with the Brahman-murderer: the re-marrying man, the re-married man, the younger sister that marries before the elder (agredidhishu), and the husband of an elder sister that marries after the younger sister (didhishupati); another statement is in Manu, iii, 173.[37]

In consonance with this rule it comes about that the five sons of Pāṇḍu in the order of their ages take Draupadi to wife on five following days. If on the other hand, the elder brother has been expelled from his caste *(patita)* or has become an ascetic *(pravrajita),* then the younger brother is free to wed.[38]

As is well known the polygamy of the man in Aryan India does noit form the slightest offence in the Brahmanic system, although since Vedic times, indeed, one wife is seen to be the usual, often the obvious thing. On the other hand, polyandry is utterly repugnant to Indian feelings, and in the Epic only one or two cases of it are found, and these are exclusively cases of a community of wives among brothers.

It is a remarkable fact that the chief heroes of the Mahābharata, the five brothers, have one wife or head-wife in common, Draupadī. Yet this is not so wonderful if we bear in mind the origin of the Pandavas. In very many places the Epic shows with the utmost clearness that the Kauravas are the original heroes of the poem, and, as I hold, not, so to say, only those of "ballads or ballad cycles" which came before the putting together of the actual Epic, but those of a greater poem, of an epic of the Bharatas. No less clearly does the present text also show us what unauthorised stranger intruders of a later date the Pandavas are. Nothing could be more evident, whatever one's attitude may be to Holtzmann's theory in detail. To all seeming, the Pandavas were even of non-Aryan stock; and no one with an open mind can let himself think that they were any cousins of the Kauravas, as the later revision would have us believe. Polyandry must probably be called non-Aryan, in spite of the objection raised by Jolly (*Recht und Sitte,* p. 48), and the five brothers, too, were certainly non-Aryan. They may very well have belonged to one of the many aboriginal peoples or tribes which dwelt and still dwell in India and on its boundaries, and have kept polyandry down to this day.[39] It then was a task of heavy toil to justify this shocking moral defect of the chief heroes and the pillars of the Brahmanic Mahabharata. The one explanation is this: When the five brothers, who are going about in Brahman garb, bring Draupadī to their mother, and show her to her, the mother does not notice what this *bhikshā* (alms) is, that the supposes has been brought home from the begging they ply, and says: "Enjoy it together." The mistake has now been made once for all, and both she and her band of sons now think that the word of a mother is holy and must be held to, absolutely and after the letter. Moreover, they are all aflame with love for the wonderfully fair one, and so Yudhisṭhira deems that therefore they would rather all possess her together than that through her, strife should come about among the brothers. When now they tell Draupadī's father of their polyandric intentions, who has naturally thought that Arjuna has won her and shall marry her, he alongwith his kinsfolk is deeply wounded in his moral feelings. He makes the strongest protest against such an unheard of *adharma* (lawlessness, wrong), conflicting with wordly custom and the *Veda.*

Once the gods made a great sacrifice Yama was the slaying priest; he now utterly neglected his office as god of death; creatures no longer died, and their numbers brought anxiety. There was no longer any distinction between mortals and immortals. Then went the gods to Brahma to complain to him of this distress. He consoled them by telling them that Yama would split up his personality, and they were now to fill this second half with their power, and thus it would bring death to beings. In content the gods went to the sacrifice. Then they saw on the Ganga a lotus-flower. The hero among them, Indra, was sent off to find out whence it came. He saw a glorious woman weeping at the source of the Ganga, and her tears as they dropped became golden lotus-flowers. He asked her the reason of her sorrow. She led him on to the mountain top. There he saw a handsome youth playing dice together with a young lady; as the youth, however, in his eagerness to play gave him no heed whatever, the king of the gods grew angered, and boasted of being lord of the world. The youth laughed at him, and looked at him. At this Indra became as stiff as a tree-stump Civa (this was the dicing hero) bade the woman that shed tears of golden lotuses to take the haughty one into a cave in the mountain.[40] There he saw four shining figures sitting, like him down to the last hair. At the sight of them he was gripped by sorrow: "Shall I perhaps become like these?" Angrily Civa told him that these were four earlier Indras that had been as haughty, too, as he. For this they had all had to come into human life, and would bring about great deeds in it. The four Indras begged: "May the gods of right and of the wind, Indra and the two Acvins, beget us." Indra promised to give them a fifth as fellow, sprung from his seed. Now this is Arjuna, and his four brothers are the four former Indras. In kindness of heart Civa also granted them the boon that the weeping woman, the goddess Lakshmi, should be their wife in mankind. She was then born in wondrous wise to Drupad out of the ground (mahitalat). Vyasa through his ascetic powers then endowed the king Drupada with the eye of a god; so Drupada saw the five brothers and Draupadi in their heavenly forms, and was now fully contended.

Then quite needlessly Vyasa told him the same tale he had told (i, 169) the five brothers before their wooing of Draupadi, and in more or less the same words; the trishtubh metre goes over into the cloka at the beginning of this piece: There was once the daughter of a Rishi, who because of her deeds in an earlier existence found no husband in spite of her beauty. Then she gave herself up to hard penance, and when the rejoiced Civa asked her what she would have, in her fierce yearning she uttered five times: "Give me a proper man." "Good; five shalt thou have, since thou hast said it five times." And her remonstrance that she only wanted one was of no help (i., 191 ff.)[41]

The state of things brought about by this marriage now gave rise to some difficulty. The divine Rishi Narada, the wandering journalist of the Indian heaven comes up and begs the brothers in heartrending words not to quarrel among themselves because of the woman, as the over-fierce Daitya brothers Sunda and Upasunda once had done; and as a warning example he tells them the tale of these demon giants, who held all three worlds in the ban of their rule of terror until the Apsaras Tilottama through her peerless loveliness so strongly fired them both that they slew one another (i, 209-212). Then the Pandavas settle it between themselves: if one of us comes to another while the latter is with Draupadi, then he must live in chastity twelve years in forest.[42] Now one day a Brahman comes who has just had his cows stolen, and sets up a truly priestlike outcry before the rulers forgetful of their duty, the Pandavas. Arjuna is at once ready to punish, and only wants to fetch his arms quickly. But alas! these are in a room where, at this very moment, Yudhishthira is with Draupadi. He has also the holy duty to take leave of his eldest brother. After long wrestling with his conscience Arjuna decides for the higher duty; he goes in and fetches the weapons. After he has run the robbers to earth, he comes home again to the sound o᷾ rejoicings, and makes ready for his long exile in chastity. Yudhishthira is utterly overwhelmed, declares he bears him no anger whatever, and that all is well. . "For if the younger goes in to the elder (while the latter is with the woman) then that is no harm or wrong (upaghata); but if the elder goes in to the younger, then that is a breach of the holy ordinance." But Arjuna in his true boyish way rises proudly up, and shouts: "How should I swerve frorn the truth!" For Draupadi this parade of virtue must have been the more upleasing in that she did not fully share in the disinterestedness of the brothers; she is accused of having preferred Arjuna, and has to atone for it at the great departure for heaven (xiv, 87.10; xvii, 2.3 ff).

It is in harmony with Yudhisṭhira's words that even Dhṛishṭadyumna only protests against one thing, that the younger brother Arjuna, to whom Draupadī really belongs, has to share with the elder. But that the younger brothers have access to the wife of the elder one seems to appear to him not at all unnatural. This exactly corresponds with the well-known arrangement in group-marriage, or better, fellowship marriage of brothers, and is reflected, too, in a mythical tale in the *Mahābhārata*. Once a famous wise Rishi, called Utathya. Mamata was the name of his much-prized wife. But Utathya's younger brother, the sacrificial priest of the heaven-dwellers, Brihaspati the majestic, forced himself on Mamata. But Mamata said to her brother-in-law, best among speakers: 'But I am with child by thine elder brother Desist. And this offspring of Utathya within my body has already studied the Veda with its six auxiliary sciences. But thou art a man of irresistibly powerful seed. Two cannot find room here. But as things are so, do thou therefore now withdraw.' Though thus addressed by her aright, yet the noble-minded Brihaspati could not hold back his soul filled with love's urge. Then, with love's longing full, he united himself with her, who had none of love's longing. But as he ejaculated the seed, he that was in the womb said to him: 'Listen, father dear, do not give way to love's heat, there is no room here for two, the space is small.[43] And I came here first. And withal, thy seed, O holy one, is not barren; I pray thee not crowd me.' But Brihaspati listened not to these words of the child in the womb, but only forced this way into the lovely-eyed Mamata to beget. When he that rested in the womb marked the spurting seed, with his feet he barred the way against Brihaspati's seed. Then the seed fell swiftly onto the earth, driven back without reaching its place. At this Brihaspati was angered; when he saw the seed fall down, filled with rage he cursed Utathya's son that was in the womb, he the holy seer, did abuse him: 'Since thou hast spoken such words to me at a time like this, which all beings yarn after, thou shalt go into a long darkness (dirghatamas). The Rishi was of a truth born under the name of Dirghatamas, blind from his birth owing to the curse of the high-famed Brihaspati, equal to Brihaspati in strength and power (i, 104.9 ff.).[44]

It is a strange thing to find a usage, which aroused the moral feelings of the Indian, unhestitatingly ascribed to this priest of the gods, Bṛihaspati, and to his brother, as also to other *ṛishis* and holy women; and one feels tempted to look on such things as echoes from a time when, among even the Aryans also, group-marriage may have been a recognized institution.

But such a conclusion would seem to be at least a highly uncertain one; for what stories are not told among the different peoples of gods and holy men! The Indian has often declared, in the Epic, too, that such divine figures as these are not tied down to the laws of earth, that mankind indeed must follow a loftier ethic than they. True, enlightened views such as these belong to a later time, of noble spiritual and emotional culture, and can hardly be assumed in the age when such myths were being shaped, or in the day before it. And if for that earlier period, too, the same lofty character of at least some minds were to be assumed, such as shows itself already in the oldest *Upanishad,* that would prove nothing for or against the conditions that might be actually existing. Thus there is left always a certain doubt. But it is quite clear that, as it was Draupadī's marriage was reluctantly taken; and the words of Karṇa, the bitter foe, indeed, oif the princess of Paṇcāla, may not have stood so isolated in a more primitive form of the Epic:

Like these legendary traditions of polyandric marriages is the evidence in the Epic as to earlier or still existing conditions of hetaerism.[45] The gospel of unrestricted free love, from the lips of the sun god—in this case, indeed, not unprejudiced—has already been listened to by us. The Indians tell many tales of the Uttarakurus dwelling in the north, an ideal people in an ideal land that is a real Utopia. There, we are told, the women follow their own inclinations (kamacara bhavanti), and neither man nor woman knows jealousy (irshya nasti narinaranam, xiii, 102.26; cp. xiii, 2.13 ff).[46] In the thirty-first chapter of Book ii there is a description of how Sahadeva, Yudhishthira's brother, when on his world-conquering expedition (digvijaya), reaches the farthest south. Before Mahishmati, the city of the king there, Nila,[47] he finds himself in very great distress, for the god of fire is standing by Nila, and everything in Sahadeva's army, man and beast, goes up in flames. "For it is learned that the uplifter of sacrifices (Agni) that dwells in Mihishmati had once been found out as an adulterer.[48] The daughter of King Nila was fair beyond everything. She always came to kindle the burnt sacrifice. But the fire would not blaze up, even when fanned with fans, until it was set alight with wind coming from the lovely rounded lips. Then the holy Agni fell in love with this maiden, who was sweet to look on, for King Nila and all, and she took him to her.[49] But once when he happened to be sporting in love (with her) in the form of a Brahman, the just king chastied him according to the precept. Then the glorious uplifter of sacrifices blazed up in wrath. When the king saw him he was filled with wonder, and bent his head to the ground. Then, in time, the prince, with head bent likewise,[50] gave this maiden as wife to the fire god with the Brahman form. Then when the shining one had accepted this lovely-browed daughter of King Nila, he bestowed his favour on the king. The most excelling fulfiller of wishes offered the prince a favour, and the lord of earth chose invulnerableness in his army. From that time all that through want of understanding (or: knowledge) try to take this city are forcibly burned by the fire god. And in this city of Mahishmati, as is well known, the women, too, were then freed from interference as to their wishes.[51] Thus Agni granted women the favour that they are not to be held back; for there the women are wholly free, and go the way that pleases them."

In the Mahabharata i, 122 King Pandu makes the following speech to his wife, "harmonizing with law and virtue." "Now will I make known to thee the true essence of dharma (law, custom, virtue), listen unto me, the ancient dharma perceived by the lofty-minded knowers of it. In former times, as it well known, women were left unhindered.[52] O thou of the lovely face, going the way of their desires, in freedom, O sweet-smiling one. When they, from the years of maidenhood on, did trick their husbands,[53] that was nothing wrongs, O lovely-hipped one, but rather that was the right thing in former times. And the same moral law of early times is followed still to-day, free from love and anger, by the beings that linger in an animal-birth. This is the moral order laid down by the rule of conduct;[54] it was honoured by the great Rishi through observance and to-day is still honoured among the Uttarakurus, O thou with the banana-like thighs. For this is the eternal law that shows favour to women. By whom, however, and on what grounds, a short while ago the barrier of to-day was set up in our world—learn this now at full length, O brightly-smiling one, from me. There was once a great Rishi, Uddalaka by name, thus we have heard. Cvetaketu was his famous son, the Muni. This Cvetaketu set up this barrier of the moral law, and from anger, O thou with lotus-leaf eyes. Hear from me why. Once, then, a Brahman took Cvetaketu's mother by the hand, before his father's eyes, and said: 'Let us go.' Driven by displeasure, the Rishi's son gave himself up to wrath, when he saw his mother thus led away as though by force. To the angry Cvetaketu his father spoke, when he saw him thus: 'Do not yield thyself up to wrath, O dear one. This is the eternal law. For the female beings of all kinds are unhindered (anavrita). As the cows stand before our eyes, dear one, so are all creatures in their various kinds.'[55] But the Rishi's son would not bear with this law, and he laid down the following moral order for woman and man, among human beings only, O excellent one, but not among other creatures; and since that time this moral rule has been in existence, and so we have heard: 'if a woman is unfaithful to her husband, then, from to-day onwards, that is a crime leading to loss of caste, like the killing of a child in the womb, gruesome and bringing down evil. And in like wise it is a crime leading to loss of caste, if a man unfaithful to his wife, that has walked in maidenly chastity and keeps faith with her husband. A wife lays the same burden on herself, if she be charged by her husband for the sake of a son,[56] and does it not.' With these words, O timid one, did Cvetaketu, the son of Uddalaka, set up by force the barrier of the moral law . . . At the time of the Ritu,[57] O king's daughter, thou so faithful to thy husband, the wife shall not go afield from her husband; these are the words of the law recognised by the law-learned. At all other times the woman has free independence (svatantryam stri kilarhati) for herself. It is such a law that good men call the old one."[58]

Another account of the origin of to-day's conditions is given in i, 104-22 ff. The blind seer, Dirghatamas, who had already been disturbed in the womb by the unbridled passion of his uncle, and possibly was thereby already disposed this way—one of the Vedic singers—finds a young and lovely Brahmanic wife, by name Pradveshi, and begets several sons by her. "The Muni, filled with righteousness and virtue, noble-minded, and who had reached the further shore of the Veda and Vedanga, learned fully from Saurabheya (the son of the divine cow of wishes) the "custom of the cattle", and he set about practising it, full of yearning and without fear. As the excellent Munis now looked on him as one that was following a wrong ordinance, they were all angered, we dwelt there in the hermitage, and overcome by a foolish blindness, speaking thus of the Muni Dirghatamas:[59] "Alas! this man hath broken the moral rule, and therefore must not live in the hermitage. Therefore will we all shun this evil-minded one." And since his wife had won sons, she was then not at his call and bidding. And to the hating wife the husband said: "Wherefore dost thou hate me?" Pradveshi spoke: "Because the husband gives food to the wife, therefore, after the tradition, is he called husband; and because he offers her shelter, he is called her lord.[60] I that have not power to maintain thee will not be ever drudging and keeping thee, blind from birth, together with thy children, O great penitent." When the Rishi had heard her words, he spoke, filled with wrath, to Pradveshi and her sons: "Lead me into the house of a Kshattriya, and wealth of possessions will be ourlot." Pradveshi spoke: "Possessions given by thee, O Brahman, I would not have; they bring sorrow. Do as thou wilt, O prince among the Brahmans; I shall not keep thee as hitherto." Dirghatamas spoke: "From this day on the course of law in the world is laid down by me. One husband is for the woman the first thing and the last (parayana) so long as she lives. Whether he be dead or alive, she shall have no other man. But if a wife goes to another man, then unfailingly she sinks out of her caste. And for unwedded women, too, it is from to-day a crime leading to loss of caste.[61] But if copulation does come about, then all men must give money; the women withal are not to have any profit from the pleasure, but it shall ever be dishonour and shame for them."[62] His wife is now overcome with anger, and in obedience to her bidding, the sons bind the blind man onto a raft, and leave him to be carried away by the Ganga. Thus at last he comes into the land of King Bali, who rescues him, and, having heard his story, makes use of him in a way corresponding with the peculiar strength of the holy man and of which we shall hear later. We thus learn, too, from this episode who it is that has prostitution for money—that pillar of shame among mankind—on his conscience.

We are often told that the Madras in north-western India, the Sindhusauvīrakas, dwelling on the Indus, and the Punjāb peoples had an evil reputation among the Brahmans of the post-Vedic age. Even if, indeed, both these views, and Karṇa's words in the *Mahābhārata*, which among other things mock at the women and the promiscuity prevailing in these places, are to be perhaps taken with caution, yet it is not impossible that they were not altogether without foundation. Father and son, mother and mother-in-law, father-in-law and maternal uncle, son-in-law, daughter, brother, nephew, and other kindred, friends, guests, and others, slave-men and slave-women—all pair, one with the other. With the men the women mingle, known or unknown, just as the longing comes on them. How should there be virtue among the befouled[63] Madras, a byword for their unlovely deeds, among these untutored eaters of groats and fish, who drink heady drink in their houses, and with it eat cow's flesh, and then shout and laugh, sing unrhymed rubbish, follow their lusts, and chatter such things at one another as they choose? How should the Madra man speak of virtue, the son of women that throw off their clothes, and so dance, clouded by heady drink, that pair without heed of any barrier, and live as their lusts lead them;[64] that make water standing, like the camel and the ass, have lost seemliness and virtue, and in all things are without shame—the son of such as these, thou wouldst speak here of virtue! If the Madra woman is asked for sour rice gruel, she shakes her buttocks, and utters—she, infatuated with giving[65]—these dreadful words: 'Let none ask me for my beloved sour rice gruel. My son I would give, my husband I would give, but I would not give sour rice gruel.' Pale-faced (gauryas), big, shameless are the Madra women, clad in woollen wraps, greedy, and usually without cleanliness or neatness. Thus do we hear" (viii, 40).[66] In the forty-fourth canto Karna, among many other bitter draughts, knows how to pour out the following for Calya, the king of those parts (a Brahman brought it by Karna speaks): "The people dwelling between the five streams and the Indus sixth, these that are outside the law, and also the unclean Bahikas, let men shun . . . When the women have taken heady drink of corn and molasses and taken cows' flesh with garlic—they, who eat cakes, flesh, and roasted barley, and know not the ways of goodness, sing and dance, drunk and unclothed, on the earth-walls of the city and of the houses, without wreaths and unanointed, and amidst drunken, lewd songs (avagita) of various kinds, which sound like the noise of asses and camels. They know no bridle[67] in their pairing, and in all things they follow their lust. They utter fine sayings against one another, they, who hold forth maddened by the drink: 'Ho there, ye outcasts! Ho, ye outcast! Cast off by your husband, cast off by your lord!' Screaming, this refuse of women dance at the festivals, putting no restraint upon themselves. A husband of these foul, evil women of the Bahikas, one that dwelt in Kurujangala, sang with but little rejoicing soul: 'She the tall one, the fair (gauri) one, clad in a thin wool wrap, lies, I know, and thinks of me, the Bahika in Kurujangala. When I have crossed the Catadru and the delightful Iravati, and come into my home, then shall I see the great-shelled,[68] splendid women, the outward corners of whose eyes[69] shine with red-lead, the light-skinned women anointed[70] with ointment from the mountain of Trikakud, wrapped in woollen cloaks and skins, screaming, fair to look on." Then we are further told how the Bahikas strengthen themselves with cakes, groats, and butter-milk, and then mishandle and rob the wayfarers, and how their great, light-skinned women devour flesh, and soak themselves with heady drink.[71] In the forty-fifth canto, cl. II ff., we are told why the women of the Gandharas, Madras, and Bahikas are so evil. These tribes or peoples robbed and outraged a good and chaste woman, and she uttered the curse that for this their women would be loose, and they would not be able to be freed from this dreadful evil. Therefore, too, among them it is not the sons, but the sisters' sons who inherit.[72] Calya, who is thus mocked at, asserts, on the other hand, that in the land of Anga which is under the rule of Karna, they sell their children and wife (xiii, 45.40); and in the Ram. (ii, 30.8; 83.15) we are told that the cailushas (actors) hand their wife over for others' use, as Manu, viii, 362, also tells us. Neither of these, however, is really a case of hataerism, but they show the man, indeed, as the lord, free and none too tender, of the wife.[73]

Inspite of the ill-report, probably not altogether unfounded,as to the loose morals of certain districts, and in spite of occasional passages where utter freedom in things of sex is described as the primitive and as the ideal,[74] there is likewise to be seen in the Epic that earnest and strait view of wedlock which is so often manifested by the Indian; and in spite of the somewhat curious Indian garb we get a quite modern feeling of pleasure when Yudhishṭhira is wrestling with dark doubts : what is marriage, then, really? Is it a holy and divine thing, or has it only the practical purpose of begetting, or does it only serve the ends of the lowest sensuality, does it spring from evil powers? So he comes to Bhishma and asks: "But what is called married duty,[75] O bull of the Bharatas, which first arises at the time of taking the hand of women, how is it with this according to tradition? Does that which the great seers have called the rule of duty in common, spring from the holy Rishis (the compilers or the divine word, of the Veda), or from the god of procreation, or from the demons? Here, so methinks, lurks a great and conflicting doubt. And whatever wedded duty is here on earth, what becomes of it after death? For the dead in heaven,[76] is there still wedded duty? But when one (of the husband and wife) dies first, where stays then the other, tell me, since mankind, the many partake of divers fruits of their toil, are set to divers work (karman), are going towards divers hells as their destination?[77] 'Women are untrue,' is the verdict of the compilers of the Sutras.[78] If, now, women are untrue, why does the tradition speak of the duty in common?[79] 'Women are untrue,' so we read, too, in the Veda. Is dharma (duty, order) now here a first veal term? A metaphorical expression? A rule for a determined case?[80] This seems to me dark and confused, as I ponder on it ever. Therefore, do thou, O grandfather, thou so deeply wise, unfold this all to me, set beyond doubt according to revelation, and in its wholeness, when, of what kind,[81] and how it was introduced. Bhīshma's answer to these truly hard and intricate is, in more ways than one, truly Indian. He tells him as follows: The mighty one in penance, Ashtavakra, wishes to wed, and woos Suprabha, without compare on earth for loveliness, the daughter of the Rishi Vadanya, distinguished, too, on account of her excellent character and pure life, one who ravishes Ashtavakra's heart at the first sight like a flower-strewn forest in spring. The Rishi says the wooer must go up to the holy north, where Civa and Uma with their servants do dwell and take their delight, where the periods of the world's ending and the seasons of the year, the periods of men and of the gods, in bodily shape, bring the god their worship; he will at last come into a dark-leaved, glorious forest, and meet with a splendid old woman; then he is to come back home and wed. Ashtavakra now wanders ever towards the north, reaching, in the Himalaya, Kubera's abode, where he is entertained most splendidly, so that, to the sound of godlike music, he there spends a whole year of the gods.[82] Then he goes on his way and reaches that forest country, which is glorious with fruits and filled with birds at all times of the year, and a wonderful penitential grove there. Then he sees a magificent dwelling, surpassing even Kubera's, great mountains of jewels and gold, all kinds of precious stones, flowers from one of the trees of the gods, and other splendours. Seven ravishing maidens, differing in form, welcome the guest, and whichever of them he beholds, each delights him, and he can make no choice of one; but he bids his heart be still. They lead him up to an old woman who is lying on a couch, decked in magnificent ornaments. He says that they are all to go away, and only the most understanding and passionless one is to stay behind to wait on him. The seven take their leave, and only the old woman stays. But in the night she comes up into his bed, pretending that she is so cold. When she then clasps the Rishi, he lies like a log. "This she saw with sorrow, and said: 'Brahman, otherwise than through love, to women there can come no rest and content from the man.[83] I am crazed with love. Love me, her that loves. But roused, Rishi of the Brahmans, unite with me. Take me in thine arms; I am sore tried with love for thee. For thereby it is, thou that art steeped in virtue, that the fruits of thy work of mortification come into their own; and the bare sight of them gives a longing.[84] Thou art the lord over all this wealth here, and over me myself. In the entrancing forest we will daily in love together, all divine and human delights we will try. For to the woman there is never anything higher than sexual union with the man; that is her highest reward. Driven on by love, women live after their own appetites. And so they are not burned, though they walk on hot-glowing sand.' Ashtavakra spoke: 'To stranger women I never go. By those learned in the text-books of the law the touching of strange woman has been declared to be evil. Know, my dear one, that I will wed, I swear it on the truth; I know nought of the pleasures of the senses; offspring is here for the sake of the holy dispensation. So I wish through sons to come into the heavenly worlds. My dear one, acknowledge the moral good, and cease.' The woman spoke: 'Neither the god of wind, nor he of fire, nor Varuna, nor the other thirty-three gods are so dear to women as the god of love; for to women the pleasure of love is all. Among thousands of women nay, among hundreds of thousands, there is to be found only one that is faithful to her husband, if, indeed, one at all. They know not father, family, mother, brothers, husband, or brothers-in-law; given up to their pleasure, they destroy families, as great rivers destroy their banks.' Once more repelled by the Rishi, she exhorted him to stay; then would his work be done. She bathed[85] and anointed him, and gave him hospitality in the most splendid wise; thus the night and the next day went by without his noticing it. In the following night she again slipped into bed to him, but she said: 'My dear, my mind does not lean to strange women. Rise, if it please thee, and desist of thine own will.' She answered: 'I am without ties. Thou dost, then, not deal wrongly with righteousness and virtue.'[86] Ashtavakra spoke: 'There is no being without ties for women, for the fair are tied. The teaching of Prajapati is this: "Woman is not fit for independence." The woman spoke: 'I have an urge to pair, an urge that is pain, O Brahman, and do thou consider my sacrificing love. Thou dost sin against rightness and virtue in that thou scornest me.' Ashtavakra spoke: 'The drivers kinds of vices carry that man away with them, that has given himself up to his lusts. I am ever lord of my soul by my staunchness.[87] Go into thine own bed, my dear one.' The woman spoke: 'With my head I bow, O Brahman; mayest thou bestow favour on me, be thou the refuge of her that is sinking onto the ground. But if thou seest something forbidden in stranger women, then I give myself to thee, that I assure thee on oath. Know that I am free. If there is any wrong withal, then it shall fall onto me. I have set my heart on thee, and am my own lord; enjoy me.' Ashtavakra spoke: 'How shouldest thou be free? Tell me wherefore. In the three worlds is no woman capable of freedom. The father wards them in childhood, the husband in youth, the son in their old age; for women there is no freedom.' The woman spoke: 'I have kept maidenly chastity; I am still a maid; of that there is no doubt; make me thy wife; do not repel my yearning.' Ashtavakra spoke: 'It is with thee as with me, it is with me as with thee (that is, we both are in love, but not with one another).' Must this not of truth be a test, a hindrance set by that Rishi?[88] For that is a wonder beyond measure (what I now suddenly see before me). What is best for me? For it is as a maid in heavenly comeliness that she (the former old woman) hs now come to me. But how has she now the most splendid of forms? And how was it that her shape seemed aged? And whence now a maiden's form like this? What else will happen there? Yet will I call up all my strength to keep myself from sexual infidelity. For such infidelity pleases me not. By truth will I win her (the beloved)." He now asked the woman, what all this might mean, and she made acknowledgment: "To strengthen thee did I make this trial. Through thy faithfulness in love (avyutthana) thou hast won these worlds, thou truly stout and strong one (satyaparakrama). Know thou that I am the protecting goddess of the northern quarter of the heavens. Thou hast now seen the fickleness of woman. Even old women are plagued by the feverish longing for man.[89] Brahma is now content with thee, as also the gods and Indra. And as to the business on which thou, O holy one, didst come hither, sent by the Brahman the father of the maiden, to give thee instruction—that has all been carried through by me. Thou wilt come happily back home, no weariness will come on thee,[90] thou wilt get the maiden, and she will bear a son."[91] Then Ashtavakra went back home again, related, when questioned by the holy man, what he had gone through, and he (the holy man) said: "Take my daughter, for thou are most highly worthy." He wedded the maiden, and lived with her, full of joy and without sorrow.

This may seem to some extent a curious, "education for marriage"; at least, such a thing would hardly be likely to arouse very great pleasure in a wooer, and this answer to a puzzling and tangled question is shadowy enough, indeed. Yet out of this story, by no means friendly towards women, there looks forth a spirit of deep and earnest morality, and a beautiful meaning. It sounds cynical, but it is steeped in the light of an infinitely higher and purer idealism than the seemingly mystical ecstatic lifting of the eyes of the typical knight of western lands, dreaming of his "madonna". In unsullied chastity and truth, and steadfast in both—thus shall the man enter into wedlock with the beloved maiden, urged by religion, not by the lower lust of the senses, and fully aware with himself that the woman is a wavering reed. Thus he will not make too great demands on her, but rather on himself. This may then, too, have an ennobling and strengthening effect on his mate, who as a woman is so susceptible, and the husband may experience untroubled joy with her. Marriage, therefore, comes from the inspired seers, it is divine, even if men fall behind it—a great and fine thought and of deep truth.[92]

References

1. Āvāhya goes alongwith āvāha. According to Böhtlignk and Monier-Williams, this word is not found in the meaning of marriage. But it is so found in xiii, 63.33 (wrongly understood by B); and Karṇa says in v, 141, 14; āvāhac ca vivāhac ca saha sūtair mayā kṛitaḥ. It is the bringing hither, the marrying hither or acquisitive marriage (of the child-in-law), opposed to the marrying away or giving in marriage (of one's child). Anukūlataḥ might also mean: in fitting wise. The passage is a hard one. I have translated in agreement with the rest of the standpoint of the Smṛiti. By far the smoothest arrangement would be to refer the relative clause to āvāhyam. Then: "With one that in fitting wise (or: of free bent) may give a gift of honour." According to the scholiast, it is true, whom I cannot follow in this, what is referred to is the buying of a bridegroom, and the prājāpatya vivāha is here meant. But elsewhere he is otherwise described.
2. Here probably "give" = afterwards consent. Bearing in mind cloka 36, one is tempted, indeed, to translate: "Without regard to his own wish, a man shall give his daughter to him who loves her, and whom she loves. This is called the Gandharva form by those learned in the Veda." The wording also would be most naturally so translated, but there are otherr objections.
3. While, for example, Manu, iii, 13 ff., holds that for this crime there is no atonement. According to Mark.-Pur. (Mārkaṇḍeyapurāṇa), cxiii, 30ff. the man mut first take a wife from his own caste, then there is no objection to his marrying one from a lower caste; if he brings home first one of a lower caste, then he sinks down into this: and Agnipurāṇa, cl, 10-11, states that the children of mixed marriages take in general the mother's caste. There are no restrictions, in what the Vishnu, xvi, 2, lays down, as to the offspring of wives of a lower caste. The law books, indeed, do not speak well of the man's marrying below him. But Manu, ii, 238, allows the pious man an otherwise excellent wife from a lowly house (dushkulā), Vasiṣṭha, xiii, 51-3, gives more particular information. The male offspring of the casteless man is casteless, but not the female offspring. The

woman, indeed, when she weds goes out of her father's family into the husband's (this is confirmed by the other law books). A man, therefore, may marry such a girl, but without a dowry. Cp. Yājñav., iii, 261. See further Jolly, *Recht and Sitte,* p. 61 f.

So, too, Manu, ix, 90 ff.; Vasishṭha, xvii, 67 f.; Baudhāyana iv, 1.14. Others, however, give only three menstruations as the period. So Gautama, xviii, 20; Vishṇu, xxiv, 40. The last-named precept is perhaps of later date. Cp. Nārada, xii, 24; Yājñav., i, 64.

4. Dharmakopana, cp. Pali (e.g. Milindapanho, p. 266, bhutgama-vikopana; my Dacak., p. 90, line 4 of the text from the bottom); and vidhikopana, v, 29.29; prakopayati dharmam, xii, 64.3, here seems = distort; rājye sthitim akopayan, xii, 132.5; vidhiprakopa, v, 29.29; rangaprakopa (infringement of the laws holding for the stage), i, 135.4. Cp. also xii, 135.4.
5. Nothing is altogether good, and nothing altogether bad, is the anaching of Jat., No. 126; M Bh., xii, 15.50.
6. The meaning of the whole oraculary dark statement seems to be somewhat as follows: In marriage all should be agreed on with reepness and friendliness. But just as no one thing in itself represents the absolutely right, so, too, none of the various kinds of marriage is metly to be rejected. Bhishma probably has in mind the marriage by capture, which as a warrior and famous maiden-robber, he commended; and as he moreover altogether disapproved of purchase marriage, not to speak at all of marriage by stealing or fraud (paicāca), as in the end the better translation is: "In the one (that is, capture marriage) there is no absolute wrongdoing. How, then, does it rightly arise (why does one accept it), even when a man robs a woman whom, however, her kinsfolk offer, and who is bought?" Perhaps tadaikena is to be read instead of tadā kena: "There is absolutely no wrongdoing to be found in this one thing: when the kinsfolk give her away thee according to the law; through one thing (the other) it (the wrongdoing) then arises: when she is bought." But then tje way of expression would be a somewhat twisted one. Or lastly yaṃ prayacchanti might after to what follows. But then Bhishma would hardly be answering Yudhishṭhira's question. As to the question what is to be done when a man has taken a girl for himself without her kinsfolk's consent, as in capture marriage (and Gandharva marriage), we seem to be given an answer in what follows.
7. That is to say, the important persons are man and wife; and what they agree together under holy forms stands good; whereby, therefore, capture and Gandharva marriage are shown as founded on law even without taking te kinsfolk into account. Cp. Buhler's

note to Manu, as, 32, in his translation.

8. Or: at the behest of the law (of the god of justice)?
9. Probably the husband, simply by acquiring and holding the woman.
10. Or: "is a falsehood in that case something blameworthy," the fact, that is, of giving the girl to be the second? Less likely: "Need one in that case be telling a lie," that is, be disowning the earlier agreement? Perhaps the translation is to be taken according to Nārada. xii, 30: "Shall a man then declare (the agreement) as invalid (anṛita or not?" Is vācyam to be changed to vākyam?

    Hardly perhaps: "saying: 'Take her home, after having decked her out'; where, therefore, the purchase price would consist of ornaments for the bride, or money for these.
11. In Divyāvadāna, ed. Cowell and Neil, p. 1, we find that three things must combine together that there may be children: mātspitarau raktau saṃnipatitau (the loving begetters); 2. mātā kalyā; 3. ṛitumati gandharvapratyupasthirā. Cp. Windisch, *Buddhas Geburs.* etc., 17 f.; L. v. Schroeder, *Wurzelu d. Sage vom heil. Gral,* 84 f. On the view that in marrige one must only follow the urge of the heart see my note Daṇḍin's Dacakumāracaritam, p. 301 f., and with ii.
12. Panayos, that is, buying and selling of the girl. The word is not heard with this meaning in Bohdlingk.
13. For Bhishma thought indeed tht he had an equal right to the girl that had been taken by the hand, since he had won her by capture and fighting.
14. Lājāntaram upāsita. Bālhika is the brother of Bhishma's father. free e.g. also v, 149.14 ff.
15. Probably less likely: it is not convincing to them.
16. Were it a real, legal sale, then it would unconditionally bind.
17. K. has the less striking reading dāvsivat "like a slave".

    Then, too, nothing definitive has happened. The smoother but rather lame rendering would be: "The time leading up to the taking by the hand is that in which all happiness-bringing usages and holy sayings are put in practice."
18. When bestowing an object on anyone water is poured on hands. See, e.g. M.Bh., iii, 193.36; K., iv, 78.37; Āpast., ii, 4, 9.8, Jātaka, ii, p. 371; Raghuv, v, 59; Vetālap. (ed. Vidyasagara), p. 114 (Kathās. Tar., 93); Kathas., 113, towards the end. The object is given with the left hand, with the right the water is poured out (Angutt.-Nik, iv, p. 210; Chavannes, *Cinq cents contes et apologues,* etc., iii, pp. 367-383, 388). Hence he that gets the gift is called ardrapani or klinnapāṇi.
19. Or after the Bomb, text: "equal in birth," which is also very

indeed. K. reads anuvacām.

20. *Dubois-Beauchamp, Hindu Manners and Customs,* 3rd edit., p. 40.
21. Or referring to "verses": "which are set (written down) in the law books." With the following cp. Manu, iii, 51 ff.
22. This, of course, does not refer to capture marriage, as the scholiast holds, but to rape. That things must not be done which even gods and holy men have on their reckoning is several times stress as elsewhere, in the M bH. So xii, 291.17-18, 294.7. In xii, the well-known penitents, etc.) has quite confused the moral ideas this "way of life" (ācāra) and the books praising it are rubbish washes up together with from everywhere; a man who has some importance the world is praised by conscienceless poets greedy for fame, and everything about him is set up as an example, and so on. [N.B.—washed up chip of wood or whisp of straw of this kind, to use the language of our text, is to be seen, too, in cl. 24 and 25. They must be cast away here; then we get a sensible and clear text. Cl. 24 ii. doublet to cl. 30; cl. 25 must be put before 31. A pretty list of the lewd doings of the gods and holy men is to be found in Dacakumla caritam, p. 209 of my translation. Moreover in their case "devilish tricks" do not bring about any lessening of virtue (ii. pp. 209-10). For the holy man is still unspotted, even when he is in the service of lust and brandy. Mārk.-Pur., xvii, 17 ff. Cp. MBh., ii 141.67. The poisons of the Saṃsāra are first and foremost wine and women, and can only be driven out by wine and women (that is, the devils by Beelzebub). See Mahānirvāṇatantra, transl. by atha Avalon. p. cxvi and chap. viii, 269. But with both passages cp. was follows, as also M.N. Dutt in the introd. to his translation, pp. II. xxviii. And this is also a mystical doctrine for the initiated, and in neching to do with the sensuality of the many. We often find, too, the assertion that the Brahman who knows the Veda, and perhaps alsoi practises this or that good work, is pure, even though he were the most dreadful of sinners (e.g. Vasishṭha, xxvi, 198; xxvii, 1-9; Manu, xi, 262). By deeds that are in any, even the slightest relation with a particular god, above all Civa and Vishnu, even the most shameless offender is wholly cleansed from any stain. But this is not the place to go further into this. Cp. J. J. Meyer, *Isoldes Gottesurteil, pages* 41 and 43.
23. The law literature on this point has already been pointed out. According to this the wife's property (stridhana) is what was given her by her father, mother, brother, or other kindred, what she received before the wedding-fire, or in the wedding procession, or from her husband, whether out of love or as pain-money on his taking a second wife or what she has received

otherwise since marriage, and then her puurchase price (culka). This last came to be in Old India, as, for example, among the old Germans, a gift to the bride. See Nārada, xiii, 8; Vishṇu, xvii, 18 ff.; Manu, ix, 194 f. Yājñavalkya, ii, 143 ff.; Agnipurana. pp. 742, 925, etc. Cp. espec. Meyer, Uber das Wesend. altind. Rehtyschr., etc., 76-81; 186; Kautilya (transl.), 243.17-245.19 and addits. Benoy Kumar Sarkar, *Polit. Instit. and Theorities of the Hindu.* 28 ff. Worthy of note is Mahānirvāṇatantra, xii, 25, according to which, over and above this, all she has acquired herself is the wife's property (cp. xii, III).

24. The law books are usually less hard than the Epic against the Chir I woman's son. True, Manu, ix, 155, too, lays it down he is to lame what the fatrher finds good to give him; but otherwise, so far as I can see; this restriction is not found. Gautama, xxviii, 39, allows the Chira son, even of an otherwise sonless Brahman, only the means of (vṛittimūla); Vasiṣṭha, xvii, 48-50, pays no heed to him at all, and so on. According to Baudhāyana, ii, 2, 3.10 (=ii, 2.10) and Vājñavalkya, ii, 125, of the Brahman's sons that of the Brahman woman inherits four-tenths, that of the Kshattriyā three-tenths, that if the Cūdrā one-tenth; the sons of the Kshattriya man get three-sixths or one-sixth, those of the man two-thirds or one-third. So, too, Bṛihaspati, xxv, 27 ff.; only Vishṇu says nothing whatever about the at the Vaccya man. Baudhayana and Manu, ix, 153 ff., deem only Brahman's sons worthy of a detailed treatment. Bṛihaspati, xxv, 32, lay down that the Cudra woman's son can have one of the ten shares only where land is not in question. Cp. Buhler's note to Manu, ix, Kautilya (transl.) 259.1-19 and addit. 259.27-28.
25. In the twenty-sixth chap. of the 5th book of the Vishnupur. and elsewhere the song is sung of how Kṛishṇa carried off Rukmini on the eve of her solemn wedding with Çiçupāla.
26. Wishing to have the maiden in marriage (prārthitā)—in the Praja patya form. Cp. Agnipur., 154.10b; Vishṇu's law-book, xxiv, 22.
27. The Gandharva marriage, anyhow, not, as the comm. has the Rākshasa form. It would be possible, of course, to find the Gandharva form already in anumānya, as K. indeed does. Then the meaning would be: "Know now that this is the eighth kind of taking home chosen by the wise." Kavi as a matter of fact in the M.Bh. quite usually means 'the wise man, seer, master".
28. The armour, too, was ornamented with gold and precious stones. When Yudhisthira's armour was shot to pieces with arrows in the fight by night, we read: "It fell down in tatters like a swarm of star from the sky" (vii,m 165.39; cp. viii, 49.42 f.).

29. Bhishma here speaks as a true Indian: what is traditional, the custom of the fathers, is holy. Ask a Hindu wh he follows this custom or that, and he will immediately say that his father taught him to do so and that it was handed down to him from time immemorial. Rāmakrishṇa, *Life in an Indian Village,* London, 1891, p. 27. So, too, Dubois, *Hindu Manners,* etc., p. 100. Whether the buying of a wife is in itself bad or good is left undiscussed withal. In different parts, or even families in India there prevailed in olden times, and still prevail to-day, very varying customs and laws. Moreover, as is well known, the Indus populations have never fitted themselves to unbending Brahmanism, and were therefore held in ill repute; and that the Madras, Vāhikas, etc. under Çalya's rule were held not to be ethicallly polished is to be seen easily from Karṇa's scornful scandalous chronicle of these, at least so-called, moral barbarians (vii, 40 ff.). But anyhow Bhishma Bhishma does not hesitate to take part in this business as the buyer.
30. Or: with ears black on one side. So Nil.
31. Cp. Bhāgavatapurāṇa, ix, 15; Vishṇurāṇa, iv, 7 (Wilson, Vol. 4, pp. 13 ff.)
32. But it would seem seriously meant in the case of Citrāngadā, the daughter of the king in Maṇipūra. The father demands, and Arjuna grants him the only son that is possible of the marriage instead of the purchase price (i, 215.25; 217.25). In this family after Çiva's ordinance only one child is ever born, and the present king has a daughter.
33. It is to be noted, too, that King Yayāti, who is moreover called a "Rishi" and "Rishi's son", wins the brahman's daughter devayāni because she has had the curse laid on her that no Brahman shall wet her. But in the tale there can be heard that clear note of the caste pride of the priest, often sorely humbled by the nobility. So probably that curse was purposely invented into bargain.
34. Vasati with acc. "to have to look forward to, to fall into something, to experience, to obtain" is also found elsewhere in the Epic. Cp. v, 35.30; Ram., iv, 20.17.
35. According to the comm. as a woman unenjoyed (abhuktā).
36. In Assam the younger brother cannot marry before the still unwedded elder one has given leave in writing. But the latter now cannot marry any longer, and is shunned as one without a caste (Starcke, *The Primitive Family in its Origin and Development,* New York, 1889, pp. 135-136). Among the German people, too, ridicule and contempt even now fall on such a luckless fellow or lover of freedom: at the younger brother's wedding "he has to dance in the swine's trough", an expression I have heard

Heaven knows how many times.

37. The law books are no less severe. Both the brothers and both the husbands in case of a new marriage must for their defiling offence undertake penances. Āpastamba, ii, 5, 12.22. Brothers stained by re-marriage, the husband of the younger but first-married sister, and the the athiest, the man expelled from his caste, etc., not be invited to a Çrāddha or sacrifice to the dead. Gautama, xv, 16, 18. Cp. xviii, 18, 19. According to Baudhāyana, ii, I, 1.40 the two brothers, the priest who acted at the wedding, and he that bestowed the bride, must cleanse themselves by a twelve days' Kṛicchra penance; for the wife a three days' fast is enough. According to iv, 6.5-7 pañcagavya (a mixture of butter, milk, sour milk, dung and urine of the cow) mixed with rice-gruel is a help. All these four men participators fall into a bad offence, like the murder of one that is not a Brahman, or into a bad offence, the murder of one that is not a Brahman, or of a cow, like blaspheming the Veda, adultery, etc. Vishnu, xxxvii, 13 ff. So, too, Yājñav., iii, 234 ff. Cp. Manu, xi, 6. Vishṇu, liv, 16, lays down for the participators just named and the re-married elder sister the Cāndrāyaṇa penance. Parāçara, iv, 24, prescribes for the elder brother, the priest, the bride and her guardian variously graduated mortifications (Kricchra, Atikṛicchra, and Cāndrāyaṇa). For the MBh., Vasishṭha, xx, 7-10 is particularly enlightening: The two brothers must undergo certain defined penances (Kṛicchra and Atikṛicchra), the younger one hand over his wife to the elder, and the latter take her as his own wife (Probably in form, as the expositor says), and then give her back to the other; then the younger must get married to her again. The man who carries a younger sister before the elder has to carry out twelve days' Kṛicchra, and then wed the elder (probably over and above the other one). The husband of an elder sister married after the younger one must do atonement with Kṛicchra), and hand over his wife to the husband of the younger one (probably only in form, but see Bühler's note SBE, xiv, p. 103). That the greater shame should lie mostly on the elder brother and the husband of the re-married sister seems understandable. The snushāṃ in MBh. (in itself remarkable) might be therefore a later garbling for an earlier Jāyām. In the end, however, it would be better to take Nilakantha's snushātvena to be wrong, and to translate: "The re-married man shall offer (in marriage) this daughter-in-law (to the elder brother)." The elder brother, indeed, is like the father.

Winternitz in *Wiener Zschr. f.d. Kunde d. Morgenlandes,* xiv, 65f. brings forward MBh, i, 191 and Arjuna's speech there as a leading proof of the reality of polyandric marriage, and says:

"Arjuna therefore holds it as quite wrong even to think of making Draupadi the wife of him alone. He, Yudhishṭhira, must, he says, marry her first," etc. But although this reading is also no doubt about the polyandry of the Pāṇḍavas, yet this latter cannot be deducted from that passage. Niviç means simply: to found household for oneself, and not at all: to wed a certain person. Arjuna says only this: "First Y. must take a wife, then we four brothers come in the order of our ages, and as he is the lord of us all, so he is, too, of Draupadi whom I have won." He might quite well mean here: "If he wishes to marry her for himself only, that is right and good." In any case what is here expressed is only the dread of the sin of "re-marriage".

38. According to Parācara, iv, 25 the younger may marry without regard to the elder, if the latter is hunchbacked, a dwarf, impotent, weak-witted, gadgada (stutterer?), blind, deaf, or dumb from birth. Those mentioned here and in our Mahābhārata passage, together with some other afflicted ones, are not entitled either to inherit or to have law dealings. They may, indeed, marry, at least as a general rule, and their offspring can inherit, if this offspring have no defects. See Manu, ix, 201-203, and the parallels given by Bühler in his transl. (according to Vishṇu, xv, 35 ff., the exceptions are the offspring of those deprived of caste, if born after the criminal offence, and that of the child, likewise outside the law, which was begotten of a woman of higher caste. Cp. Gautama, xxviii, 45, and especially Kauṭilya (transl.) 257-3 ff. and addits.) Among the South Slaves also it is held to be "a firm-based principle of customary law"—and this prevails among them as among the Indians, and among all primitive peoples and tribes—"that younger brothers and sisters must not marry before the elder ones." But exceptions are made, when the elder brother has a mental or serious bodily illness, or becomes a priest, or expressely gives his leave. Krauss, *Sitte und Brauch,* etc. 334 f.

39. A good short account of them in Jolly, *Recht und Sitte,* p. 48. Cp. Hardland, *Primitive Paternity,* ii, 155 ff. The above words, too, were written wholly under the influence of reading the MBh. itself. Afterwards I saw to my satisfaction that other investigators had long ago uttered such views. Thus Winternitz leans towards the view that the Pāṇḍavas were a "non-Aryan mountain tribe" (WZKM, xiv, 71). So Hopkins, *The Great Epic,* pp. 376, 400. On the other hand I do not believe that from the passages brought forward by Winternitz and others polyandry for India can really be deduced. Cp. also Jacobi, *Gottinger Gel. Auzeigen 1899,* p. 885.

40. The world as the dice-game of a god, and Çiva and his wife as players, are often-recurring Indian thoughts.
41. The two last legends are clearly marked as being very late, childish inventions. See, too, Winternitz, JRAS, 1897, pp. 733 ff. An explanation that is partly more sensible nonsense is given in Mārkaṇḍeyapur., v.
42. The first half of the cloka (212.29) is =Draupadyā sahāsinam anyam no 'nyo 'bhidarçayet. Böhtlingk's rendering: "to betray" is quite a mistaken one. Cp. 213.19, 27, 31, 32. It an be sen how foreign to the Aryan Indians polyandric relations are. Where polyandry prevails the matter is mostly very easily arranged. Either each sharer in the marriage then takes his turn on his fixed days, or a sign before the entrance to the woman warns the others. Such a *cave canem* before the gate to the common love-paradise was among the Massagetae the quiver, of the man who was with her, hanging to the wife's waggon; among the Nasamones in Libya the happy man left his staff at the door; so, too, in Arabia Felix and among the Sabæans. Hartland, *Primitive Paternity,* ii, 130; Ed. Meyer, *Geschichte des Altertums,* i, I^3, pp. 25, 30; Lippert, *Kulturgesch,* ii, 11-12. The staff, arrow, or shoe among the old Arabs had to be shown to keep away him that was not called. Welhausen, *Gött. Nachr.* 1893, p. 462. Cp. 464. The Tiyan in Malabar make use of a knife in the doorframe as a warning sign, the Izhuva or Taudan in South Malabar make use of a vessel with water before the entrance. Hartland, l.c., ii, pp. 165 f. As is well known it is not only poverty that is the cause of polyandry, as has been asserted. Rather the wife of many is just as proud of her wealth in husbands as the polygamist is of his crowd of wives; and the Tibetan woman, for instance, pities her poor European sister who has to be satisfied with only one representative of manhood. No: the more husbands, the greater happiness. Hardland, ii, 161 ff. Cp. 182.
43. Less likely: "for two, with the narrow space, there is no being begotten" (literally: there is no being begotten in small space).
44. The same ancient legend, which of course has been devised as an explanation of the name of the seer and singer Dirghatamas, is found again, told shortly, in the xiith book, chap. 341, çl. 49 ff. Cp. also Winternitz, WZKM, xx, 31 ff.
45. Such mythical tales of earlier times oftne seem to me to be altogether too bold to be used as wholly credible grounds of proof. Like other peoples, the Indians too—and especially often and gloomily—speak of an earlier "time without a ruler and filed with terror": there was at that time utter lawlessnss, they ate one another, all crimes were daily evnets, until men met together,

-and chose themselves a king (from thue Epic cp. for instance MBh., xii, 67; Rām., 76.33 ff. under the text as çlokāh prakshiptāḥ). To say nothing of the fact that this picture does not correspond with more primitive conditions, the Indians who told such tales had at any rate no longer any memory of such misty far-off days. A pet theory set the powers of imagination at work. The Aino, who are well known to be monogamic, relate in their tales that men were allowed in olden days to have more wives than their one (Chamberlain, *Aino Folk Tales,* p. 48). Here it is a quite natural sophistication of the understanding that is speaking, or the knowledge that such a thing is customary among other peoples. Polyandry is nowhere found in the Veda, but probably, as already pointed out, it was to be found among the primitive population in and about India. The conditions among them have, anyhow, been the leading cause of such suggestions. But then, mainly under their influence, polyandry may have been found in isolated cases among the Aryan Indians also. The Aino just mentioned believe that, in the far past, girls enjoyed full freedom in sexual intercourse (*Anthoropas,* Bd. v, p. 770). Among them it is not so, but it is so among a vast number of peoples and tribes of older times and of today, and in the most different lands. The Kanakas have a tradition that originally a man had always but one wife (*Anthropos,* ii, p. 385), a shrewd blow against current "proofs" of the development of marriage, by way of promiscuity and other horrors, into monogamy. Those who play about with survivals often seem quite to have forgotten that man, and above all, more primitive man and the child, has not only his actual experience and his memory (which is, however, exceedingly weak) of it, but still more a heart filled with yearnings, an inquisitive understanding, and unchecked powers of imagination. And in the name of Heaven what would be the good of poor mortal man making himself gods, legendary heroes, and saints, if they could not do things which the everyday child cannot allow himself to do!

Horace Man reports a remarkable case of polyandry in the Nicobars. The woman had no children by her first husband; she therefore married a second, and could then prove the truth of her suspicion as to number one; both the husbands lived peacefully together, but everyone laughed at the family (*Transactions of the 9th Internat. Congr. of Orientalists,* Vol. ii, p. 891).

46. There, indeed, the "beauteous maidens grow on trees", and all live only for the pleasure of love, as the Epic, too, relates (see, for instance, Rām., ii, 91.19; iv, 43.37 ff.). [From Melanesia for

plants turning into women cp. G.C. Wheeler, *Mono-Alu Folklore* (London, 1926), pp. 25-26 (Translator).]

47. "Blue-black."
48. Pāradārika, therefore, here used of wrongful behaviour with a woman who is not (here even: not yet) wedded to a man. As to the position of Māhishmati, "sacred to Agni," see Pargiter, Mārkaṇḍeya Purāṇa (Calcutta, 1904), p. 333, note.
49. Hardly: "While Nila, yet, was king of all." We might perhaps read: Nilasyājñasya sarveshām, or better still: Nilasyājñāte sarveshām "without Nila (and) all knowing anything of it, she took him to her". The genitive too in -sya is sometimes, however, used as an ablat. in the MBh. (i, 228.17; ii, 81.37; xii, 1986, II; 218.28; fate). See further x, 10.14; xiii, 216.8. If taken so, the traditional text, "without Nila (and) all," would come to the same thing. That is to say, therefore: "without N. or anyone else having known of it." Fire, moreover, must not be blown up by the mouth. Mārk.-Pur., xxxiv, 112; Manu, iv, 53; Gautama, ix, 32; Āpast., ii, 5, 15.20; Vasishṭha, xii, 27. Nor must the feet be warmed at fire, nor put over or under it, nor must one jump over it. Vishnu, lxxi, 37; Yājñav, i, 137; Manu, iv, 53 f. Of course, it must not be touched with the foot (MBh., vii, 73.30; K., xiv, 108.13 ff.; Yājñav., i, 155).
50. Or perhaps: as it should be, in the right way (tathaiva).
51. Babbhūvur anatigrāhyā yoshitaç chandataḥ kila. More exactly, that is to say: freed from encroachments. I take the word as = avinigrāhya. "Not to be outdone in their sexual longing" (according to a meaning given by Pāṇini) would not go well here.
52. Anāvrita unhindered, not forbidden, accessible to all, not restrained, unbridled, free. This word is often found in the MBh., particularly as applied to woman, and always with this meaning. As a commentary take only i, 229.9, 13: anāvṛita = apratishiddhabhoga; vii, 40.30 compared with 44.13 = asamyata. It has also the meaning: unclad, naked, and so Jacobi takes it here. Context, use of words, and çl. 14 forbid this rendering, important as this further statement would be.
53. A maiden, who does not keep her chastity, sins against her future husband. While this view is rooted in the rough conception that the man's right of property has even a retrospective force, yet in a noble and beautiful meaning it is true; only it must likewise be applied, too, to the man's behaviour before marriage. Agni is perhaps accordingly accused of adultery for lying with a maiden.
54. Pramāna. This word is rendered by Nil. in an earlier passage by veda. Na cirat, in the following, might perhaps mean; after a short time (instead of: a short while ago).

55. The Old Indians have indeed here too, fully anticipated the theories of modern science: In the beginning all the men of the clan, the horde, or the tribe had the right to enjoy all the women of the community; then came marriage, whether polyandric, polygamic, or monogamic, "simple or mixed," but at first always with the very actual consciousness still (and one that was often obeyed) that, in spite of it, access to a woman was not barred to the other men. In perfect harmony with our tale, for example, is the custom among the polygamous Nasamones and the monogamic Massagetae, among whom even after marriage the wife could be freely visited by all the men. Withal, in all probability, father-right prevailed in the original indo-Germanic people, not, as has been held, mother-right. Yet among many Indo-Germanic peoples in later times there is evidence even of a community of wives not to speak of other loose customs. See Ed. Meyer, *Gesch. d. Altertumsn,* i, I, pp. 26 f. And the patriarchate is in itself consistent with the greatest unconcern as to the woman's chasteness, and even after marriage. Cp. for this chapter, among the moderns, Hartland, *Primitive Paternity,* especially the second volume, and in this especially 101-248; H. Schurtz, *Urgesch. d. Kultur* (1900), pp. 105 ff.; Ed. Meyer, loc.cit., pp. 15-30. I name these three excellent works, too, because they are written from differing standpoints. Schurtz, indeed, believes that he finds the "way out of the dilemma" in the highly important theory arising out of his studies on "age-classes and men's associations" (1902, see espec. pp. 54-56), namely, that the "general course of development was this, that the younger men had the utmost freedom of sexual intercourse with all the girls of the tribe, but the olden men married" (*Urgesch d. Kultur,* espec. 123 f.). In which case therefore only the cripples of love, so to say, would have agreed to marriage—just as it happens so often among us. Eduard Meyer, who here often finds himself with Schurtz, even makes the monstrous assertion that "the free union of the sexes, and therefore, promiscuous likewise, exists without exception among all peoples and in every community, whether it be that intercourse is left fully free, or whether it is put under fixed regulations, and, fcr instance, is only allowed between members of certain groups, or whether it is allowed to the girls before marriage, or, as with the widespread religious prostitution, is directly enjoined . . . Among Christian peoples, in direct contrast to this, free sexual intercourse . . . is officially forbidden, but it is not thereby the less zealously practised" (*Gesch. d. Altertums,* i, I. 3, pp. 17 f.). Things, indeed, are bad enough on this point, but such words give an untrue and distorted picture; in olden

and modern times there are plenty of peoples who give much heed to the girl's chastity, to say nothing of the married woman; and in civilized Christian mankind there are, in spite of everything, very many chaste wives, and unspotted maids. Here we are not speaking of the men.

56. To let offspring be begotten of herself by another man. Niyukta and niyoga (charged, ordering) is the technical term for begetting in another's stead, especially when the brother-in-law or some other kinsman raises up, with the widow, children or the dead man. On this see below.

57. The days immediately following the enses, which are proper for conception. The husband, therefore, shall not then be injured in this title to beget children. Cp. Kautilya (transl.) addit. 252.26; MBh. K., xiii, 58-59.

58. The teaching here set forth is anyhow more acceptable than the actual custom of the Hassanieh Arabs, of whom, J. Patherick (*Egypt, the Souden and Central Africa, p.* 151) reports that the wives in this tribe are only bound to be faithful to their husbands for three or four days out of the seven in the week and that the latter feel themselves highly flattered if their fairer halves have a great many love adventures during the marriage holiday; for they would look on this as a proof that their wives were attracting (Finck, *Primitive Love Stories,* p. 92; Henne am Rhyn, *Die Frau in der Kulturgesch.,* Berlin, 1892, p. 20; Hartland, ii, 222). The Bahuana in the Congo area demand faithfuulness of their wives only during pregnancy: they believe that at this time other sexual intercourse harms the child. Not only is the husband, among not a few peoples, left cold if his wife bestows her favours on others, but often it is even the greatest honour for the wife if she is embraced by a great many; her owner then basks, like the Hassanieh just mentioned, in the consciousness of calling such a treasure his own. So the Brame in Africa is proud when his wife has many lovers; the Kamchadale women plume themselves on the number of their lovers; among the Gindans the fair, like the Hassanieh just mentioned, in the consciousness of calling such a treasure his own.' So the Brame in Africa is proud when his wife has many lovers; the Kamchadale women plume themselves on the number of their lovers; among the Gindans the fair, like the "lady in the chest", who is especially known from the Arabian story-book, used to wear, as a token of each man conquered and embraced by them, a leathern anklet; among the Bullam, Bago, and Timmaney in West Africa held ass extremely uncivil and badly brought up; and Timmaney in West Africa the married woman who should repel a man she had kindled

would be held as extremely uncivil and badly brought up; and among the inhabitants of the island of Augila, and the Nasamones, the more men lay with a newly-wedded wife on the wedding night, the greater the brilliance in which she shone. Hartland, ii, 119, 183, 131, 118; Ed. Meyer, loc. cit., p. 24; Lippert, *Kulturgesch.,* ii, 14; cp. J.J. Meyer, *Isoldes Gottesurteil,* p. 15 and note 9, and on this Hartland, ii, 174; Müller-Lyer, *Phasen d. Liebe* (München, 1913), pp. 7 ff.

The women is only a chattel; her good points or her defects have their meaning and being only with reference to the man: to his sexual pleasure, his feelings of power, his vanity, and so forth. The virginity of girls is very generally, among the ruder peoples and tribes, not in the slightest an object of desire. Prostitution as a matter of course for the as yet unmarried woman is what may be really called the rule among them. Of course, there are many exceptions. Indeed, what is there for the man in such a comfortless "fiction of the brain", as Brantome calls the maidenhead! Maidenly purity, indeed, often is looked on as a shame, even a crime, plenty of intercourse as an honour for the girl—anyhow a more consistent view for all that than that found among us, which one sidedly so appraises only the man. See, e.g. Daçakumāracaritam (in my transl.), p. 45, n. 2; Ploss-Bartels, Rp. 172, 349, 429, 459; ii, 429; Finck, *Prim. Love,* 44; 543 ff.; Engels, *Ursprung d. Familie,* etc. (1894), pp. 35 f.; Westermarck, *Human Marriage*[3], p. 81; Starcke, *Prim. Family,* 121 ff.: Hartland, i, 31; ii, 102 ff. (the whole of the 6th chapter with numberless examples), 254 ff., and elsewhere in the 7th chapter; Schurtz, *Urgesch. d. Kultur,* ch. ii, espec. p. 123 ff.; *Altersklassen u. Männerbünde,* 91-93; Reitzenstein, *Zeitschr. f. Ethnolog.,* Bd. 41, p. 676; *Anthropos,* vi, 372; vii, 100; Yule's *Macro Polo,* ii, 44 (in Tebet [Tibet] every girl got a ring from each man that had enjoyed her, and unless she could show at least twenty she did not find a husband; cp. the further examples there p. 48). And so on *ad infinitum.* This may then not seldom lead to such incidents as the Finnish peasant writer Alkio describes in *Puukojunkarit* ("Knife Heroes"), his great picture of life in Österbotten in the sixties of last century: here too, many girls at least find a pride in letting as many young men as possible have a share in their bed. If a new love candidate then comes while one is already lying in the fair one's arms, then there is a proper fight in which the knife, too, is often used, till one of them is beaten and thrown down the stairs. Then while the loser is picking up his bones down below as well as he can, the one favoured by the god of battle refreshes himself upstairs in the bosom of the large-hearted country girl. The same thing is also often found elsewhere among the peasantry. Cp. for instance Jeremias Gottelf's great novel *Anne Bäbi Fowäger,* espec. i, ch. 13-15. That retrospective proprietory feeling of the man is either not yet to be found there, or it is satisfied by the vanity of the owner of a wife that formerly was so run after, feeling itself highly gratified; he it is that has carried off such a pearl and cut the others out! How, then, should this vanity not be just as delightfully puffed up, when she that is already married has a strong attraction for others ! If we read this sentence (already, indeed, anticipated by Rousseau) in Engels, *Der Ursprung d. Familie,* etc. (1894), p. 17: "If anything is sure, it is this, that jealousy is a feeling developed relatively late," then at first we call such a thing monstrous beyond words. And yet, Finck above all (pp. 82 ff.; 438 ff. and elsewhere, as also Hartland, *Primitive Paternity,* especially ch. vi) has brought together overwhelming evidence that real jealousy is hardly to be met with among more primitive peoples; among the men we can only speak, at most, of anger at the infringement of their rights of property, among the women, of envy for her that is favoured by the husband with better treatment. Here and there outward circumstances may have contributed towards men and women manifesting an indifference like this—lower than among the beasts—in things of love. Thus among the Eskimos there is the stress of life (Dr. H.C. Stratz, *Die Frauen* prince, or priest drinks from the same cup as ordinary mortals, the men thus favoured feel the most devout, nay, proudest joy, and that not only among the Kalmucks (Westermarck, p. 79; Finck, 44-45). *Tout comme chez nnous* is what even the civilized European must acknowledge, who is familiar with history and the present day.

The "cattle girl" in Johannes Schalf and her sly mate *in spe* is often far outdone. So, for instance, by many tribes in Algiers. There the father sends the daughter who is ripe out into the world, that she may gather as much together by her charms as possible. Then the girls get married, and those get a husband the quickest who can show by plenty of jungling money how greatly the treasuures of their love have been sought after. This is reported particularly of the Uled Nail, and indeed the father, so it is said there takes the money brought home (Robert, *XIV. Internat. Orientalistenkongress.* 3rd Sect., pp. 572 ff.; Schweiger-Lerchenfeld, *Die Fräuen d. Orients.* p. 296). In the same way the fathers in Nicaragua used to send their daughters through the land for them to get themselves a dowry by way of prostitution

(Finck, 565, note; 610). And in old Grecian times on the island of Cyprus the girls earned their wedding-portion by going to the shore and giving themselves to seafarers and travellers (Brantome, vol. ii, 375a). Cp. Lippert, *Kulturgesch.,* ii, 13-19; Ploss-Bartels, i, 413-15; ii, 17. Of very many peoples it is reported that the men make a full use of their wives as a source of income by giving them up to others. There is a particularly rich collection again in Finck, passim, and in the 6th chapter of Hartland's *Primitive Paternity.* The old king Pāṇḍu was therefore on the right track.

But it is another question whether we can regard as proof his and the other statements in the MBh. as to promiscuity in the Aryan pre-history of India. The theory of hetærism or promiscuity as the primary stage of mankind is, indeed, now given up by the most competent investigators, and since the Indo-Europeans evidently already had a well-ordered family life before their dispersal, and the Veda, too, knows, nothing of any hatærism, we cannot put our trust in such legends for taking so break-neck a leap into the greyest dawn of time. The Greeks and probably other peoples, too, spin tales in the same way, of certain men having introduced marriage, the women having been up till then in common.

According to Nil. This is public copulation. But whuy should D. have to "fully learn" such a usage? One would be inclined to think of the joyous heat, painted by Boccaccio, of the stallions and mares on the Thessalian plains, which the woman described to us by him (and before that by Apuleius in the *Golden Ass*) imitates with her lover, as she stands by the great vat in which her good, scouring husband is toiling away. The amorous enjoyment pacuvat is of course looked on as orthodox. There were also probably other special "refinements" in this case. Of course, D. likewise did the thing publicly, as we must conclude. On the public sexual act cp. Müller-Lyer, *Phasen d. Liebe,* 16 f.; 65; Schrader, *Die Indogermanen,* 76.

This would seem to be the translation. Otherwise craddhavant usually means "he that is filled with belief".

59. The accus. with *verbis dicendi* in the meaning: of, about is often found in the MBh. (e.g. i, 48.20; 123.14; 124.17; 127.5; 165.6; 167.47, 48; 192.11; 193.12; iii, 61.17; 105.20; 191.50; 294.20; vi, 120.13, 15; vii, 72.23 f.; 155.41; viii, 40.38; ix, 59.20; x, 9.26; xi, 24.21; xii, 156.3; 249.29). Cp. evaṃ taṃ vadati, so he speaks of thee, Jāt., iii, p. 150, 1.14.

60. The well-known, often-found, etymology: bhāryāyā bharaṇād bharātā pālanāc ca patiḥ smṛitah, that is, from keeping her that

must be kept (that is, the wife) he is called the keeper (that is, the husband), and from sheltering, the lord (or husband, given as also = shelterer).

61. That is, if they copulate, and thereby sin against their future husband.
62. The double conditional particle (yadi and ced) also in ix, 27.25, cp. xii, 34.32; 152.6; xiii, 115.3; xiv, 48.2.
63. Avalipta, probably not "haughty": cp. viii, 44.15.
64. So, if we read—carāç. According to the text with—varāç: "who woo (themselves) according to their lusts."
65. Ready to give.
66. But how can one look for anything better of them? "They are non-Aryans (barbarians) born in a bad land, who know nothing of the holy laws." The allusion to such people being like the Mlecchas, that is, belonging tothe aboriginal population is worthy, however, of notice. Cp. for instance, Pargiter, Mārkaṇḍeya Purāṇa, p. 311, and what is there said.
67. Anāvṛita.
68. Çankha is here an expression for vulva, though the dictionaries do not show anything of this kind. In the "gallant" time of German literature also, "Muschel" (shell) was used for the woman's pudenda.
69. Or: forehead marks (apanga)?
70. Cp. Caland, *Die altind. Toten-u. Bestattuungsgebräuche,* pp. 123f. So far as I know this ointment does not seemj to be particularly valuable otherwise, and if we take our passage in the Mahābhārata, it was looked on, indeed, as something vulgar. The Hindu, indeed, has often declared that "what mankind eats its gods eat". And yet we know that often only the worthless is dedicated to gods and spirits and their service; they are cheated.k Thus, to keep the dead, these in Old India get fringes of garments to clothe themselves, and have to nourish themselves with only the hot steam of the cakes (Caland, *Altind. Ahnenkult,* 9; 64; 180; the same *Totenverehrung,* 6). If now what is worse ways, in an earlier culture, looked on as altogether excellent, to the supernatural powers it is, as something old, doubly pleasing (cp. Schurtz, *Urgesch. d. Kultur,* 3060. When the Indian Aryans learned how to prepare a better drink, the soma was therefore left for the gods. So this ointment which is so highly prized in the ritual of the dead in "pre-Epic" times may also have seemed a thing of excellence to the ritually pure Aryans. K. for trikakudañjanāḥ has the easier reading: gauryas tāḥ kākūjitaḥ "these mournfully cooing".
71. Their beloved rice gruel is naturally one such heady drink. Sir

Bampfylde Fuller writes that the mountain tribes make a gruel from a dwarf-rice, that quickly changes to an alcoholic state; even that which has only been boiled a short time before is, he says, a mild intoxicant (*Studies of Indian Life and Sentiment,* p. 152).

72. Traces of the matriarchate cannot be proved from the Epic. ix, 4.9 gives the list of the dearest kindred: son, brother, sister's son, and uncle on the mother's side; ix, 9.46, likewise: son, brother, grandfather, maternal uncle, sister's son, friend. Cp. vi, 46.2 f. In ix, 5.12 Kṛishṇa's great grief for the dead son of his sister is referred to. But he is also the son of his dearest friend. The relation between mother's brother and sister's son is looked on as naturally a very close one in viii, 7.9 f.; ix, 7.20, 39 too: Çalya has even left his bhāgineya, and is fighting for the Kurus. But the mātula is also often missing where a list of dearest kinsfolk is given. So, for instance, in x, 8.98. 121; xi, 12.7; 16.19, 55; 27.2 f. And that the particularly near relation to the mother's brother does not in itself give any proof of mother-right is stressed by Ed. Meyer, loc. cit., p. 29. According to Hopkins, *Forun. Americ. Orient. Soc.,* xiii, note, pp. 141 f., the importance of the mātula in the MBh. would even be a later phenomenon. See too *Forun. Roy. Asiatic Soc.,* xiii, 139, note, and Jacobi, *Gött. Gel. Anzeig,* 1899, pp. 882 ff. WZKM, xxiii, 165; Schrader, *D. Indogermanen,* 75, 107. On the other hand the matriarchate is often found among the primitive population of India. Thus according to Dalton among the Pani-Koch the property belongs to the wife her daughters inherit it, the husband lives with his mother-in-law and must obey her and his wife; if he commits adultery he pays 60 rupees, or is sold as a slave (*Zschr. f. Ethnol.,* vol. v, p. 336). Among the Khasi in the mountains of Assam the matriarchate is found remarkably developed. See Fuller, *Indian Life and Sentiment,* 171-174, and *Anthropos,* iv, 892 f.

73. The law books make, of actors and singers, the same statements as something which is a matter of course and known to all, and therefore, in the case of their wives there is neither the strict prohibition against a man speaking to another's wife or having connection with her, nor does the general principle hold that the husband is not responsible for his wife's debts. For these wives have intercourse elsewhere with the knowledge and will of their lords; these are hidden near by, and then naturally come forward to claim the rent of love: they live on their wives. Baudhāyana, ii, 2, 4.3; Manu, viii, 362; Yājñavalkya, ii, 48. Cp. Kauṭilya (transl.), 252.12 ff.; 196.7 ff. They are thus like the men of so many

peoples, who are overoyed when a man flirts with their wives, and they can thereby get something out of him. Many examples, for instance, in Finck, passim, and Hartland, especially ii, 120, 127, 129, 203, 205, 208, 215 ff. Cp. *Anthropos,* i, p. 935; iv, 619.

74. It is this very fact, that promiscuity is set before us so persistently as the primitive state, which must be puzzling to the reader. Here we have the sensual and the thinking Hindu: how then could it be but that his glowing passionate love, his boundless, eager fantasy, and his piercing understanding should have led to such thoughts? Thus, too, the sexual freedom among the more primitive peoples, dwelling around the Indian Aryans and among them, may well have led to the conception that these were indeed the more primitive conditions; and what is old, is also, to the Hindu, that which is perfection. It should also be borne in mind that among the Uttarakurus, dwelling far to the north, and the people of King "Blue-Black", dwelling in the farthest south, a love paradise of this kind is to be found. And it is the women that have pleasure and profit from these loose sexual ways, they who compared with men have so little freedom, and according to the Indian view are yet by nature so infinitely more sensual. Here the philosopher has the word. Here and there, anyhow, there may have been in "Epic times", too, great immorality and hetæristic abominations, it may be, not without the influence of the non-Aryan tribes. The people and culture of India is, indeed, from earliest times, a mixture, ever growing in complexity, of what is Aryan and what is due to the aboriginal population. But this is the exact opposite of "survivals" and memory, of the far past of the Aryans. It is truely Indian to find Bṛihaspati, ii, 28 ff. saying that, in the East, the women practised promiscuity, and that there this was, as the custom of the land, right.
75. Sahadharma, the common duty, ordering of life, virtue.
76. Read svarge for svargo.
77. All men, especially kings, save those wholly without sin, must go to hell; either they first enjoy in heaven the fruits of their good works, and then in hell those of their evil works, or the other way about. MBh. xviii, 3.12 ff.; Agnipurāṇa, 369.15-18.
78. According to a saying, which is very often found, giving the list of women's detects and beginning with anṛitam. Translated in Kressler, *Stimmen indischer Lebensklugheit,* p. 31; Böhtlingk, *Ind. Sprüche*[2], 328; cp. my *Hindu Tales,* 256, note.
79. Because of the falseness of womenfolk one could not even be sure with them of one's own begotten children; as Kshemendra,

Darpadalana, i, 15 very well reminds us, no one must be proud of his origin, for none knows indeed who his father is. How then could women take any share in the higher, religious things?

80. I do not know whether this translation is the right one. K. (50.7) has: dharmo yaḥ pūrviko drishṭa etc. I would therefore translate: "Is then the dharma (order, system) that one which is looked on as first (that is, procreation)? (Or) eroticism (upacāra)? (Or) the carrying out of the action of divine service? Then Yudhisṭhira would seem to come back to his first thought: Is it (duty) founded by the Rishis, that is, for the fellowship in religious and holy life? Or by Prajapati, that is, for begetting? Or by the demons, that is, for satisfying sensuality? But there is nothing said here of three ways of solemnizing marriage, which have been supposed.

81. Yādṛiçam "how constituted".

82. That is, 128,600 human years (see Manu, i, 65 ff.; Mārkpur, xivi; Vishnupur, i, 3, etc.). Naturally with the heavenly sounds he did not notice the time going by, any more than, in Pauli's *Schimpf und Ernst,* the Monk of Heisterbach (so well known especially through Wolfgang Müller's poem) amid the sweet notes of the small bird—a motive which has a vast number of parallels. Thus the king Raivata with his daughter listens to the song of the Gandharvas in praise of Brahma; an endless time goes by in this, but seems to him like an instant, and when he gets back he finds everything on earth changed. Wilson's Vishṇupurāṇa, Vol. iii, pp. 249 ff.

83. K. reads: Brahmann, akamakaro 'sti, for which read—karāsti: "Brahman, staunchness of mind (as towards sensuality) arouses displeasure in women," or: "staunchness of mind in the man is of no use to women."

84. The enjoyment of women is, countless times in Indian literature, praised as the most glorious thing in heaven and on earth, as the one meaning and end of living, or anyhow of the years of youth. The ascetic, too, often sees the love of many and lovely women, shining before him as the goal and reward in the world beyond, or in a future incarnation. In in grave, deeply ethnical writings the like view breaks through. So, for instance, Uvāsagadasāo, § 246 with comment., praises bliss with women as the one happiness, the goal of asceticism; redemption (mokkho) without it is but a threefold captivity and only it is the Real in the empty world. Indeed, he that is melted together with his beloved in the spell of delight has come into Brahma, into Nirvana (cp. Kuṭṭananimatam, 558, and my Daçakumārac, pp. 3 and 356, where many further parallels could be given). Couplation, this highest of the five things (paramatattva) leading to perfection,

or being as the gods (siddhi), according to the Tantra writings even brings about siddhi and the knowledge of Brahman.

85. For arriving heroes, guests, etc., to be bathed by women is quite epic in India, too. Cp. Rām, vi 121.I ff.
86. Na dharmacchalam asti te.
87. Or: I am ever lord of my staunchness, it is ever in my grasp.
88. Less likely: "I would fain know whether it is a (testing) hindrance, and one to be overcome, set by the Rishi, and not the truth."
89. So Brantôme in his *Dames galantes* has a lengthy dissertation on the theme: Woman never grows old below the girdle.
90. Holtzmann gives a small section on the relation of Brahma to wedlock, as it is found in the MBh. (ZDMG, 38, p. 184).
91. Or: "sons". For the whole adventure with the old woman cp. the 61st Jātaka.
92. With this ordeal of chastity imposed on the man before marriage cp. Hartland, *Prim. Paternity,* ii, 80-82; 90-91 (the last case, however, reminds us rather of the Finnish custom, where the youth and maid lie together by night without consummating the sexual union, which is well known as a feat of Christian and other saints and of medieval love). The law literature in marriage demands from the man not only the like love and faithfulness as from the wife, but also unsulliedness before the wedding. Since the various books of rules for the behaviour of the Indian make complete sexual continence a holy duty of the scholar, and he must enter into wedlock at once after this period of life is over, this insistence on chastity is to be really found in them all. But Yājñavalkya, i, 52ff. also lays it down expressely that: Without ever having spotted his chastity, thus shall he that is discharged by his teacher take home s wife a young woman *beloved* by him, and that has as yet belonged to no man, is healthy, and so on. And Baudhāy., iv, 1.11 gives this guiding thread: Let a man betroth his daughter as nagnikā to one that has not broken his vow of chastity. For the Brahma marriage particularly, he demands such an unspotted wooer in i, II, 20.2. Cp. Manu, iii, 2. It is true that a good deal can happen between the consummation of the marriage and a marriage of this kind with a child-bride, as prescribed by some at least of the legal writings. Cp. too R. Schmidt, *Ind. Erotik*[1], pp. 632 ff.—Besides the tale from the MBh. there is Mārkaṇḍeyapur., lxi, 5 ff.: A young Brahman obtains a magic salve for the feet by whose help he covers 1,000 yojanas in one day. In the far-off Himālaya the melting snow washes it off him, he cannot get home again, and an Apsaras falls in love with him. He repels her advances in spite of the loveliness of the heavenly fay: "Dear to me is the hearth, and my beloved wife is

my divinity dwelling about me (ramyaṃmāgniçaraṇam, devivistaraṇi priyā 65). He calls on Agni, who sets him home again in an instant of time. And happiness comes, too, for the poor loving woman; a Gandharva named Kali has long been in love with her, but has never been listened to by her. As she now sits there in her disconsolate abandonment, he thousand joys; for the suspects nothing of the trick. During union, however, she has always, at the Gandharva's bidding, to shut her eyes; for at such times and in his sleep he that is magically changed must appear in his true shape, as indeed is seen from the tale of Amor and Psyche (the mark of an Indian origin?). Cp. Mahāvagga, i, 63;

9

Motherhood and Widowhood

Women's exclusive confinement to reproductive function and the attendant emphasis on nurturance have made the domain of motherhood specially vulnerable to patriarchal control. The idea of an original matriarchate conceived by Bachofen and Morgan that was taken up by Engels is no longer acceptable as historical reality. However, is Meillasoux has pointed out this myth of an original matriarchate is an acknowledgement of the power of reproductive arena and its later appropriation by the patriarchal. This appropriation has taken many different forms in different societies which display little similarities with the European model with which Bachofen had originally conceived his study of mother-right. Patriarchy, whether in its more traditional or modern form constantly tries to glorify motherhood as the most prized vocation for women.

The ideology of motherland has been held by Aryan patriarchal social system as the natural and primary destination and responsibility of women. Women's mothering has continued to be basic to women's lives and organisation of the family and fundamental to the genesis of ideology about women. Conceptualization of motherhood determine values and norms with regard to what women ought to do and offer ideal patterns of maternal behaviour and nature. Indian mythology and cultural symbols glorify women's role as mother—she is benevolent mother—goddess, the food giver but without actual control over external factors which govern the food supply to the home. The concept of motherhood demonstrates dichotomy that while on the one hand the mother is extolled in the Ancient Indian literature with every available adjectives, on the other, she is denied of basic right of determining even the fortune of her own children. Because motherhood being very much under male control and it operates strictly within the marital framework and is not autonomous. The concept of motherhood was often used to unify the diverse forces to fight for the liberation and protection of mother, since mother always looks at her son to protect her because she neither has the power nor strength of her own. The cultural artefact of *Deshmata,* the country as motherland that gained legitimacy during nationalist movement, substantiate our argument—the very earth mother which has given life.

Motherhood played most significant part in the social like of ancient India. It was obligatory for girl to be a good wife and a good mother and be blessed with 'the motherhood of sons'. At the time of wedding a prayer was offered on behalf of the bride that 'she may never have an empty lap. Immediately after the wedding ceremony the newly wedded couple prayed, that the wife silently joined the husband who said: 'Come let us join together that we may generate a male child, a son for the sake of the increase of wealth'; so marriage was primarily for male child.

A barren women was considered to be an abominable creature, was most pitiable in Aryan family system. It is ordained that' A barren woman could be cast away (parivritti or parivrikti) because she was possessed by Nirrti. While the barren women could be discarded after ten years, a women who gives birth to daughter only after twelve years and the mother of still born children after fifteen years. The husband of a sonless wife should marry again. The defination of a good women is one who pleases her husband, gives birth to male children and never speaks back to her husband. The poignant desire for avoiding the slur of sonlessness' or the stigma of barrenness is a universal phenomena/ All over the worldland down the ages women have craved for sons and have practised austerities, observed vows, prayed and supplicated for fertility. Here in India these vows have multiplied with time, the later texts have the more numerous prescriptions for conception of, and giving birth to, sons. Childnessness was regarded as a great misfortune. Motherhood thus has been the cherished ideal of every Hindu women. The birth of a son immediately heightens her status. Kisa Gautami was called nobody's daughter when married, and was disdainfully treated by the neighbours, until she bore a son, then they paid her honour. Since as far as is known, this constitute a unique record in Buddhist literature of such a complete change of front from the attitude taken to the mere wife to that taken to the mother.

But the mother relegated to the background soon after she attained motherhood, at least until the next cleverly. She should offer worship, oblations, observe vows for the health, longevity and well being of her children, she could give up certain delicious articles of food and drink. It is presumed that she was delegated the charge of her children's clothes, toys, ornaments and other belongings. In sickness, she more than the father nursed them and took every necessary care for their comfort.

However, unlike the father the mother had scant reason to prefer a son to a daughter unless when her response was not personal but social and, theref re conditioned and conventional. In a peritracheal form of society that we have, the property owned by father goes to his son and not to the daughter; she being the transitory member of the family; she was to be transplanted from the house of hearturance to the houses of procreation. Hence, not only immovable property but even craft trade or profession was inherited by son alone. One likes to guess that her emotional preference was for the daughter whose company she would enjoy only for a short while, until the daughter's marriage. Besides, she could emotionally and imaginatively Project herself in the daughter alone. In later literature we sometimes ass the mother pleading with the father for the daughter's happiness. But basically society looked upon the daughter as a cure:

Parents love their children but at times of distress when they fail to procure food for them they are sometimes forced to given them away to other for adoption; the scriptures enjoin that both the parents together or either of them take such a decision. Thus in some matter the mother had say.

The mother was entitled to honour from the son: "The professor is equivalent ten teachers, the father is equal to hundred professors, the mother exceeds a thousand fathers in honour". "One conquers this world through respect for the mother, the middle region (the firmament) through respect for the father, and through service to the perceptor one gains the region of Brahman". A son must always serve his mother even if she has been an outcast (for some sin), since for him she undertake numerous (troublesome) actions. A son should maination his mother even though she is an outcast (but) without speaking to her". "An outcast father may be forsaken, but not the mother, she is never an outcast to the son". The Pandava says, "All other sins are expiable but he who is cursed by the mother is never liberated." "Only then does one grow old, only then is he in grief, only then does his world become comity when he loses his mother". When Ajatasatru wanted to kill his mother because she had succoured her husband in prison against Ajatsatru's order, his minister told him: "there are records of 18000 bad Kings who were patricides but there is no record of matricide". A *Jataka* passage says that "A mother like a sire should be reverned honour crowned". The above admiring references to the mother is society's indebtedness to woman's role of procreation. It reminds the children of the trial and troubulation that a mother undergoes during patturition and of her subsequent duty to bring them up.

The early literature were replate with such references where motherhood was imposed on unwilling women. In the Mahabharata both Ambika and Ambalika shuddered at the sight of the sage Vyasa, yet then were obliged to submit to him and bear his children. This kind of references can be added to any limit.

Not only was motherhood often imposed on women,—but women were conditioned to regard it as the summum bonum of life, they deplored barrenness and suffered untold torture from rituals directed towards fertilisation of the womb. Male impotence was known only hazily, it was always the women who paid socially and emotionally for childlessness. It as also the women who condemned and ridiculed the unfortunate childless women because women had internalised the male social values regarding the merits of having a son. Thus each girl was looked upon as a potential mother of sons, was trained and conditioned for this. "divinely allotted role and woe to her if she failed to fulfil this function; she felt and was regarded by the society as a wholly inauspicious, incomplete and futile-being.

The attitude to women in general and the norms of behaviour prescribed for a mother in particular is conditioned by the prevailing socio-economic condition in which it rises. An agriculturally primitive society needs many hands for tilling because it cannot always ensure good harvest because of many natural calamities that beset farming and also the use of primitive tools for ploughing minimises production. It also needs sons to leave property to. And incidentally, it needs girls, too, who will wed and bring forth children. Hence a huge premium was laid on female fertility percse and it will not be wrong to surmise that women themselves used fertility as a power in early stages. In a polygamic family the mother of children enjoyed and flaunted a social superiority over the or childless co-wife. For many retails only a women whose husband and children are living were eligible for an auspicious rite. But her social captivity usurped her power and used her fertility to achieve its own interest. Then for her motherhood was suffering, pure and simple because she could not claim the offspring of her womb as her own. She suffered in the process butobviously derived some gratification emotionally in terms of social recognation of her fertility, and derivatically, of her auspiciousness. "Women's capacities for mothering and ability to get gratification from it are strongly internalised, and psychologically enforced and are built developmentally into the feminine psychic structure." Social motivation for increase of female fertility was thoroughly assimilated, 'imbibed and unconsciously internalised by women. Another factor helped this internalised by women. Another factor helped this internalisation. Married women were denied the opportunity for education, a personal vocation, independent social and political identity; most fine arts and many enjoyments were forbidden to them; child bearing was the one avenue left open to her whereby she could prove her social utility and command some respect within the familial and social context. Keeping the women in abject subjugation was made possible by denying them the opportunity to earn their livelihood; the husband was their Lord. Therefore, they were totally dependent on the bread winner and felt that by bearing children to the husband they were but practically repaying their debt to their masters. The scriptures say that if a wife refuses to oblige a husband's sexual advances, he should coax and cajole her; if she still refuses he should offer her gifts; but if she persists in her refusal, he should thrash her with his bare fist or with rods.

Another aspect fundamental to the question of motherhood also needs mention here. The religious needs of women are often defined in terms of their 'emotional' nature and their dependency on others. In recognising women as religious being within certain strict boundaries, the majority of patriarchal religious interpret motherhood as sacred.

Widowhood

Widow is a women whose husband is dead and who has not married again. It is a very old word which can be traced beyond the Vedic language to Indo-European origin, and exists with little modifications in most of the languages of the Indo-European family. Thus we get in Latin *vidua,* Italian *vedova,* spanish *viuda,* French *veuve,* old Slavonic vidova, Russian vidova, old German wituwa, Gothic *widuwo,* old English *widewe* and *widuwe,* and Persian beva. In Latin the word *viduus* in the masculine means bereft, widowed, and in Greek the corresponding word nioeos, means an unmarried man.

Sanskrit grammarians derive the world *vidhavā* from the base *dhava* meaning a woman whose husband has died. According to their derivation a married women whose husband is alive is *sadhavā*. Curiously, *sadhavā* is a comparatively new word, which does not occur in the whole Vedic literature. On the other hand, the word *avidhavā* in the sense of a women not widowed was commonly used in Vedic times. Again, the word *dhava* meaning a husband is not found in the Vedic literature, and its first mention is met with in the *Nirukta;* but even there the meaning given is a man and not a husband, except by implication. In the *Atharvaveda, Dhava* is the name of a tree mentioned together with Plakśa, Aāvattha and Khadira. Thus we see that the word *vidhavā* was neither in general use, nor the basic word *dhava* was known, and that instead of using a positive word like *sadhavā* a double negative form like *avidhavā* was current. Then again, no word similar to the Sanskrit *dhava* in the sense of a man or a husband is met with in any of the European languages.

This naturally awakens a suspicion that the etymological meaning given by Indian grammarians is not correct. Evidently the *vi* of the word *vidhava* is not a prefix but part of the main root word. It must therefore be derived from a root like Teutonic *wid,* to lack, Latin *videre,* to separate, as in *di-videre,* and Sanskrit *vidh,* to be bereft. When the true derivative meaning was lost in India, the word dhava in the sense of a husband came into existence in the Sanskrit language by a wrong splitting-up of the word *vidhava.* Yaska is the first writer known to make a suggestion like that, though he gives priority to the views of earlier grammarians who derived it otherwise without reference to *dhava*[1].

The life of a Hindu widow is hard indeed. A widow, according to the current Smṛti works, is "either to mount the funeral pyre with the dead body of her husband, or to lead the life of a *brahṃacāriṇī,* till death.—Like a *brahṃacāriṇī,* she must not indulge in the luxuries of betel-chewing, oiling the body and using bell-metal vessels for eating. She must take only one meal a day and never twice, and must not lie on a couch, nor use scents. She should offer daily oblations to her dead husband. She should observe some religious vow *(vrata)* in the months of Vaiśākha and Kārtika, and always take ceremonial baths, make gifts and recite the name of Viśṇu. "A widow should either enter the fire with the dead body of her husband, or wear herself by asceticism with the hair shorn."

Such rigid rules for a widow did not exist in the Vedic period. No aversion is expressed anywhere in the Rigveda to the remarriage of widowed women. Indeed, the custom of a widow marrying the brother of her deceased husband seemed to be common, and hence the word *devara.* literally meaning second husband, according to Yāska, came to denote a women's brother-in-law. When the dead body was going to be burnt, the dead man's brother seized the hand of the widow lying beside and asked her to be his wife.[2] The *Atharvaveda* declares that in case of the remarriage of a woman she would region that husband in the next world who had offered the Paṇcaudanam oblation in this world. The Taittirīya Samhitā regards it undesirable for a women to have two husband at the same time. This opinion is repeated in the Aitareya Brāhmaṇa which states that "one women cannot have more than one husband at the same time." This passage, according to even later commentators like Mitramisra in the *Viramitrodaya, Adhivedana Prakarna,* and Nilakantha in his commentary on the *Mahabharata,* indirectly recognises the marriage of a woman a second time after the death of her husband.[3]

Pointed reference to a chaotic state of society in the Vedic period is made in the Mahābhārata, Adiparva, where the sage Svetaketu, son of Uddālaka, is said to have for the first time laid down the law of strict womanly chastity. Another story of lax sexual morals is that of *Dirghatamā*, who was the first to prohibit the marriage of widows by decreeing that "a women must remain faithful to, and dependent upon, one husband only, alive or dead, and must not marry a second time." These stories may be fanciful but they are clearly reminiscent of a period, that of the Vedic rsis, when for a women to marry a second time was not looked upon as unusual. That it is was common for a woman to marry her husband's brother after his death is alluded to in the *Mahābhārata*. Santiparva, "As a woman marries her brother-in-law after the death of her husband, so the brahmana having failed to protect her, the earth made the ksatriya her husband." This passage finds repetition in Anusasanaparva, which proves that the sentiment underlying it was quite familiar in those days.

Epics Period

One of the grounds of objection to the marrying of a widow in modern times is the feeling of repugnance to taking for wife an anyapūrvā, i.e., a women who had been possessed by one another person. Thus Yajnavalkya advises a man to marry a woman "that has as yet belonged to no man." Yet in the age of the Epics virginhood was not always regarded as an indispensable factor in choosing a wife. Jayadratha wanted to make Draupadi "his wife." Trisanku took the wife of a Vidarbha prince killed by him and had by her a son. King Rtuparna was eager to marry Damayanti at her second *svayamvara* knowing her to be the wife of a former husband. Satyavati was sought in marriage by king Ugrayudha shortly after the death of her husband Santanu. Arjuna accepted as wife the widowed daughter of Airavata, the Naga king, and had by her a son. It is not surprising that references to remarriage of women are meagre in the Epic literature. The wonder is that after the successive expurgations and revisions in the hands of later orthodox brahmanas so much evidence of this custom has been allowed to survive. In later times it was declared that in the sacred texts which refer to marriage the *niyoga,* or levirate, is nowhere mentioned, nor is the marriage of widows prescribed in the rules concerning marriage. The practice of *niyoga* was quite legal and common in the period referred to, and the two, *niyoga* and marriage of widows, being bracketted together by Manu, may lead to the supposition, apart from other evidences, that one was as much in existence as the other, though brāhmaṇical opinion represented by puritan law-makers like Āpastamba and Manu was growing more and more pronounced against them.

At the end of the Vedic period the remarriage of women was getting out of fashion and was spoken disapprovingly of even in the earlier Dharmaśāstras. Thus Apastamba decrees that "if a man unites with a woman who had been once married before, or belongs to a different caste, they both commit a sin." The putting of widow-marriage in the same category with inter-caste marriage by Āpstamba shows that it was still in existence at the time, though its total abolition was a thing to be devoutly wished. Manu, too, indirectly recognises such marriage, for according to him a son born of a remarried widow, *punarbhava,* by a brāhmāna father does not cease to be a brāhmāna, and is regarded only as much degraded as a brāhmāna living by trade. Gautama acknowledges its existence by admitting the right of the son of a widow by her second husband to inherit one-fourth of his father's property in the absence of ordinary legitimate heirs. According to Vasiśṭha and Viśṇu, the son of a married widow by her second husband is fourth in order of preference in the matter of inheritance among the twelve kinds of sons, and is regarded as better than an adopted son.

Vasistha, one of the liberal of the law-givers, lays down: "if a damsel has been abducted by force, and not wedded with sacred texts, she may lawfully be given to another man; she is even like a maiden. If a damsel at the death of her husband had been merely wedded by the recitation of sacred texts, and if the marriage had not been consummated, she may be married again (cf. *Baudhayana*) The wife of a person gone abroad shall wait for five years. After five years have passed, she may go to seek a husband. In this manner (after the death of her husband) a wife of the Brahmana caste who has issue shall wait five years and one who has no issue, four years; a wife of the Ksatriya caste who has issue, five years, and one who has no issue, three years; a wife of the Vaisya caste who has issue, four years, and one who has no issue, three years, a wife of the *Sudra* caste who has issue, three years, and one who has no issue, one year. But while a member of her family is living, she shall certainly not go to a stranger (for marrying)". Not only widows but unwidowed wives also could take second husbands and that the marriage tie was dissoluble in certain circumstances. Divorce was recognised by law in ancient India, the equivalent expression used in Kauṭilya's Arthaśāstra being mokśa. Kautilya's rules on the subject will be discussed later on.

> "When the husband is lost, or dead, or turned a recluse, or impotent or an outcast, in these five kinds of distress a woman can take a second husband. The Brahmana wife shall wait for eight years for her husband who is gone abroad; if she has no issue she shall wait for four years, after which period she may marry another. The Ksatriya woman having issue shall wait for six years, and without issue, for three years. The Vaisya woman who has issue, four years, and without issue, two years. The Sudra woman has no rule for waiting. If it be heard that the husband is alive, the waiting period should be twice as long. Such is the order of Prajapati. So in these circumstances the remarriage of a woman is not an offence." These rules are given also in the *Devala Smrti* with little change of language.

It is further stated by Narada that "woman have been created for the sake of propagation, woman being the field, and man the giver of the seed. The field must be given to him who has the seed. He who has no seed is not entitled to possess the field," and that "when a woman after the death of her husband rejects her brother-in-law or other kinsmen who have approached her (for marrying), and goes to a stranger through lust, she is a wanton woman." Katyayana, too, follows Vasistha and Narada and decrees that if the bridegroom be of different caste, an outcast impotent, of vicious occupation, of the same *gotra,* a Dasa, a constant invalid, the bride even married, should be given to another." (Quoted in *Nirnayasindhu*). occurs not only in the law-book of Parasara but also in that of Narada. It is found also in some of the Puranas, such as *Garuda* and *Agni.* From the rules laid down by Vaśiṣṭha, Nārada and Devala regarding the remarriage of a women with or without children in the case of a husband gone abroad, it is clear that this verse was not meant only for girls betrothed and not married, as is sought to be explained by more modern commentators. (The law-givers of the period were trying to set up ideals and at the same time had to acknowledge the existing usages. At a later time when the practices of the higher castes became more and more conformed to the ideals, the necessity of recording conflicting statements disappeared and many of the anachronistic passages were expurgated in the course of time. Hemādri and Raghunandana forbid entirely the practice of widow-marriage in modern times.

There are reasons to believe that this verse occurred fomerly even in the law-book of Manu, as is noticed by Mitramisra in the *Viramitrodaya, Adhivedana Prakarna,* though it has dropped out from the modern editions. When we see that Manu enjoined a strict life of asceticism for widows and set his face even against the long standing practices of *niyoga* as in, doubts may be expressed if the above-mentioned passage permitting remarriage of women could find place in his book. But such conflicting statements reflecting differences between ideals and practices, or between the past and present usages, are met with in many of the law-books, including those of Manu and Parasara. Thus Parasara in the verse immediately following the above-mentioned passage states, "that woman, who when the husband is dead, observes the vow of chastity, goes to heaven after death like a brahmacarin. "This is almost similar to the verse 160 in Manu, V. Even the waiting periods for the wives of husbands gone abroad are stated by Manu, as by Vasistha and Narada, though it is not clear what to do after the expiry of those periods. The commentator Nandanacarya says that the implication is that they may take second husbands.

Therein also it is admitted that in ancient times the marriage of widows, like *niyoga* and inter-caste marriage, was prevalent. The supporters of the custom, on the other hand, quote a verse from the *Vyasa Samhita,* which states that in case of a difference of opinion between Sruti, Smrti and Purana, the authority is first of all Sruti and then Smrti, Purana being the last. In this matter Vedic texts supporting the custom must be given first consideration, prohibition in the Smrtis notwithstanding. Then it is admitted that of the Smrtis the *Parasara Samhita* is meant for the people of the Kali age, Manu being of the Satya age, Gautama of Treta, and Sankha and Lakhita of Dvapara. The text approving of remarriage of women under certain circumstances in the *Parasara Samhita* cannot therefore be annulled for the Kali age by a different texts from any other Smrti, not to speak of a text from a Purana, nay, an Upapurana. Moreover, as many of the practices banned by the *Adityapurana* are known to have currency in the present Kali age, e.g., the Asvamedha sacrifice, life-long brahmacarya, pilgrimage to distant places, ending one's life by burning in fire acknowledgment of Putrika-putra, and sea-voyage, why should the prohibition of remarriage of women given so much sanctity? (Vidyasagara, *Marriage of Hindu Widows.)*

There are evidences other than those gleaned from the sacred literatures to show that this custom of a second marriage for women under certain circumstances existed in India even among the highest caste about two thousand years ago. Vātsyāyana admits its existence and sums up the attitude of the religious teachers towards this custom when he states that "union with a women of lower caste and a twice-married woman is neither desirable nor forbidden. Kautilya lays down elaborate rules stating the various circumstances in which a women can legally marry a second time at the death or during the life-time of her first husband. "On the death of her husband a women wishing to lead a virtuous life shall at once receive not only her endowment money and jewellery but also the balance of dowry due to her. If she is desirous of a second marriage she shall be given on the occasion of her marriage whatever her father-in-law or her husband or both had given to her. If a widow marries any man other than that selected by her father-in-law, she shall forfeit whatever had been given to her by her father-in-law, and her husband . . . . If a husband is of bad character, or is long gone abroad, or is guilty of high treason, or is dangerous to his wife, or has become outcast, or has lost virility, he may be abandoned by his wife . . . If the wife of an absent husband lacks maintenance and is not taken care of by the well-to-do kinsmen of her husband, she may remarry anyone whom she likes and who is in a position to maintain her and save her from misery . . . Childless wives belonging to Sudra, Vaisya, Ksatriya or Brahmana caste should wait for a year for their husbands who have gone abroad for a short time. Wives with children should wait in such cases for more than a year. If they are provided with maintenance they should wait for twice the length of that period. If they are not so provided, their kinsmen should maintain them, for four or eight years. Then the kinsmen should leave them to merry after taking from them what had been given to them at the time of marriage." *(Arthasastra,* III 2-4).

Another evidence of the existence of this custom is supplied by references in the Jātaka literature. From the Asātarūpa Jātaka we learn that a king of Kośala killed the king of Kāśi and made the widowed queen, who was already a mother, his chief queen.A similar story is related in the Kunala Jataka. According to tradition as preserved in the introduction to the *Candakinnara Jataka,* many princes were desirous of marrying the wife of Gautama Buddha, who had already a son then, when he renounced his home and became an ascetic. In the *Ucchhanga Jataka* a woman prays for the release of her brother, who alongwith her husband and son has been sentenced to death, saying that of these three she can get a new husband and a new son but never a new brother, whatever she can do.

An interesting instance of the marrying of a widow by her brother-in-law is known from the history of the Imperial *Guptas.* Chandragupta II Vikramāditya, son of Samudragupta, murdered his elder brother Rāmagupta and made widow Dhruvadevī his chief queen. "The conduct of Chandragupta in marrying her thus not at all opposed to the law laid down by the *Smriti.* If widow marriage and marrying the wife of a dead elder brother had been prohibited by the Dharmaśāstra, he would not have been able to perform the ceremony and, above all, his son Kumāragupta I by that queen would never have been allowed to succeed him to the throne..... But when we find, as we do now, that no less a personage than Vikramāditya, who made the *Gupta* period a Golden Age in the ancient history of India, himself married a widow who was again the wife of his elder brother killed by himself, it cannot but shock the orthodox susceptibilities of most of us, howsoever we may like to contemplate his learning and the patronage he gave to Sanskrit literature.

From Merutunga's *Prabandhacintamani* we learn that king Viradhavala's mother married her deceased sister's husband though her first husband was alive. Viradhavala lived for some time in the house of his step-father before he became a ruler in Gujarat in the 13th century A.D. His famous ministers were Tejahpala and Vastupala, who were the sons of a twice-married woman by her second husband, and who achieved great fame for administrative qualities, learning and righteousness.

Tod's *Annals and Antiquities of Rajasthan* gives an account of the marriage of Hamir, king of Mewar, with the widowed daughter of Maldeo, governor of Chittor. Though Hamir was ignorant of the fact at the time of marriage, it did not prevent the issue Khaitsi from becoming the ruler of the proudest Rajput clan on the death of his father without any difficulty in 1365 A.D.

It may be remarked that the hard ascetic life prescribed for widows by later law-givers had not come into fashion before the time of Manu. There is no such regulation in the whole Vedic literature. One of the earliest Sūtra-writers, Gautama, does not make any mention of it. Baudhāyana and Vaśiṣṭha prescribe a rigid life for widows for a short period only, and that also in the case of those who seek children by *niyoga.* A widow shall avoid during a year the use of honey, meat, spirituous liquor and salt, and sleep on the ground. Maudgalya declares that she shall do so during six months. After the expiration of that time she may, with the permission of her Gurus, bear a son to her brother-in-law, in case she has no son" (Baudh., II. 2. 4. 7-9). "The widow of a deceased person shall sleep on the ground during six months, practising religious vows and abstain from pungent condiments and salt. After the completion of six months she shall bathe . . . Then her father . . . shall appoint her to raise issue to her deceased husband" (Vas., XVII. 55-56). Manu is the first law-giver to regard life-long asceticism as a desirable practice for widows. "Let her rather emaciate her body by (living on) pure flowers, roots and fruits; but she must never even mention the name of another man after her husband has died. Till her death she should remain forbearing and restrained, and live the life of a brahmacarini. A virtuous wife, who after the death of her husband remains chaste and established in the life of brahmacarya, goes to heaven, though she may have no son, as do the brahmacarinis. A woman who from a desire to have off-spring proves unfaithful to her dead husband earns infamy in this world and loses her place with her husband in heaven"

(V. 157-161). Manu thus condemns *niyoga,* though he could not entirely forbid it, as he states in another place, "A woman without a child can raise a son by her brother-in-law or a *Sapinda,* if duly appointed" (IX. 59). A life of rigid brahmacarya for a widow being constantly praised by the later law-givers after Manu, such as Yajnavalkya (I. 75), Parasara (IV. 31), Visnu (XXXV. 14) etc., it gradually became in the course of centuries a religious duty for her from which there was no exemption.

An alternative to such a hard life was self-immolation of a widow on the funeral pyre of the dead husband. Many scholars have expressed their disbelief in the existence of this dreadful custom during the Vedic period. Their is no direct reference to it in the Vedic literature. The Gṛahya Sūtras, which do not leave any important ceremony of domestic life untouched, are singularly silent about it. While minutest details are given about the cremation ceremony and the purificatory rites consequent upon bereavement, no directions are given as to how *Suttee* is to be performed, or what is to be done for a woman thus burnt, though such directions are found in profusion in the later law-books. The authors of law-books up to the time of Manu and Yāṇavalkya do not refer to it.

There however is one significant passage which indicates that the performance of *Suttee* was gone through symbolically in the Vedic period. It did not in ordinary cases have a tragic end, like the practice of human sacrifice which though actually performed at one time in some rites had, as we know, by the time of the Yajurveda, the Satapatha and Taittirīya Brāhmaṇas, become purely emblematic. After sacrificial grass and a black antelope's skin with the hair outside have been spread out on the pile of fuel they place the dead body thereon . . . To the north of the body they place the wife of the deceased . . . Her brother-in-law, being a representative of her husband, or pupil of her husband, or an aged servant, should cause her to rise from that place with the verse, "Arise, O woman, to the world of living (of the *Rgveda*)." There is no mention anywhere, either in the *Rgveda* or in the Sutras, that this verse was addressed to a pregnant woman not entitled to immolate herself, as is explained by later commentators supporting Suttee. Originally this verse was addressed to the widowed woman only by her brother-in-law, who ordinarily married cohabited with her. In the course of time when widowmarriage and *niyoga* had become objects of disapproval the recital of the verse became meaningless, and so a substitute for the brother-in-law might formally recite, "Arise, woman, thou art lying by one whose life is gone; come to the world of living away from thy husband, and become the wife of him who grasps thy hand and woos thee as a lover." (*Rgveda,* X. 18.8). This verse occurs also in *Atharvaveda* (XVIII. 3.2), and the meaning becomes clear if the verse preceding it be studied alongwith it. "This woman, choosing her husband's world, lies down by thee that art departed, O mortal, continuing to keep her ancient duty; to her assign thou here progeny and property." (XVIII. 3. I). The question is whether the woman who is described as lying by the side of the dead body of her husband was actually burnt and made to follow him to the other world. The above two verses indicate that first of all the blessing of the dead man was invoked for progeny and property to her in this world and then she was led away from the funeral pyre by her wooing (*didhisu*) brother-in-law to fulfil the blessing of the departed husband. The supporters of the practice of Suttee, on the other hand, interpret *iha* as *asmin bhuloke janmantare* (in this world on being born again), which is no doubt a laboured explanation and is at variance with the meaning of the verse following. It is referred to as *dharmam puranam* in this verse, and was followed only to the extent of the widow lying on the pile but not being burnt at the time when these verses were composed.

Later commentators and law-givers quote a verse of the *Rgveda* (X.18.7), which also occurs in the *Atharvaveda* (XII. 2. 31) and *Tai iriya Aranyaka* (VI. 10.2), as recommending the rite of Suttee *(vide* Raghunandana*'s Suddhitattva*). Some of them seek to read *agneh* (of fire) in place of *agre* (first), while others explain *yonim* to mean 'to fire' instead of 'to house'. The verse is as follows:[4] "Let those women, who are not widowed, who have good husbands, applying the collyrious butter to their eyes enter; without tears, without disease, and full of ornaments, let these wives first enter the house." The question is to whom the verse was addressed, is it, to the recently widowed wives of the dead husband ready to accompany him by entering into fire, or to the assembled young women around ready to go back home from the cremation ground. If it were addressed to the widow, as is done in the verse following,[5] why is the plural number used without any reason?

Yet me may believe that the custom of Suttee, inspite of general silence of the early Sūtra-writers, persisted among certain sections of the people, especially among the princely class. In many savage communities we find the existence of a custom of sacrificing wives and a slaves at the time of burial of a dead chieftain with the intention of securing to him the same service and ministration in other world as he had been used to in this. We read in Herodotus (V. 5) that amongst the Thracians it was usual, after the death of a man, to find out who had been the most beloved of his wives, and to sacrifice her upon his tomb. Mela (II. 2) gives the same as the general custom of the Getae. Herodotus (IV. 71) asserts a similar fact of the Scythians, and Pausanius (IV. 2) of the Greeks, while our own Teutonic mythology is full of instances of the same feeling" (Max Miller, *History of Ancient Sanskrit Literature,* p. 48). From the prevalence of this custom among several branches of the Indo-Germanic race in Asia and Europe, it may be presumed that it existed in some form or other among the early Indo-Aryans. With the advancement of civilisation in the time of rigveda, it was regraded with disapproval, and the Brāhmaṇa sages of the time began to treat is as a symbolical function and to discontinue the actual execution. The practice, however, persisted to a certain extent among he princely class, with whom it was sometimes a necessity in view of the miserable lot to which the wives of a slain chieftain were consigned by the victor. Almost all the cases of Suttee recorded in the Epic and Paurāṇic literature occurred in the families of kings and generals. The *Mahābhārata* mentions two instances of Suttee; one of Mādri immolating herself on the funeral pyre of her husband Pāndu and another of the four wives of Vasudeva, including Devaki, mother of Kṛśna. But so rare was the custom even among the Kśatriyas that no Suttee took place after the carnage of Kurukśetra in which over a million combatants are said to have been killed and in which almost all the princely families of India took part. The widowed women of the Kuru family are seen duly performing the Srāddha ceremonies after the cremation of the dead bodies. The fragmentary Greek accounts regarding Suttee leave an impression that it was a peculiar custom with certain military tribes of North-Western India and not a general custom throughout the country in the 4th century B.C. "A Peculiar custom is mentioned as existing among the Kathaians—that the husband and wife choose each other, and that the wives burn themselves alongwith their deceased husbands." (Diodoros XVII. 91). A similar notice of the custom is made in connection with Taxila alongwith other "strange and unusual customs."

The first sanction of the custom by a Brahmana law-giver is to be found in the *Visnu Smrti* which states that the duty of a woman "after the death of her husband is to observe *brahmacarya* or to ascend the funeral pyre with him" (XXV. 14). Similarly the *Brhaspatisamhita* decrees, "A wife is considered half the body of her husband, equally sharing the result of his good or wicked deeds; whether she burns herself with him, or chooses to survive him leading a virtuous life, she promotes the welfare of her husband" (XXV. II). The reasons for Brahmana legislators gradually giving religious sanction to this horrible custom after the time of Manu and yajnavalkya are that probably they found it more difficult to prevent moral lapses in widowed women after they had decreed the abolition of widow-marriage and *niyoga.* The introduction of Suttee is only a logical corolloary to the total prohibition of widow-marriage and the maintenance of a high standard of womanly chastity. An additional factor was the great havoc and disruption caused by the barbarian invasions led by the Sakas and Hunas in the first six centuries of the Christian era. The princely families at least were sometimes compelled to resort to this dreadful practice to save the honour of their womenfolk from the hands of the victorious barbarians. Moreover, it is likely that such a practice was prevalent among the Scythians or Sakas, as has been mentioned before, and that the attempts of the Brahmana legislators to establish Suttee in the fifth and sixth centuries A.D. were helped as much by the circumstances of the time as by the continuance of this practice in the families of those barbaric chiefs who were admitted into the rank of Ksatriyas.

Yet it must be observed that the legislation of this custom by Brahmana writers was not effected without strong protests. The poet Bana in the *Kadambari* regards it as "utterly fruitless. This is a path followed by the illiterate, is a manifestation of infatuation, a course of ignorance, an act of foolhardiness and shortsightedness, a stumbling through stupidity, that life is put to an end when a parent, brother, friend or husband is dead. Life should not be ended if it does not leave itself. If it be properly considered, this suicide has, indeed, a selfish object because it is intended to obviate the unendurable sorrow of bereavement." Medhatithi writes, 'One shall not die before the span of one's life is run out'[6] and condemns *Suttee* as an act of suicide and not *dharma* (V. 157). It required a good deal of explanation on the part of later commentators to refute the argument of Medhatithi. Thus Madhavacarya in his commentary on Parasarasamhita states, "The Smrti text approving of the self-immolation of a widow remains in force, otherwise it has no use. So the Sruti text relating to suicide has indeed application everywhere except in the case of women desirous of accompanying their husbands to heaven." *Raghunandana,* as has been mentioned before, following *Brahmapurana* misinterprets the Vedic text *ima nariravidhavah* to support the self-immolation of widows.

Widows are regarded as inauspicious sights whose presence is disliked at any auspicious ceremony like marriage. The sentiment is a very old which can be traced to Vedic times. The repeated use of the word avidhavā in connexion with such ceremonies, as in Kauśitaki Gṛbya Sūtra, indicates that widows were not welcomed on such occasions. The association of wine and dancing with this part of the ceremony probably became disagreeable to the more puritan taste of later writers, and hence we find the substitution of unwidowed twice born women by Sūtra widows for this function in the Śāṇkhāyana Gṛhya Saṃgraba.[7] When the bridegroom has arrived at the house of the bride for marriage, "he is to be ushered into the hall by young women of good luck who are not widowed" (avibhavāḥ sūbagā yuvatyaḥ). In Bengal at the present time the young women who take part in the various rites in connexion with the marriage ceremony are called *eyo* and suyo, which is nothing but a corruption of the expression avidhavā and subhagā, and must not include widows. However closely related they may be to the bride or the bridegroom.[8]

References

1. विधवनाद्वा । विधावनाद्वेति चर्मशिराः । अपि वा धव इति मनुष्यनाम । तद्वियो-गाद्विधवा । (Nirukta, III. 15).
2. X, 18. 8. See *infra,* p. 674.
3. Ait., Br., III. 12—तस्मात् एकस्य बह्यो जाया नवन्ति नैकस्यै बहवः सहपतयः । Mitramisra—सहशब्दसामर्थ्यात् क्रमेण पत्यन्तरं भवति इति गम्यते । *Nilakanṭha*—सह इति युगपत् बहुपतित्वनिषेधो विहितो न तु समयभेदेन ।
4. इमा नारीरविधवाः सुपत्नीरांजनेन सर्पिषा सं विशन्तु ।
अनश्रवोऽनमीवाः सुरत्ना आ रोहंतु जनयो योनिमग्रे ।।
5. उदीर्ष्व नार्य्यभि जीवलोकं गतासुमेतमुप शेष एहि ।
हस्तग्राभस्य दिधिषोस्तवेदं पत्युर्जनित्वमभि सं बभूव ।। (X. 18. 8)
6. तस्मादु ह न पुरायुषः स्वर्गकामी प्रेयात् ।
7. That the drinking of intoxicating liquor was indulged in by Brahmana women, not to speak of women of the lower varnas, as late as the seventh and eight centuries A.D. in the central region of Āryāvarta, is known from Kumārila Bhaṭṭa's *Tantra-vartika,* I. III. 4, which states, "Among the people of modern days we find the Brāhmaṇa women of the countries of Ahicchatra and Mathurā to be addicted to drinking." The reformer Kumārila condemns this practice in the case of Brāhmaṇas only, but not of Kṣatriya and Vaiśya men and women, if the liquor was distilled from fruits or flowers (Mādhvi), and molasses (Gauḍi) and not from grains (Surā).
8. For a more detailed discussions of the marriage rules and of the causes of the progressive deterioration of the position of women in India reference may be made to the writers' *Origin and Growth of Caste in India.*

10

Punarbhū: Her Social Status

The word *punarbhū* means a widow who has remarried. Nārada says that there are seven types of wives who have been previously married to another man *(parapūrvā);* among them, the *punarbhū* is of three kinds and the svairinī (wanton woman) is of four kinds.[1] The three *punarbhus* are: (1) a maiden whose hand was taken in marriage but whose marriage was consummated; in her case the marriage ceremony has to be performed once more; (2) a woman who first deserts the husband of her youth, betakes herself to another man and then returns to the house of her husband; (3) a woman who is given by the husband's relatives (when the husband dies) to a sapiṇḍa of the deceased husband or a person of the same caste, on failure of brothers-in-law (this is *nigoya* and no ceremony is to be perfomed). The four svairiṇīs are:

(1) a woman, whether childless or not, who goes to live with another man through love while the husband is alive;
(2) a woman who rejects after her husband's death his brothers and the like and unites herself with another through passion for him;
(3) a woman, coming from a foreign country or purchased with money or oppressed by hunger or thirst, gives herself to a man saying 'I am yours';
(4) a woman who is given to a stranger by the elders relying on the usages of the country, but who incurs the blame of wantonness.[2] Nārada says that each preceding one of the punarbhūs and svairiṇis enumerated is inferior to the next in order.

It is the second husband and the son of the second marriage

that bear the appellation 'paunarbhava' (*pati* or *putra* respectively) and not the first husband. According to Kaśyapa the seven kinds of punarbhū are (1) the girl who had been promised in marriage, (2) one who was intended to be given; (3) one on whose wrist the auspicious band was tied by the bridegroom, (4) whose gift had been made with water (by the fāther), (5) whose hand was held by the bridegroom, (6) who went round the fire, (7) who had given birth to a child after marriage. In the first five cases it is to be supposed that the bridegroom either immediately died or left the further prosecution of the marriage rites. Even such girls would be styled punarbhūs, when they married another person later on, though the first marriage was not complete because the saptapadī had not been performed. The sixth case is one of completed marriage (though it refers to only going round fire). Baudhāyana's seven varieties are slightly different, the first two being the same as Kaśyapa's: the others are (3) one who went round the fire (with the bridegroom); (4) one who took the seventh step; (5) one who has had sexual intercourse (either after marriage or even without it); (6) one who has conceived; (7) one who has borne a child.[3] These meanings of the word punarbhū must be borne in mind when one meets with the word punarbhū in Vedic texts. That even the promise to give in marriage without the performance of any ceremonies was looked upon as tantamount in its consequences to marriage follows from the words of Sukanya quoted above (in note 1306) from the Sat. Br., where she had been only offered to the sage Cyavana by her father, but where no ceremonies had been performed as none are described or referred to therein. Manu (IX. 69–70) confines the rules of niyoga to a girl who was only promised (vagdatta); while Vas. Dh. S. XVII. 72 speaks of the vagdatta and one given with water as still a maiden, if no Vedic mantras have been repeated.[4] Vas. Dh. S. XVII. 74 refers to the 4th variety of Baudhayana. Yaj. I. 67 when he speaks of *aksata* refers to all the six varieties of Kasyapa or the first four varieties of Baudhayana and when he speaks of 'ksata' he refers to the seventh variety of Kasyapa and last three of Baudhayana. Vas. Dh. S.[5] 17 19–20 describes *paunarbham* as the son of a woman, who leaves the husband of her youth and after having lived with another person, re-enters the house of the husband or as the son of a woman who takes another husband after leaving an impotent, outcast or lunatic husband or after the death of the first husband. Baud. Dh. S. II. 2. 31 describes paunarbhava as the son of a woman who after abandoning an impotent or outcast husband goes to another husband. Narada (stripumsa, v. 97), Parasara IV. 30 and Agnipurana 154. 5–6 have the same verse 'another husband is ordained for women in five calamities viz. when the husband is lost (unheard of), is dead, has become a samnyasin, is impotent or is *patita.*'[6] Great controversies have raged round this verse. Some like the Par. M. (II. part I, p. 53) give the easy explanation (always given about inconvenient texts) that this verse refers to the state of society in another *yuga* (age) and has no application to the Kali age. Others like Medhatithi (on Manu V. 157) explain that the word pati means only 'palaka' (guardian). Medhatithi[7] (on Manu III. 10 and V. 163) is not dead against niyoga, but he is opposed to the remarriage of widows. Even the Smṛtyarthasara (which belongs to about 1150 to 1200 A.D.) mentions several views viz. some hold that a girl may be married to another if the bride-groom dies before saptapadi, others hold that she may be remarried if the first husband dies before consummating the marriage, while still others are of opinion that if after marriage the husband dies before she begins to menstruate she may be remarried and some hold that remarriage is allowed before conception.[8]

Remarriage of Women

Āp. Dh. S. II. 6. 13. 3–4 condemns remarriage 'if one has intercourse with a woman who had already another husband, or with a woman on whom no marriage samskara has taken place or who is of a different varna, then sin is incurred; in that case the son also is sinful'. Haradatta says that the son procreated on another's wife is called kuṇḍa if the husband is living, and *golaka* if the husband is dead. Manu is opposed to the remarriage of widows 'nowhere is a second husband declared for virtuous women'. The Brahmapurāṇa and other purāṇas forbid remarriage of widows in the Kali age. A girl, who has gone through the ceremony of marriage with a sagotra, may be married again and remarks that the text refers to the state of society in another *yuga.* This is the view of all the commentators and *nibandha* writers. Manu itself expressely allows the saṃskāra of remarriage in the case of a girl, whose first marriage has not been consummated or who left the husband of her youth, went to live with another and returned to the first husband. In this the author of the *Manusmriti* probably only reiterates popular usage which was too much for him in spite of his own view denouncing remarriages. So it may be taken that Manu does not forbid the use of *mantras* in remarriage, but holds that even after the *mantras* are recited the remarriage of a widow is not *dharmya* (approved). It is said in the *Mahābhārata* that *Dirghatamas* forbade remarriage and also *niyoga.*[9] Manu himself speaks of the samskara of a pregnant girl (IX. 172–173). Baud. Dh. S. IV. 1.18, Vas. Dh. S. 17.74, Yaj. I. 167 speak of the samskara of remarriage (paunarbhava samskara). Manu III. 155 and Yaj. I. 222 include the paunarbhava (the son of a punarbhu) among brahmanas that are not to be invited at a sraddha. Apararka (p. 97) quotes a passage from the Brahmapurana itself which speaks of a fresh samskara of marriage for child widow or for one who was forcibly abandoned or carried away by somebody.[10]

Remarriage When Husband Unheard of

Several *smritis* contain certain rules about that what the wife was to do when the husband had gone abroad for many years after marriage. Nārada gives the following directions.[11] 'If the husband has gone to a foreign country a Brāhmana wife should wait for eight years, but four years if she has not given birth to another man (then Nārada lays down lesser number of years for kśatriya and vaiśya wives). If the husband is known to be living then the periods are double of those stated above; this is thue view of Prajāpati when no news can be had of persons and hence there is no sin if a woman resorts to another man (in such cases).' If a man has gone to a foreign land for doing some religious duty the wife should wait for him for eight years, six years if he has gone for acquiring knowledge or fame, or three years if he has gone on a love affair (or for another wife).' Manu does not state what the wife is to do after these years of waiting. Vas. (17. 75–76) requires that 'the wife of one who has gone to a foreign land should wait for five years and after five years she should go near her husband.' This may be all right as far as it will go. But if the husband is unheard of how is she to reach him? Vasistha says nothing on that point. Viśvarūpa says that the periods of waiting prescribed for the wife of an emigrant are meant not for permitting niyoga thereafter, but for calling upon her to repair to her husband. Kauṭilya prescribes some interesting rules: 'the wife of one, who has long gone abroad, or who has become a recluse or who is dead, should wait for seven menstrual periods and for a year if she has a child already. Thereafter she may marry the full brother of the husband. If there be many brothers she should marry one who is near in age (to the first husband), who is virtuous, capable of maintaining her or who is the youngest or unmarried. If no such brother exists she may marry a sapiṇḍa of the husband or one of the same caste.' The story of Damayanti suggests that when the husband was not heard of for many years, a wife could marry again. Damayanti is said to have sent a message to Rtuparna that, as Nala was not heard of for many years, Damayanti was going to celebrate a svayamvara and Rtuparna hurries for it and does not think it a strange thing (Vanaparva 70.24).

One question[12] raised by Dr. Banerjee is: what is to be regarded as the *gotra* of a widow when she is to be remarried (is it to be her father's *gotra* or of the first husband's?). There are hardly any indications in the ancient smṛtis or commentaries on this point. Viśvarūpa[13] commenting on Yāj. I.63 (on the word *'kanyaprada'*) observes that according to some the father gives away the bride even if she is not a virgin. So it appears that the father's *gotra* should be looked to in the remarriage of a widow. Vidyasagar, whom Dr. Banerjee follows, held the same opinion.

Remarriage of Widows

Certain passages of the *Atharvaveda* may be considered in connection with the question of the remarriage of widows-Atharva-Veda V.17. 8–9 are[14] 'when a woman has at first even ten husbands, who are not brahmanas, if a brahmana takes hold of her hand (i.e. marries her), he alone is her (real) husband. A brahmana alone is (a real) husband, not a ksatriya or a vaisya—the sun goes proclaiming this to the five (tribes of) men' T[illegible] first verse is not to be taken literally in the sense th[illegible] married ten persons in succession and that the 11th was a brahmana; the first verse contains rather what is called *praudhivada* (pompous assertion or boast) and this is indicated by the word 'uta'. The verse may at the most mean that if a woman has first a ksatriya or Vaisya as husband, and she marries on his death a brahmana, then the brahmana is the real husband. The word 'pati' may also have been used loosely and all that is meant may be that if a girl is promised to ten persons one after another and then lastly to a brahmana, the latter is to be accepted as the best. Another passage[15] of the *Atharvaveda* (IX. 5. 27-28) is 'whatever woman, having first married one husband, marries another, if they (two offer) a goat with five rice dishes they would not be separated (from each other). The second husband secures the same world with his remarried wife, when he offers a goat accompanied with five rice dishes and with the light of fees'. Here the word *punarbhu* occurs. It is possible to hold that this may refer to the promise of a girl in marriage, subsequent death of the intended bridegroom before the marriage ceremonies take place and then the bestowal of her on another. Whatever the meaning of *punarbhu* here may be, it is clear that some sort of sin or inferiority attached to her and that such sin or opprobrium had to be removed by sacrifices. Other passages are discussed later on. But it must be admitted. Remarriage of women was not prohibited in the times of the *Atharvaveda.* The gṛhyasūtras are silent about remarriage; so probably by that time it had come to be prohibited generally, though soradic instances might have occurred. Among the brāhmaṇas and castes similar to them and holding or endeavouring to hold a high place in the hierarchy of castes widow remarriage has been forbidden for centuries. One of the earliest historical instances is the remarriage of Dhruvadevī, queen of Rāmagupta, who was after Ramagupta's death, married by her brother-in-law Chandragupta. Among Śūdras and other lower castes widow remarriage has been allowed by custom, though it is held to be somewhat inferior to the marriage of a maiden.[16] Among these castes remarriage is allowed after the death of the husband or during his life-time with the consent of the husband who gives a writing called *farkhat* or *sod-chitti* (a deed of release). Such marriage are called pat in Mahārāśṭra, *natra* in Gujarat, *udki* in the Kanarese districts. In some cases the caste in a meeting assembled takes upon itself to bring an end a marriage and allows the wife to remarry.

Certain verses of the *Rigveda* and the *Atharvaveda* have given rise to various explanations and opinion is divided as to whether they refer to *niyoga,* to the remarriage of widows or to the practice of the immolation of widows. First the two verses Rig. X. 18. 7–8[19] which are part of a funeral hymn will be set out: 'Let these women, who are not widows and who have good husbands, sit down with clarified butter used as collyrium; may the wives who are tearless, free from disease and wearing fine jewels (or clothes) occupy the seat in front (first). O woman! raise yourself towards the world of the living; you lie down near this departed (husband); come, this your wifehood of the husband who (formerly) held your hand and who loved you has (now) been fulfilled'. It is somewhat strange that Sayana understands the latter half as an invitation by the husband's brother to the wife of the departed to remarry him. But that meaning is far-fetched and does not bring out the proper force of 'hastagrabhasya', 'patyuh' and 'babhutha'. The Asv. gr.[20] (IV. 6. 11–12) prescribes that (in the expiatory rite performed on the death of an elder) the young women relatives should salve their eyes with butter with their thumb and fourth finger and with tender darbha blades and then throw the blades away, when the performer of the rite should look at them while they are salving their eyes with the verse 'ima narir &e.'. The same sutra (IV. 2. 16–18) says that "(when a dead body is to be cremated) they should place the wife to the north of the body and a bow for a ksatriya (if he be the dead person) and then her brother-in-law or some one else who can be the representative of her husband or pupil or an old servant should make her rise up with the mantra 'udirsva'". The San. Sr. S. IV. 16.16 also directs that the verse Rig. X. 18.7 is repeated when the eyes of women are touched with blades of kusa grass and XVI 13.13 says that Rig. X. 18.8 and Rig. X. 85. 21–22 are called utthapinyah (verses addressed for making one rise). There is another mantra in the Atharvaveda (18.3.1) and Taj. Ar. VI. 1[21] 'Oh (dead) man! this woman choosing the world of the husband lies down by thee, the deceased, observing the old universal custom; bestow on her in this world offspring and wealth'. The first verse (i.e. Rig. X. 18.7) contains nothing about niyoga or remarriage. It has been made use of for giving Vedic authority to the practice of *sati* (which will be dealt with later on). That verse refers to the practice that young women of the household of the departed used to go to the cemetery and applied clarified butter to their eyes (by way of purification and santi); this practice continued to the days of the Asv. gr, the Brhad-devata (VII. 12) and the Baud. pitrmedhasutra (I.21.11). The two verses 'iyam nari' and Rig. X. 18.8 are employed by the Baudhayana-Pitrmedhasutra[22] in the funeral rites, the first to be repeated when the wife is made to sit near the corpse and the next for making her rise. It is to be noted that Baud. directs that the corpse is placed on the funeral pile after the wife is made to rise from the vicinity of the corpse; while the Brhad-devata appears to suggest that the wife ascends the funeral pile after the corpse is placed theron and then the younger brother forbids her with the verse 'udirsva & co.' But the Brhad-devata[23] does not mean that the wife burns herself on the funeral pyre and the brother-in-law contents himself with only repeating a verse to dissuade her. The Rigvidhana[24] (III. 8.4) says that the brother-in-law should call back the wife of his sonless brother when she is about to ascend the funeral pyre for procreating a son on her with Rig. X. 18.8. It appears that the verse Rig. X. 18.8 symbolically describes what even in the days of the Rigveda was probably only a tradition *viz.,* that in hoary antiquity a wife burnt herself with her husband. In the times of the Rgveda this practice had altogether ceased, but a symbolical imitation of it had come into vogue, viz. that the wife lay near the corpse in the cemetery and then she was asked to get up and was told that by following her husband to the very doors of death she had fulfilled all that was expected of her and that she should return. The same idea is referred to by the verse 'iyam nari', but the latter half appears to refer to the practice of niyoga when it calls upon the departed to bestow on the wife offspring and wealth. It is possible to argue that Rig. X. 18.8 also impliedly has niyoga in view. But both these verses do not expressly refer to the practice of *sati* at all. They at the most might lead to the inference that the woman had either to marry the deceased husband's brother or go in for niyoga because the husband died sonless. The latter appears to me to be the more probable of the two hypotheses, if those are the only explanations. The symbolic use made in the grhyasutras and in the Brhad-devata of Rig. X. 18.8 shows that they practically are against the burning of widows. It is probable that these authors knew of the custom of niyoga, that it was not then much approved of and so they are silent about it, while the Rgvidhana which appears to be comparatively a late work takes the verse 'udirsva' 'as referring to niyoga (which is most probably referred to in Rig. X. 40.2 to vam sayutra vidhaveva devaram). The consideration of the practice of widow burning naturally arises here from the above discussion and will be dealt with in a separate chapter.

Divorce

In the Vedic literature there are at least some texts capable of being interpreted as relating to the remarriage of widows and we have the word *'punarbhu'*. But as regards divorce there is absolutely nothing in the Vedic texts nor is there much in post-vedic literature. The theory of Dharma-śāstra writers is that marriage when completed by *homa* and Saptapadī is indissoluble. Manu IX 101 says 'Let mutual fidelity (between husband and wife) continue till death; this in brief may be understood to be the highest *dharma* of man and wife.' In another place Manu (IX. 46) declares 'neither by sale nor by desertion is the wife released from the husband; we understand that this is the law ordained by the Creator in former times.

The position of the writers on Dharmaśāstra is that marriage is a saṃskāra, that the status of wife-hood arises from that samskāra, that even if the husband or wife became *patita,* the saṃskāra already performed is not annulled by that fact, that even if a wife committed adultery she still remains a wife and that when she performs a penance for her lapse, it is not necessary to have a fresh saṃskāra of marriage performed on her.[25] A man was allowed to supersede a wife and marry another or others or to abandon his wife altogether in certain circumstances but that does not amount to divorce the marriage is still there intact. According to Nārada, Parāśara and a few a woman are allowed to remarry in case the husband died, or was unheard of; but according to the digests and commentaries these rules apply to a former *yuga* (age). Therefore divorce in the ordinary sense of the word has been unknown to the

Dharmaśāstras and to Hindu society for about two thousand years (except on the ground of custom among the lower castes). Even when the husband was allowed to abandon the wife for her lapse, still she was in most cases entitled to at least starving maintenance. Therefore tyāga (abandonment) was not only no divorce a *vinculo* at all but was not even a divorce a *mensa et thoro* (divorce from board and bed). Later *smṛtis* and medieval digests could hardly conceive of any ground for which the wife could desert her husband altogether, though Nārada and a few others allowed her to desert one husband and marry another if he was impotent, or became a saṃnyāsin or an outcast. A wife is not under the control of her husband as long as he remains *patita* (outcast or excommunicated) and that she should wait till he is purified by penance and restored to caste and that thereafter she again becomes dependent on him. The gravest sins can be expiated by penance; therefore it follows that a wife could not for ever desert even a *patita* husband.

The *Arthaśāstra* of Kauṭilya contains some interesting observations bearing on divorce.[27] A wife hating her husband cannot be released from the husband if he is unwilling (to let her go), nor can the husband release himself from the wife (if she is unwilling); but if there is mutual hatred then release is possible. If a man fearing danger (or injury) from his wife desires release from her, he shall return to her whatever was given to her (at the time of marriage); marriage in the approved form cannot be dissolved.' If the marriage was in the *gandharva,* āsura or Rākśasa from, then the tie may be dissolved by mutual consent, if both have come to hate each other. But he seems to hold that there can be no release at the instance of only one party to the marriage who has begun to feel aversion to the other party in whatever form the marriage may have been performed. Even in this latter case he apparently makes an exception, where physical danger is apprehended by one party from the other.

References

1. Compare Manu IX. 176 and Visnu 15, 8 for the first punarbhū, Manu IX. 176, Vas. Dh. S. 17.19 and Viṣṇu 15. 9 for the second punarbhū.

2. Dr. Jolly in his translation of Narada (S.B.E. Vol. 33 pp. 175-76) renders this verse of Narada differently; but his rendering appears to me to be incorrect. The 3rd kind of punarbhu refers to the practice of niyoga; the 4th kind of svaīriṇī is one who is allowed to have intercourse by her elders for procreating a son for her deceased husband but without observing the strict rules of niyoga laid down in the smṛtis. That is the difference between the two. The action of the स्वैरिणी is described as साहस as it is no more than *vyabhicara,* though with the elder's permission.
3. वागदत्ता मनोदत्ता अग्नि परिगता सप्तमं पदं नीता भुक्ता गृहीतगर्भा प्रसूता चेति सप्तविद्या पुनर्भूर्भवति । अतस्तां गृहीत्वा न प्रजां धर्मे च विन्देत । बौधायन quoted in स्मृतिच० I. p. 75, सं.प्र. p. 735.
4. अग्दिर्वाचा च दत्तायां म्रियेतादौ वरो यदि । न च मन्त्रोपनीता स्यात्कुमारी पितुरेव सा ।। पाणिग्राहे मृते वाला केवलं मन्त्रसंस्कृता । सा चेदक्षतयोनिः स्यात्पुनः संस्कारमर्हति ।। वसिष्ठ 17, 72 and 74.
5. पौनर्भवश्चतुर्थः । या कौमारं भर्तारमुत्सृज्यान्यैः सह चरित्वा तस्यैव कुटुम्बमाश्रयति सा पुनर्भूर्भवति । या च क्लीचं पतितमुन्मत्तं वा भर्तारमुत्सृज्यान्यं पतिं विन्दते मृते या सा पुनर्भूर्भवति । वसिष्ठ 17, 18-20.
6. नष्टे मृते प्रवजिते क्लीचे च पतिते पतौ । पन्चास्वापत्सु नारीणां पतिरन्यो विधीयते ।। नारद (स्त्रीपुंसप्रकरण 97).
7. यत्तु नष्टे . . . विधीयते इति तत्र पालनात्पतिमन्यमाश्रयेत सैरन्द्रकर्मादिनालवृत्त्यर्थम् । मेधातिथि on मनु V. 157; तथा स्वर्गे गच्छत्यपुत्रापीत्यनेनापत्यजननमापदि प्रतिषिध्यते नियोगस्मृत्या तु तत्पुनरभयनुज्ञास्यते । तदेतदपत्योत्पादनमुक्तप्रतिषिद्धत्वाद्विकल्पते । मेधा. on मनु V. 163.
8. मृतेऽन्यस्मै तथा देया वरे सप्तपदात्पुरा । पुरा पुरुषसंयोगान्मृते देयेति केचन ।। ऋतावदृष्टे कन्यैव पुनर्देयेति केचन । आगर्भधारणात्कन्या पुनर्देयति चापरे । देशकालादिमा धर्मा अनुष्ठेया विजानता ।। स्मृत्यर्थसार p. 12.
9. एक एव पतिर्नार्या यावज्जीवं परायणम् । मृते जीवति वा पस्मिन्नापरं प्राप्नुवात्पतिम् ।। अभिगम्य परं नारी पतिष्यति न संशयः । आपतीनां तु नारीणामद्यप्रभृति पातकम् । आदि 104. 35-36.
10. यदि सा बालविधवा बलात्यक्ताथवा क्वचित् । तदा भूयस्तु संस्कार्यगृहीता येन फेनचित् ।। ब्रह्मपुराण quoted by अपरार्क p. 97.
11. अष्टौ वर्षाण्युदीक्षेत ब्राह्मणी प्रोषितं पतिम् । अप्रसूता तु चत्वारि परतोऽन्यं समाश्रयेत् ।। अप्रवृत्तौ तु भूतानां दृष्टिरेषा प्रजापतेः । अतोन्यगमने स्त्रीणामेष दोषो न विद्यते । नारद (स्त्रीपुंस vv. 98-101).
12. Vide 'Marriage and Stridhana' (5th ed.) p. 309 'one of these rules of selection requires that the parties to marriage should be of different *gotras;* but what is to be regarded as the *gotra* of a widow-the *gotra* of her father in which she was born or that of

her deceased husband to which she has been transferred by marriage?'

13. कन्याप्रद इति वचनादक्षताया एव नैयमिकं दानम् । पिता त्वकन्यामपि दद्यादिति केचित् । विश्वरूप on या I. 63.
14. उत यत्पतयो दश स्त्रियाः पूर्वे अब्राह्मणाः । ब्रह्मा चेद्धस्तमग्रहीत्स एव पतिरेकधा ।। ब्राह्मण एवं पतिर्न राजन्यो न वैश्यः । तत्सूर्यः प्रबुदन्नेति पंचभ्यो मानवेभ्यः ।। अथर्ववेद V. 17. 8-9. उत is explained by the निरुक्त, (e.g., I. 19) generally as अपि, whatever it is at the beginning of a verse or pāda.
15. या पूर्वे पतिं विश्वाऽथान्यं विन्दतेऽपरम् । पन्चौदनं च तावजं ददातो न वि योषतः ।। समानलोको भवति पुनर्भुवापरः पतिः । योऽजं पंचौदनं दक्षिणाज्योतिषं ददाति ।। अथर्ववेद IX. 5. 27-28.
16. Vide Steel's 'Law and Custom of Hindu Castes' pp. 26, 168-169.
17. इमा नारीरविधवाः सुपत्नीरांज्नेन सर्पिषा सं विशन्तु । अनश्रवोऽनमीबाः सुरत्ना आरोहन्तु जनयो योनिमग्ने ।। उदीर्ष्व नार्यभि जीवलोकं गतासुमेतमुप शेष एहि । हस्तग्राभस्य दिधिषोस्तवेदं पत्युर्जनित्वमाभि सं बभूथ ।। ऋ. X. 18. 7-8. अर्थर्ववेद (XII. 2. 31 and XVIII. 3.57) has the verse इमा नारीः, but reads संस्पृशन्ताम् for संविशन्तु. तै. आ. VI. 1 and अथर्ववेद 18.3.2. have उदीर्ष्व etc. but तै. आ. reads इतासुं for गतांसु, त्वमेतत् for त्वेदं and बभूव for बभूथ. The most difficult words are the last quarter of Rg X. 18.8. बभूथ requires a subject in the 2nd person which does not occur in the latter half of the verse.
18. इमा नारीरविधवाः सुपत्नीरित्यंजाना ईक्षेत । आश्व. गृ. IV. 6.12; उत्तरत पत्नीम् । धनुश्व क्षत्रियाय । तामुत्थापयेद्देश्वरः पतिस्थानीयोऽन्तेवासी जरद्यासो वोदीर्ष्व नार्याभि जीवलोकमिति । आश्व. गृ. IV. 2. 16-18. These sutras are referred to by अपरार्क p. 112. The com. on Tai. Ār. holds that the latter galf the calls upon the wife of the deceased to remarry.
19. इयं नारी पतिलोक वृणाना निपद्यत उप त्वा मर्त्य प्रेतम् । विश्वं पुराणमनु पालयन्ती तस्यै प्रजां द्रविगं चेह धेहि ।। तै.आ. VI. 1; अथास्य भार्यामुपसंवेशयति । इयं नारी . . . धेहि इति । तां प्रति हितः सव्ये पाणावभिपाद्योत्थापयति उदीर्ष्व . . . बभूव इति । बौ. पितृमेधसूत्र 1.8. 1-2.
20. अथैनमेतयासन्द्या सह चितायामादधाति । चौ. पितृमेधसूत्र I. 8.7.
21. उदीर्ष्व नारीत्यनया मृतं पत्यनुरोहति । भ्राता कनीयान् प्रेतस्य निगद्य प्रतिषेधति ।। वृहद्देवता VII. 13.
22. भ्रातुर्भार्यामपुत्रस्य संतानार्थे मृते पतौ । देवरोऽन्वारुरुक्षन्तीमुदोर्ष्वेति निदर्तयेत् । ऋग्विधान III.8.4 (ed. by Meyer).
23. Vide विश्वरूप on या. III. 253-54 केचित्तु परित्यक्तासु पारदारप्रायश्चित्तं नेच्छान्ति संबन्धिनिमित्तत्वाद्दारशब्दस्य । .... तथा च सति विधवास्वपि पारदाये न स्यात् । न च व्यभिचारादिभिस्तस्यापगमो युक्तः संस्कारनिमित्तत्वाद् द्वारशब्दस्य । तस्य च पतनेप्यनपगमात् ।

अत एव पतिता योषितः कृतप्रायश्चित्ताः पुनर्न संस्क्रियन्ते । अन्यथा तु पतनेन संस्कारस्यापगमात् कृतप्रायश्चित्ता अप्यदाराः स्युः । अतो व्यभिचारिणीष्वप्यस्त्येव पारदार्यम् ।

24. अमोक्ष्या भर्तुस्कामस्य द्विषती भार्या । भार्यायाश्च भर्ता । परस्परं द्वेषान्मोक्षः श्रीविप्रकाराद्वा पुरुषश्चेन्मोक्षमिच्छेद्यथागृहीतनस्ये दद्यात् । पुरुषविप्रकाराद्वा स्त्री चेन्मोक्ष-मिच्छेन्नास्ये यथागृहीतं दद्यात् । अमोक्षो धर्मविवाहानामिति । अर्थशास्त्र 111.3.

11

Foreign Accounts of Marital Arrangements

The importance of marriage does not require any emphasis. As Al Biruni aptly observes, "no nation can exist without a regular married life, for it prevents the uproar of passions abhorred by the cultivated mind, and it removes all those causes which excite the animal to the fury always leading to harm.[1] He also observes that "considering the life of the animals by pairs, how the one member of the pair helps the other and how the lust of other animals of the same species is kept aloof from them, you cannot help declaring matrimony to be a necessary institution;[2] whilst disorderly cohabitation or harlotry on the part of a man is a shameful proceeding, that does not even attain to the standing of the development of animals, which in every other respect stand far below him. It is well known that the system of marriage is not the same in all countries. In India, where marriage is held not as a mere contract, but as a religious sacrament from the days of the *Rigveda.*

According to Megasthenes polygamy was the norm. Thus, it is stated that the Indians marry many wives, marrying some of them for the sake of prompt obedience and the others for the sake of pleasure and numerous offspring. Megasthenes' statement was not entirely a fiction is apparent from the fact that although monogamy had always been held as ideal and fines were prescribed for marrying a second wife without sufficient cause.

Al Bīrūni says that the number of wives a man could marry depended upon the caste to which a man belonged; a *Brāhmaṇa* being allowed to have four wives, a *Kshtriya* three, a Vaisya two and a *Sūdra* one.

Al Bīrūni speaks of certain Hindu customs which were abolished and abrogated and infers that the abrogation of a law is allowable. One of the customs referred to by him was that which allowed the different sons of a man to have one wife in common. The custom of allowing a woman to have different brothers as husbands was already abolished, while referring to the 'unnatural kinds of marriage' which were still prevalent, he remarks that' the people inhabiting the mountains stretching from the region of Panchir into the neighbourhood of Kashmir live under the rule that several brothers have one wife in common'.

The Vedic literature does not contain any reference to a woman having several husbands, i.e., polyandry. Draupadī's marriage, with the five Pāṇḍava brothers in the *Mahābhārata* is the most famous instance of polyandry in *Sanskrit* literature.[3] Although the *Mahābhārata* clearly shows that all were shocked to hear that Yudhiśṭhira resolved to make Draupadi the wife of five brothers and vehement attempts were made to dissuade Yudhiṣṭhira by Dhṛśṭadyumna.[4] Yudhisthira, however, cited two instances in favour of this practice,[5] viz. of Jatila Gautami (who had seven sages as husbands) and of Varksi who had ten Pracetasa brothers as husbands. But, the instances are considered rather mythical, and in explaining away this puzzling occurrence, some scholars have gone to such an extent as to regard the Pandavas as a Nonaryan tribe somehow grafted on the Aryan stock[6] or as a branch of the Aryans different from the Kauravas.[7] It has also been argued that there were several Draupadis very similar to each other and the epic figuratively speaks of one Draupadi only, and that 'Draupadi was not a lady in flesh and blood, but stood for royal glory (*rajya-laksmi*) and her marriage with five brothers is only intended to show that they were jointly ruling their kingdom with absolute accord'.[8]

Generally two types of polyandry are referred to, 'one matriarchal (where a man forms simultaneous alliances with two or more men who are not necessarily relations of each other and therefore succession is traced through the female) and the other fraternal, where a woman becomes the wife of several brothers.[9] The former type of polyandry has gone out of practice, and the latter one still survives to some extent in

Kumaun and Garhwal and among peoples in the Himalayan areas upto Assam.[10]

Niyoga

Al Bīrūnī refers to another custom of the Hindus which also was abolished and abrogated. He describes it as follows: 'if a stranger has a child by a married woman, the child belongs to her husband, since the wife being, as it were, the soil in which the child has grown, is the property of the husband, always presupposing that the sowing, i.e. the cohabitation, takes place with his consent.

It is apparent that the custom referred to by Al Bīrūnī is *nigoya,* i.e., appointment of a wife or a widow to procreate a son from intercourse with an appointed man. While some *smṛiti* writers allowed *niyoga* specifying certain conditions, the violation of which made one liable to be punished,[11] others[12] condemned and forbade it. The conditions which were to be fulfilled to allow *niyoga* are: (1) the husband, whether living or dead, must have no sons; (2) the *gurus* in a family council should decide to appoint the widow to raise issue for the husband; (3) the person appointed must be either the husband's brother, or a *sapiṇḍa* or *sagotra* of the husband (according to Gautama, a *sapravara* or a person of the same caste); (4) the person appointed and the widow must be actuated by no lust, but only by a sense of duty; (5) the person appointed must be anointed with *ghee* or oil, must not speak with or kiss her or engage in sportive dalliance with the woman; (6) this relationship was to last till one son was born (or two according to some); (7) the widow must be comparatively young, she should not be old or sterile or past child-bearing age or sickly or unwilling or pregnant; (8) after the birth of a son they were to regard themselves as father-in-law and daughter-in-law. As Kane points out, the Smṛtis also make it clear that 'if a brother-in-law has intercourse with his sister-in-law without appointment by elders, but the other circumstances do not exist, (e.g., if the husband has a son), he would be guilty of the sin of incest and a son, born of such intercourse, would be a bastard and not entitled to any wealth and that he would belong to the begetter.'

The school condemning *niyoga* begun to grow stronger and stronger and public opinion became very strong against it.

This is apparent from the fact that while Viśvarūpa[13] says that the procreation of sons by Vyāsa from the queens of Vicitravirya mentioned in the *Mahābhārata*[14] should not be paid any heed like the marriage of Draupadī with five Pāṇḍava brothers, Medhatithi clearly states that the *niyoga,* though permitted by the *Smṛtis,* should not be practised as it is considered blameworthy by the people.[15] Medhātithi's statement that the practice of *niyoga* was void shows that the practice no longer received popular support and legal sanction, and therefore tallies with the evidence of Al Bīrūni that *niyoga* was no longer in vogue in his days.

According to the classical authors, intermarriage between the castes was prohibited.[16] Hiuen-tsang also stated that 'the members of a caste marry within the caste.'[17] This is also indicated by the *Apastamba Dharmasutra,* according to which one should marry a girl of the same *varna,* who was not given before to another and marriage with whom is in accordance with the Śāstra, and which remarks that by violating these rules sin is incurred.[18] It may, however, be pointed out that Gautama,[19] Vasistha,[20] Manu[21] and Yajnavalkya[22] prescribe that a person should by preference marry a girl of his own *varna,* but also allow the marriage of a person with a girl of a *varna* lower than his own. In fact, the best course (*purva-kalpa*) in a marriage, according to some of the Smrtis, is to marry a virgin of one's own caste, the less advisable course (*anukalpa*) being that which allows a Brahmana to marry a girl of any other caste, a Kshtriya, a woman of his own caste or a Vaisya or Sudra woman, a Vaisya, a Vaisya or Sudra girl and a Sudra only a Sudra girl.[23] Though a Brahmana is permitted to marry a Sudra girl by the *Visnudharmasutra* and *Manusmrti*, such a marriage has, however, been denounced in the strongest words in the same works. According to Yajnavalkya, 'a *dvijati* should not marry a Sudra girl.[24] Therefore, the Smrtis ungrudgingly recognised marriages between a Brahmana and Kshtriya or a Vaisya girl', although 'opinion was not unanimous about the marriage of a *dvijati* with a Sudra woman'.[25] Hiuen-tsang himself made note of the existence of numerous offspring of mixed marriages, though he did not describe them.[26] While commenting on a passage of Yajnavalkya, Visvarupa[27] states that, in his days, a Brahmana was allowed to marry a Kshtriya girl. During the time of Medhātithi,[28] marriage of Brāhmaṇas with Kshtriya and Vaisya girls took place, though such marriages were not very frequent, though marriage of Brāhmaṇas with Śūdra girls was no longer in vogue.

Ibn Khurdādba says that a Brāhmaṇa could marry the daughter of a Kshtriya, but a Kshtriya was not allowed to marry the daughter of a Brāhmaṇa. Al Idrīsī made some confusion while reproducing Ibn Khurdādba; or, the pratiloma marriage, i.e. the marriage of the male of the lower order with a female of the higher varṇa, the property of which has been recognised by the law-givers, although they resented[29] such marriage, was a practice in the society. Al Bīrūnī, however, stated that 'every man of a caste may marry a woman of his own caste or one of the castes or caste below his; but nobody is allowed to marry a woman of a caste superior to his own.[30] Like Al Bīrūnī, Kulluka[31] while commenting on a passage of Manu states that no marriage is legally possible between a female of a higher *varṇa* and a male of a lower order. An important information is, supplied by Al Bīrūnī when he states that, although permitted by the Smrītis, intercaste marriages of Brāhmanas in the *anuloma* order never took place in his time. The veracity of Al Biruni's testimony, however, appears a little doubtful when we take into consideration the large number of instances of intermarriage[32] among castes as furnished by our literary and epigraphic records. As it will be seen below, some of these marriages took place during the days of Al Biruni.

Of the examples of intercaste marriage known from the Classical Sanskrit literature, mention may be made of the marriage of Agnimitra, son of Senāpati Puśyamitra of the Ŝuṇga dynasty and a Brāhmana, with the Ksatriya princess Mālavikā, as recorded by Kālidāsa in his Mālavikāgnimitra, and the marriage of Bāṇa's father with a Śūdra woman[33] who gave birth to Candrasena and Matṛsena, known from the Harśacarita. According to Hiuen-tsang, the reigning king of Fa-la-pi (Valabhi), who was a Kshtriya by birth, married the daughter of Sīlāditya,[34] i.e. Harśa[35] a Vaiśya. Reference may now be made to some of the numerous instances of inter-caste marriage gathered from our epigraphs. A Kanheri inscription[36] reveals that Vasisthiputra Satakarni of the Satavahana family, the members of which were Dravidians claiming the status of Brahmana apparently owing to a little

Brahmana blood in their veins, married the daughter of Saka *Mahaksatrapa Rudra,* i.e., Rudradaman. Leaving aside this example where a Brahmana is involved in a marriage with the girl of a foreign family, the caste of which is not known with certainty, although, in placing the foreigners in the social structure of our country, Manu describes the Sakas as degraded Kshtriya[37] and Patanjali as *aniravasita* Sudra,[38] attention may be drawn to the well-known marriage of Prabhavatigupta, daughter of Candragupta II, with the Brahmana king Rudrasena II of the Vakataka family of the Visnuvrddha-gotra.[39] The Ghatotkaca inscription of Yasodharman and Visnuvardhana[40] states that Brahmana Soma, ancestor of Hastibhoja, the minister of the Vakataka king Devasena, married Brahmana and Kshtriya[41] wives. From the Tippera copper-plate grant of Lokanatha, we come to know that Brahmana Vira married a Sudra wife and begot a son named Kesava who was the maternal grandfather of Lokanatha. An inscription dated in Vikrama 894 refers to the Pratihara kings being descended from the Brahmana Haricandra and the latter's Kshtriya wife.[42] It is stated in the Atpur inscription of Saktikumara, dated in 977 A.D., that Bhartipatta, a descendant of the Brahmana Guhadatta, progenitor of the Guhila dynasty, married a Rastrakuta princess.[43] Kane[44] also draws our attention to the marriage of a Brahmana named Brahma or Bomanna Wodeya, the governor of Āraga,[45] with Virupadevi, a daughter of the famous Vijayanagara king Bukka I (1268–98 A.D.).* A reference is often made[46] to the marriage of a daughter of *Kakusthavarman* of the Kadamba family, which originally claimed the status of the Brahmana and later that of the Kshtriya, with a Gupta king recorded in the Talagunda inscription.[47] Though mostly scholars believe that the Guptas were not Brahmanas, some taking them as Kshtriyas[48] and others[49] as Vaisyas, recently an attempt[50] has been made to show that they could have been Brahmanas as well.**

While referring to the fact that in his time the Brāhmaṇas did 'not marry a woman except one of their own caste', Al Bīrūni[51] throws interesting light on the position of the offspring of the *anuloma* marriage. According to him, the child belonged

* [The reign of Bukka I is now assigned to 1344-77 A.D.—Ed.]

** [Caste practically played little part in the matrimonial alliances of Indian rulers (above, Vol. I, p. 91).—Ed.]

to the caste of the mother and not to that of the father, and he illustrates this by mentioning that if the wife of a Brāhmaṇa was a Brāhmaṇa, her child also was a Brāhmana, and if she was a Śūdra, her child was a Śūdra. On the issue of the status of the progeny, our law-givers, however, differ. According to some, if a man of one *varṇa* marries a women of the *varṇa* immediately after it, the progeny belongs to the *varṇa* of the father,[52] while others think that the progeny of *anulorna* union is in status lower than the father, but higher than the mother.[53] There is a third group that believes that the progeny of *anuloma* marriage is of the same *varṇa* as the mother's.[54] The authorities used by Al Birūnī appear to have belonged to the third group. Huen-tsang says that no marriages were contracted between the relatives of the father and those of the mother. The pilgrim's observation while revealing the well-known endogamous character of Indian marriage shows that within the same caste there were certain groups which were forbidden for marriage to a person belonging to another group of the same caste. Hiven-tsang's short account of the prohibited degrees of marriage may, however, be explained in a better way with the help of a more detailed account given by Al Bīrūnī. The latter states that, according to the marriage law of the Hindus, 'it is better to marry a stranger than a relative.' "The more distant the relationship of a woman with regard to her husband the better. It is absolutely forbidden to marry related women both of the direct descending line. It is also forbidden to marry collateral relations, viz. a sister, a niece, a maternal or paternal aunt and their daughters, except in case, the couple of relations who want to marry each other be removed from each other by five consecutive generations." In that case the prohibition is waived, but, notwithstanding, such a marriage is an object of dislike to the Hindus.[55]

The restrictions in choosing a girl for marriage, spoken of by Hiuen-tsang and Al Biruni are based on the prescriptions of ancient Indian authorities. Some of these authorities require that the bride must not be a sapinda or blood relation of the mother of the bridegroom[56] while others[57] restrict the prohibition against marrying a *sapiṇḍa* girl to seven degrees on the father's side and five degrees on the mother's side.[58] There were also others who not only 'prohibited marriage with a girl who had the same *gotra* as the bridegroom's, but prohibited marriage with a girl whose mother's *gotra* was the same as the bridegroom's.[59] Al Bīrūni's observation is applicable to the conditions prevalent in North India which did not favour marriage with collateral relations. But that marriage with one's maternal uncle's daughter or paternal aunt's daughter was in vogue in the southern part of India from quite early times is clearly borne out by the Baudhāyana Dharmasūtra[60] which mentions it as one of the five peculiar practices of the part of India. The Apastamba Dharamsūtra[61] forbids marriage with one's maternal uncle's or paternal aunt's daughter, and, according to Manu, 'on approaching [for carnal intercourse] the daughter of one's father's sister or of one's mother's sister or of mother's full brother a man must undergo the penance called Cāndrāyana.' A wise man should not take as his wife (any one of) these; they are not fit to be wedded because they are *sapinda* relatives, for by wedding them one sinks low (i.e. falls into hell or loses caste).[62] The prohibition against marriage with a *sapiṇḍa* girl applies to all *varṇas* including the Śūdra.[63] Regarding the meaning of *sapiṇḍa*, there are, however, two schools, one represented by the Mitākśarā and the other by Jīmūtāvāhana, the author of the Dāyabhāga. According to the Mitākśara, *sapiṇḍa* means one who has the same *piṇḍa*, i.e., body (or particles of the body), and *sapiṇḍa* relationship between two persons arises from their being connected by having particles of the same body.[64] According to the Dāyabhāga, *piṇḍa* is 'the ball of rice' and *sapiṇḍa* means 'one who is connected with another through oblations of food'.[65] Both the schools, however, agree in prohibiting a man's marriage with a *sapiṇḍa* girl. Various attempts have been made by scholars to find out the causes for the prohibition of marriage between near sapiṇḍas.[66] It is believed by some that the prohibition was due to abhorence which men in primitive times felt for incest. The prohibition was due to two causes; firstly if near relatives marry, their defects are transmitted with aggravation to their offspring and secondly the fear that, if marriages between near relatives by blood were allowed, there may be clandestine love affairs and consequent loss of morals and it would be difficult to secure husbands for girls who would be living under the same roof with several near or distant cousins'.[67]

According to Strabo and Diodorus it was an ancient law among the Indians that when youngmen and maidens were minded to wed, they did not marry according to the judgement of their parents, but by mutual consent.[68] The information of Strabo and Diodorus on the liberty-enjoyed by the Indian bride in choosing her husband in ancient times, however, does not appear baseless when we remember a verse of the *Rigveda,* which states that 'when a bride is fine looking and well adorned, she by herself seeks her friend from among men',[69] and take into account the numerous reference to the gāndharva and svayaṃvara marriages.[70] The mutual settlement of marriage and the selection of the husband by the bride doubtlessly suggest an advanced age for girl at the time of wedding. Further, some of the verses in the marriage hymn of the *Rigveda* show that married girls could not have been child-wives, but must have been grown up.[71] There are, however, also verses in the *Rgveda* which are sometimes taken to reveal that 'girls were married before they had attained puberty'.[72] Thus in one place, a wife is found asserting to her husband that she is fully developed physically and has abundant marks of complete puberty on her persons.[73] But according to Altekar, 'this statement is not, however, made to remove the misapprehension of an ignorant husband; the wife makes it in the privacy of the bedroom to exeite the passion of her husband, who had previously expressed his exuberant appreciation of her amorous skill.' He, therefore, believes that there is nothing to disprove that marriage in the Vedic age took place when the parties were sufficiently grown up.[74] Altekar also analyses the evidence of the epics and the Buddhist literature and remarks that 'brides in cultured families used to be about sixteen at the time of their marriage.[75]

Diodorus, however, also states that 'when in these old times espousals were made between persons of immature age, mistakes of judgement were of frequent occurrence, and when both sides repented their union, many of the women became depraved, and through incontinence fell in love with other men, and when at last they wished to leave the husbands they had first chosen, but could not in decency do so openly, they got rid of them by poison'.[76] Sometimes marriages were settled by persons who were not mature, and as a result, the choice was often unwise and the union unhappy. Nothing has, however, been stated regarding the age of maturity of either of the parties in the marriage, and at what age the girls were actually married. But, on the basis of certain statements of Megasthenes, it is sometimes believed that girls were married at the age of six or seven. Thus, as Phlegon records, it is stated by Megasthenes that women of the Pandaian realm bear children at the age of six.[77] Referring to the statement of Megasthenes that the very fruits of the country ripened faster than fruits elsewhere and decayed faster, he remarks that 'if the age at which the women there are marriageable is correctly stated, this is quite consistent . . . with what is said of the men's age,—that those who live longest die at forty; for men who come so much sooner to old age, and with old age to death, must of course flower into full manhood as much earlier as their life ends earlier.' According to him, therefore, it is quite usual 'that men of thirty would there be in their green old age, and young men would at twenty be past puberty, while the stage of full puberty would be reached about fifteen. And, quite compatibly with this, the women might be marriageable at the age of seven.'

A.S. Altekar, however, does not attach any importance to the information supplied by the Greek ambassador as the latter made the statement about girls of a place which he had never visited. Accoding to him, 'the marriage at the age of six (sic) and conception at the age of seven (sic) are as true as Heracles visit to South India.[78] R.C. Majumdar considers the statements, referred to by Phlegon and Arrian, as altogether unnatural and absurd.[79] Altekar also observes that the data supplied by the Greek authors do not show that girls were married before they were grown up. Most of the Gṛhyasūtras speak of a rite called *chaturthi-karman* (rite on the fourth day after marriage), which corresponds to garbh-ādhāna of later writers, and says[80] that as cohabitation is expressely mentioned in connection with this rite performed on the fourth day after marriage, it follows that girls must have generally been quite grown up at the time of marriage.' There was a conflict of opinion in society durıng the period 400 B.C.-100 A.D. about the desirability of pre-puberty marriages.[81] The contentions of these scholars are, however, based on the Dharmaśāstras of Gautama, Baudhāyana and Vasiṣṭha. Though Gautama prefers pre-puberty marriage, he prescribes that 'a marriageable girl should allow three monthly periods to pass and afterwards unite herself to a blameless man of her own will.[82] Baudhayana[83] and Vasistha[84] recommend that a girl may be kept unmarried for a period of three years after she attains puberty if there is any difficulty in settling her marriage. Reference is also made to Manu[85] who lays down that 'a maiden after attaining her puberty may wait for three years (to see if she is given away by her father or brother, etc.); but after this period, she should seek a husband who is similar to her.' Manu also goes to the extent of allowing the father to keep the daughter unmarried even to the end of her life, if no suitable husband is available.[86] Gautama also describes a man as committing a sin if he neglects to give his daughter in marriage before she attains puberty, and further that Baudhāyana[87] and Vasistha[88] add that the father or guardian incurs the sin of destroying an embryo at each appearance of menses as long as the girl remains unmarried after puberty.

Yājṇavalkya *smṛti* composed about 200 A.D. prescribes the same,[89] but never says a word allowing one to keep a girl unmarried after the attainment of her puberty. Both Kane[90] and Altekar,[91] therefore, think that from about 200 A.D. 'popular feeling had become insistent on pre-puberty marriages' and in their support they refer to Vaikhanasa,[92] Parasara,[93] Samvarta,[94] Yama,[95] Vyasa,[96] Sankha[97] and many other law-givers,[98] all of whom are well known advocates of pre-puberty marriage. As Altekar points out. It was not possible always to give away girls just on the eve of their attaining puberty. "If it was postponed to the last moment, there was the danger of crossing the fateful line." Therefore, some of the said *smṛti* writers were not satisfied only by forbidding post-puberty marriages, but started encouraging marriage of Brāhmaṇa girls well ahead of puberty. Thus, Parāśara states that, if a man does not give away a maiden when she has reached her twelfth year, his *pitṛs* have to drink every month her menstrual discharge. The parents and also the eldest brother go to hell on seeing [an unmarried] girl reaching the stage of rajasvalā.[99] He also states that a Brāhmaṇa marrying such a girl should not be conversed with or admitted to dinner in the same row in which other Brāhmaṇas dine and that he becomes the husband of a vṛśalī. According to Yama, a girl should be given away in marriage before she comes of age even to a man who is devoid of merit.

It would thus appear that while Manu allowed a girl to remain unmarried throughout her life if no suitable husband was found for her, Yama, in strict adherence to the rule of pre-puberty marriage, bothers little in attaching a girl, for her whole life, with a man unworthy and unsuitable. Samvarta highly commends the marriage of a girl of eight years old.[100] Medhatithi also states that the right time for a girl to be given in marriage is eight.[101] Further, since marriage came to be looked upon as *upanayana* in the case of women, naturally 'the age for *upanayana* (eight year) came to be looked upon as the proper age for marriage.[102] Kane observes that 'the rule that Brāhmaṇa girls were to be married between 8 to 10 years general from about the sixth or seventh century[103] and continued down to modern times',[105] though it may be pointed out that, in later times, a section of the advocates of pre-puberty marriage is found to clamour for a still lower age for the marriage of Brāhmaṇa girls.[104]

Child marriages did not come to vogue among the Kshtriyas for a long time'. Life was more ephemeral in the case of the members of the fighting classes than it was with the rest of the community; they naturally refused to follow the new custom which would have enormously increased the number of child-widows in their community.[105] Post-puberty marriages were in vogue in Kshtriya circles down to the middle ages, and hence svayamvara custom survived there till the twelfth century A.D.[106] Attention is, however, sometimes drawn to the Aranya-Kanda passage of the *Ramayana*[107] referring to Sita's age as six when she was married, and it is argued that instances of child-marriage among the Ksatriyas as not lacking. Altekar[108] and Kane,[109] however, consider the passage as a later interpolation as the Bala-kanda of the same work clearly states that Sita and her sisters enjoyed in private dalliance with their respective husbands immediately after marriage. If the evidence of the Balakanda is to be relied on, then Sita cannot be taken to have been six years old at the time of her marriage.[110] Moreover, the epics contain numerous references to girls like Kunti, Draupadi, Savitri, Damayanti, Rukmini, etc., who were sufficiently grown up at the time of the marriage of each of them. Bhavabhuti in his *Uttararamacarita*[111] represents Sita as a child at the time of her marriage. According to Altekar, Bhavabhuti 'was influenced by the practice of his age, rather than by the evidence of any earlier and genuine tradition'.[112] It may be pointed out here that even Bhavabhuti himself 'imagines that Malati, the heroine of his romantic drama *Malatimadhava,* was grown up so that it was practically a case of love at first sight'.[113] The heroines[114] including Sakuntala, Rajyasri, Kadambari, Mahasveta, Durlabhadevi, Laksmi, Kalavati, etc., of Sanskrit poems and dramas, which mostly deal with the life in royal and aristocratic families, were quite grown up at the time of marriage.

The above discussion no doubt tends to show that the rule of marrying a girl before she attains puberty was not meant for persons other than the Brāhmanas. It is, however, interesting to note that while making his observations on matrimony, menstrual courses, etc., Al Bīrūni states that 'the Hindus marry at a very young age; therefore the parents arrange the marriage of their sons.[115] If Al Bīrūnī's information is true, then it requires to be said that, at least in some parts of India, all the Hindus and not simply the Brāhmanas married 'at a very young age'. The expression 'young age' used by Al Bīrūnī, however is vague and helps little to suggest that the non-Brāhmaṇas also married girls before puberty or before twelve years of age like the Brāhmanas. But at the same time, it should be noted that, as the parents arranged the marriage of the Hindu son, probably the latter was not sufficiently grown up at the time of his marriage. The statement that marriage of a Hindu son was arranged by the parents deserves further consideration. For, it may be taken to indicate at least that marriage by mutual consent and not by the judgement of the parents, referred to by the Greeks, was no longer probably very frequent. One of the reasons for such a change might have been the considerable lowering down of the marriageable age of the girl, and the other the disastrous results of marriages arranged by the parties themselves, some light on which has been thrown by Diodorus, as we have already seen.

Arrian states that the Indians marry without either giving or taking dowries,[116] and many centuries later Al Birūni records that no gift were settled between the parents of the bride and the bridegroom and that only the husband gave a present of his choice to his wife, and also a marriage gift in advance, which he had no right to claim back, though the wife might return it to him of her own will.[117] From these statements it appears that the dowry system in the sense of something already promised was probably not very common, although references to the gift of large sums of money and valuable presents alongwith the daughter are noticed in our literary and epigraphic records.[118] The Jātaka stories also record the presentation of precious gifts to the bridegroom by rich merchants like the father of Viśākhā at the time when the bride proceeded to her husband's house. Rich presents of horses, elephants and jewels were given to Draupadī, Subhadra and Uttarā at the time of their departure from their parents' house after their marriage. Kālidāsa says that handsome presents were sent by the king of Vidarbha with his sister at the time of her departure with her husband after his marriage.[119] Horses, elephants, ornaments, costly costumes, etc., were also given with Rājyaśrī by her father Prabhākaravardhana as we know from the Harśacarita.[120] In the *Samaraiccakaha,* the description of a bride shows that she was fully decorated with costly costumes and ornaments before marriage and carried all of them to her husband's house after marriage.[121] Since these presents were made voluntarily and there was no pre-nuptial contract in this respect, they can hardly be called dowry, and Altekar remarks that if the dowry, i.e. 'a pre-nuptial contract of payment made by the bride's father with the bridegroom or his guardian', had prevailed to its present extent, it would have been very vehemently condemned by Smrti writers like the similar custom of bride-price.[122]

In his account of the origin of the name of the city of Pataliputra, Hiuen-tsang describes[123] a mock marriage in which a *patali* tree was taken to represent the bride and a young man was the bridegroom. It is stated that two couples were also chosen to stand as the parents of the bride and bridegroom respectively. 'All the ceremonies were gone through, and the man acting as the father of the bride broke off a branch of the *patali* tree and gave it to the bridegroom to be his bride' Hiuen-tsang's description of the marriage reveals two very important facts, viz.: (1) that a bride required to be given away by somebody, and (2) that certain ceremonies ought to be performed. Al Bīrūnī also lays down that, on the occasion of the marriage of the Hindus, the Brāhmaṇas perform the rites of sacrifice.[124]

These foreign observers were reproducing the actual state

affairs because in describing the ceremonies and rituals connected with vivāha, all the texts concerned refer the bride as being given away (dāna) by the father or her guardian in the family and to the observation of certain rites[125] which, however, varied with the peoples of different regions and villages, as underlined even in such an early text as the Aśvalāyana Gṛhyasūtra.[126] The essential rites are pāṇi-grahaṇa, vivāha-homa, agni parikramaṇa and saptapadi, and they are mentioned by all the Sūtrakāras although they differ with regard to the order in which they should be prformed. Thus, while the *Asvalayana Grhyasutra*[127] describes going round the fire before *saptapadi,* the *Appastamba Grhyasutra*[128] describes *saptapadi* before the act of going round the fire. The *Gobhila,*[129] *Khadira*[130] and *Baudhayana Grhyasutras*[131] describe *pani grahana* after *saptapadi* while many other Sutrakaras describe it before *saptapadi.* Moreover, certain rites, e.g., *madhuparka* (mention in *Apastamba,*[132] *Baudhayana*[133] and *Manava Grhyasutras*)[134] and *kanya-dana* (mentioned in the *Paraskara*[135] and *Manava Grhyasutras*[136] are not mentioned in the *Asvalayana Grhyasutra.* According to Kane, Aśvalāyana did not mention kanyā-dāna, because he wanted to describe ceremonies that were common to all forms'.[137]

Strabo while referring to certain customs of the Cathaeans refers to the groom and the bride choosing each other. This kind of marriage was known as gāndharva. As the Taittiriya Samhitā[138] and Aitareya Brāhmaṇa[139] state, the gāndharva form of marriage was known as such because it is prompted by mutual love. In this form of marriage, the principal object was gratification of carnal desires and so sacred rituals did not precede the union. The gāndharva form of marriage was quite common in royal families. Kālidāsa refers to this form in his Sakuntalā.[140] A passage in the *Mahabharata,* however, represents Sakuntala as calling a priest for performing religious rites before proceeding to consummate her marriage.[141] But, the passage is belived to be a later interpolation as it contradicts the definition of the *gandharva* marriage given in the epic itself.[142] As Altekar points out, 'when Kanva proceeds to express his approval, to his daughter, of her love marriage, he incidentally defines the *gandharva* marriage as a love union brought about without any recitation of the *mantras.*' The Baudhāyana

Dharmasūtra appears to approve the *gandharva* marriage when it refers to the view of certain authorities that love unions ought to be commended, as they presuppose reciprocal attachment.[143] According to Manu and Nārada, this form of marriage can be resorted to by the people of all *varnas*.[144] In his Priyadarśikā, the legality of the gāndharva marriage has ben recognised by Harśa.[145] Devala, quoted by Kulluka, however, lays down that, even in a *gandharva* marriage, the rituals should be performed after the union, and the possible objecton that the marriage *mantras* refer to a *kanya* or a virgin and so could not be recited in such a case has been explained away by stating that the term *kanya* should be taken in a general sense denoting a bride and not necessarily a virgin.[146] According to Altekar, 'the subsequent formal celebration of the marriage served the purpose of its proper announcement to society; it also gave an opportunity to relations and friends to share its joy.'[147]

Strabo further says that, among certain Indian tribes, 'the virgins are set before all as a prize for the man who wins the victory in a fist-fight'.[148] The svayaṃvara marriage, mention of which is found even in the hymns of the Rigveda,[149] is regarded as the ninth form of marriage by L. Sternbach.[150] The svayaṃvara marriages were of two types, viz. ordinary and festive, the first one occurring at the failure of the father or the lawful guardians to give away the girl after she had passed three monthly periods according to Gautama[151] and Visnu[152] and three years from the attainment of puberty according to Vasiṡtha, Baudhāyana and Manu.[153] Since the ordinry svayaṃvara 'arose out of negligence of the father or guardians, the authors of the ancient Indian legal texts, all staunch protagonists of the patriarchal form of society, were reluctant to concede it the status of a distinct form of marriage'.[154] The festive svayaṃvaras were of three types. The first type occurred when girls wandered about at will to find her suitable husband. Savitri's svayaṃvaras is an illustration of this. Festive svāyaṃvara which was applicable to girls of all castes.[155] The second, the virya-sulkā type, was that in which the girl was won by the performance of some special heroic skill. The Greek description probably refers to this type which is well illustrated by the svayaṃvaras of Draupadi and Sītā. The third type involved the real choice of the husband by the bride from among the members of a vast and splendid assembly of royal suitors. The svayaṃvaras of Damyantī and Indumatī illustrate the type.

It is clearly stated in the *Mahabharata* that even after *svayamvara* religious rites had to be performed,[156] and Kalidasa has described how after the *svayamvara of* Indumati and principal religious rites of *madhuparka, homa,* going round the fire and *pani-grahana* took place.[157] Some doubt is expressed as regards whether the festive svayamvara deserves to be called an independent form of marriage as, in it, the girl's choice was restricted to a great extent and the whole show was dominated by the father.[158] Essentially, it becomes a variety of the *brahma* or *prajapatya.* Further, when the girl was allowed to choose her husband, it partook the nature of *gandharva.* In fact, the *Viramitrodaya* states that the *svayamvara,* which is frequently mentioned in the Dharmasastras, is practically the same as *gandharva.*

According to Megasthenes the Indians married many wives whom they purchased from their parents in exchange for a yoke of oxen. Megasthenes, refers here to the ārśa form of marriage. The description of 'a yoke of oxen'[159] as the price with which an Indian purchased his wife, however, demands some consideration. According to some authorities on law, the gift of a pair of cow and bull or two pairs of these was nothing less than a bride-price, and they regard ārśa as a variety of the āsura marriage.[160] But *Smṛti* writers including Manu[161] opine that gift of a pair of cow and bull or two pairs of these by the bridegroom to the father of the bride was made as a matter of fulfilling the law *(dharmatah),* and not as a price for selling the girl *(na tu śulka-budhya).* The *Purva-mimansa* of Jaimini states that the gift given by the son-in-law, being for religious pruposes, could not be regarded as bride-price.[162] According to Sabara, prices of commodities vary in the market according to quality, but, in the *arsa* marriage, all sons-in-law offered the same gift to their fathers-in-law, and so it cannot be called bride-price.[163] Mitramisra refutes Sabara's argument by pointing out that the price that was paid for the Soma was fixed; but he defends *arsa* marriage by arguing that the gift made by the son-in-law to the father-in-law was not for making any profit (*lobha-nimittah*) but for religious purposes (*dharma-nimittah*).[164] As P.H. Prabhu points out the gift of cow and bull was to be made as a token of gratitude to the man who offered his daughter to the groom to enable him to fulfil his grhasth-asrama obligations.[165] However, the testimony of Megasthenes proves the popularity of the *arsa* marriage in the fourth century B.C.

Further, as it is known from Strabo, Aristobolus, while referring to some customs current at Taksasila observes that 'those who by reason of poverty are unable to marry off their daughters, lead them forth to the market-place in the flower of their age to the sound of both trumpets and drums (precisely the instruments used to signal the call to battle), thus assembling a crowd; and to any man who comes forward they first expose her rear parts upto the shoulder and then the front parts, and if she pleases him, and at the same time allows herself to be persuaded on approved terms, he marries her.[166] This statement is believed to refer to the *asura* form of marriage.[167] According to the Dharmaśāstra writers, a marriage is called āsura when the bridegroom receives a maiden after having given as much wealth as he can afford to her kinsmen and to the bride herself.[168] The origin of the name is not known with certainty but marriage by purchase, was the order of the day among ancient Assyrians, and this circumstances may have been responsible for the name āsura given to that form of marriage where a bride-price was paid.[169] References to the āsura form of marriage have, however, been traced in the Vedic literature.[170] The *Vasistha Dharmasutra*[171] quotes two passage of the *Maitrayaniya Samhita*[172] in support of the manusa (i.e. *asura*) form of marriage one of which states that 'she indeed commit falsehood (or sin), who being purchased by her husband, roams about with other males.' Yaska's *Nirukta*[173] while explaining a passage of the *Rgveda*[174] states that the word *vijamata* means, among the Southerners, the husband of a woman who is purchased'. Instances of the acceptance of the bride-price by the guardians of the bride are recorded in the epics and the Buddhist literature.[175] The payment of heavy bride-price made to the guardians of Kaikeyi, Madri and Gandhari at the time of their marriage is known from the epics, while the father of Isidasi, a nun of the *Therigatha,* is said to have received a bride-price for her at the time of her marriage. It should, however, be pointed out that although the custom continued to prevail in certain sections of the society, it was severely condemned by the law-givers like Apastamba,[176] Baudhāyana,[177] Manu,[178] Yājṇavalkya,[179] Yama[180] etc. The *Padma Purana* states that the face of one, who has sold his daughter in marriage, should not be seen.[181] The Peshwas[182] issued orders forbidding the Brāhmanas of Wai to accept money for giving their daughters in marriage. But, although the leaders of society condemned it in very strong terms and attempts were made to stop this social evil by prescribing fines, the custom continued in the society, and as is apparent from Aristobolous, poverty definitely played a significant part in its persistence.

As is also known from Strabo, Megasthenes referred to a peculiar custom of the inhabitants of the Caucasus. They are said to have intercourse with women in the open.[183] It is difficult to be certain whether any form of marriage is attempted to be described by the Greek Ambassador, and R.C. Majumdar considers the statement to be altogether unnatural and absurd.[184]

Interesting light is thrown on the remarriage of women Hiuen-tsang[185] and Al Biruni.[186] Thus, while the former states 'a woman never contracts a second', according to the latter if 'a wife loses her husband by death, she cannot marry another man'. Al Biruni also says that a woman had to choose between two things after the death of her husband. Either she had to remain a widow till her death or she had to burn herself, and it is also stated that the latter eventuality preferable because, as a widow, she was ill-treated as long as she lived.

The authors of the scriptures used by both Hiuen-tsang and Al Biruni seem to belong to the school of Manu and others. Manu clearly lays down that a second husband is no-where prescribed for a virtuous woman,[187] although we find that some authorities allow remarriage of a woman even when the death of her husband was only presumed and not proved. Thus, Vasiśṭha states that 'a wife of the Brāhmaṇa caste, who has issue, shall wait for five years and one who has no issue, for four years; the wife of a Ksatriya, who has issue, for five years and one who has no issue, for three years; the wife of the Vaīśya caste who has issue, for four years and without issue, for two years; the wife of a Śūdra, who has issue, for three years and who has none, for one year.[188] Kauṭilya, however, reduces the period of waiting to a few months only, and allows even a woman married by regular rites to marry again the full brother of her husband. If no brother exists, she may marry a *sapiṇḍa* of the husband or one of the same caste.[189] The story of Damayanti narrated in the *Mahabharata*[190] suggests that when the husband was not heard of for many years, a wife could marry again. Damayanti is stated to have sent a message to Rtuparna to the direction that, as Nala was not heard of for many years, Damayanti was going to celebrate a *svayamvara,* and Rtuparna hurries for it and does not think it a strange thing. In one place, however, Manu himself lays down that the remarriage *samskara* is allowed to a girl whose first marriage has not been consummated or who left the husband of her youth, went to live with another and returned to the first husband.[191] In declaring this, Manu perhaps only reiterates the popular usage which was too much to be ignored. According to Nārada, another husband is ordained for women in five calamities, viz. when the husband is lost (unheard of), is dead, has become a sanyāsin, is impotent or is *patita.*[192] The *Parasarasmrti*[193] and *Agni Purana*[194] have the same verse, the interpretation of which has given rise to a great deal of controversy. According to the *Parasara-Madhaviya,* the verse speaks of the state of society in another *yuga* (age) and has no application to the Kali age,[195] and Medhatithi takes the term *pati* to mean only *palaka* (guardian).[196] The latter is opposed to the remarriage of widows. As Altekar points out,[197] the same is the view expressed in the *Laghu-Asvalayana,* and according to the *Aditya Purana,* widow remarriage is not to be performed in the Kali age.

Remarriage of child-widows was, however, permitted by certain law givers. If merely the marriage ritual is performed and the marriage itself is not consummated, the girl should be married again.[198] Baudhāyana holds the same view,[199] and according to the Laghuśātātapa,[200] such a girl is really a virgin and should marry again as a matter of course. But, later remarriage of child-widow also was prohibited and the information of foreign observers, gains additional significance when we find that expressions like bāla-raṇda and bāla-vidhavā suggesting a child-widow keeping the vow of celibacy for the rest of her long life occur in texts of the tenth century like Karpūramaṇjari.[201]

Al Bīrūnī observes that the Hindu husband and wife can only be separated by death, as they have no divorce'.[202] The justification of Al Bīrūnī's observation is clearly borne out when it is remembered that the Dharamśāstra writers regard marriage completed by *homa* and *satapadi* as indissoluble. The evidence of Kautilya,[203] however, is often understood to allow divorce. According to him, there cannot be any dissolution of the marriage consecrated according to the Brāhma, Daiva, Ārśa or Prājāpatya form. Further, although he allows dissolution of the marriage tie if it was in the gāndharva, āsura or rākśasa form, he puts stress to mutual consent. In other words, he appears to opine that there can be no dissolution at the instance of only one party to the marriage who has begun to feel aversion to the other party. Even in the latter case, he seems to make an exception, where physical danger apprehened by one party from the other. No instance of divorce has as yet been traced in the Brahmanical literature, and although the Buddhist literature records a few cases of divorce the partners were not willing to go through the process of divorce. Thus, the *Kanhadipayana Jataka* (No. 444) speaks of a woman pointing out to her husband 'though she felt no love for him, she refrained from a new marriage because it was not the custom in the family for a wedded wife to take a new husband.' Writers on Dharmaśāstra are of the opinion that 'marriage is a saṃskāra, that the status of wife-hood arises from that saṃskāra that even if the husband or wife became *patita*, the saṃskāra, already performed is not annulled by the fact, that even if a wife committed adultery she still remains a wife and that even when she performs a penance for her lapse, it is not necessary to have a fresh saṃskāra of marriage performed on her.[204] It is noted above that Indian marriage was polygamous and 'a man was allowed to supersede a wife and marry another or others or to abandon his wife altogether in certain circumstances.[205] But, marrying a second one does not mean the dissolution of the marriage tie with the first. Even when the husband was allowed to abandon the wife for her lapse, the wife received in most cases at least the starving maintenance. As we have already seen, some Smrtis allow a woman to remarry in case the husband died, or was unheard of, etc.; but the commentaries and digests assert that these rulers are of a former age and are no longer applicable, and, what is more, Al Biruni himself records that a wife cannot marry another man even when her husband is dead. Kane, therefore, does not seem to be altogether unjustified when he makes the observation that 'divorce in the ordinary sense of the word (i.e. divorce *a vinculo matrimonii*) has been unknown to the Dharmasastras and to Hindu society for about two thousand years (except on the ground of custom among the lower castes)'.[206] The Hindu Marriage Act, 1955, however, permits divorce on the following grounds—adultery, conversion to another religion, insanity, leprosy, renunciation of the world, no trace for seven years, and non-compliance with a decree for restitution of conjugal rights for two years. The Act also permits the wife to get divorce on the ground that the husband has been guilty of rape, sodomy or bestiality, or that the husband had married again, or that any other wife of the husband is alive. However, to ensure a fair trial being given to every marriage, a petition for divorce is not permitted to be filed within three years of solemnization of a marriage. The Act also permits sagotra as well as intercaste marriages, both of the *anuloma* and *pratiloma* types, provides uniform rule for determining prohibited degrees of relationship for both schools, viz., the Mitākśarā and Dāyabhāga, and prescribes the minimum age of 18 years for the bridegroom and 15 years for the bride, which they must attain before marriage. It also introduces the rule of monogamy and prescribes no particular form of marriage or ceremonies.

References

1. Sachau, Alberuni's India, Vol. II, p. 154.
2. Whether the term 'marriage' can be used to denote a social institution complete by itself or not is a matter regarding which there is some controversy. According to W.G. Sumner (Folkways, Ginn, New York, 1906, pp. 348–49), 'although we speak of marriage as an institution, it is only an imperfect one'. "It has no structure. The family is the institution, and it was antecedent to marriage. Marriage has always been an elastic and variable usage, as it now is ...In fact the use of language reflects the vagueness

of marriage, for we use the word 'marriage' for wedding, nuptials or matrimony (wedlock). Only the last can be an institution." Watermark (History of Human Marriage, Vol. I, 5th ed., London, 1921, p. 26) points out that 'marriage is something more than a regulated sexual behaviour', and that 'it is an economic institution, which may in various ways affect the proprietary rights of the parties', and as a social institution, according to him, it should be defined 'as a relation of one or more men to one or more women which is recognised by custom or law, and involves certain rights and duties both in the case of the parties entering the union and in the case of the children born of it'. For further discussions, see P.H. Prabhu, Hindu Social Organization, 4th ed., Bombay, 1963, pp. 147–50. Prabhu remarks that 'it would be impossible to study the problem of marriage without at the same time involving ourselves into the discussion of some important and fundamental questions relating to the institution of the family' and, according to him, 'all these considerations are equally true of the Hindu social institution of *vivāha*'.

3. The *Kuṇāla Jātaka* (No. 536) also refers to a polyandrous marriage of a princess named Kaṇhā (Kṛṣṇā), i.e., Draupadī.
4. I. 195. 27–29.
5. I. 196. 1ff.
6. Cf. Kane, op. cit., p. 114.
7. Cf. Altekar, op. cit., p. 114.
8. *Tantravārttika,* p. 209.
9. Cf. Imp. Gaz. Ind., Vol. I, 1907, p. 483.
10. According to Indrajit (Ind. Ant., Vol. VIII, p. 88), in Kumaun between the Tons and Jamuna rivers about Kalsi, Rājpūts, Brāhmaṇas and Śūdras practise polyandry and the children are attributed to the eldest living brother. While commenting on the *Mahabharata,* I. 104. 35, Nīlakaṇṭha refers to the prevalence of the practice of one woman with two or three husbands among low caste people in his time. Cf. also Kane, *op. cit.,* p., 556 and notes.
11. According to Nārada (*Strīpusmsa,* 85–86), one acting contrary to the provisions about *niyoga* should be punished heavily, and in the Yajna-valkyasmrti (II. 234), a fine of one hundred panas is prescribed for such a person.
12. Āpastamba, II. 10.27. 5-7; Baudhāyana, II.2. 38; Manu, IX. 64-68; cf. also Kane, *op. cit.,* pp. 602–03; Altekar, *op. cit.,* pp. 146–48. *Brhaspati* (quoted by Aparārka on Yāj., I. 68-69) 'refers to the fact that the *Manusmṛti* first described the ancient *niyoga* and then forbade it and adds that, in former times, men possessed *tapas* and knowledge and could strictly carry out the rules while,

in the Dvapara and Kali ages, there is a great deterioration of power and so men of these times cannot now pracise *niyoga*'.

13. Cf. Kane, op. cit., pp. 602-03 and notes.
14. I. 105; cf. other cases in I. 95, I. 103, I. 126, I. 127, I. 132. Although later *smṛti* writers allow only one son to be raised by niyoga, the earlier practice was different. Kuntī raised three sons by *niyoga*. Pāṇḍu, however, was not satisfied with that number and pressed his wife to have some more. Kuntī protested against the suggestion, pointing out that the custom permitted only three sons by *niyoga* and not more (I. 132.63-64). It is said that the king bali had seventeen sons by *niyoga*, six raised on his crowned queen and eleven on a Śūdra wife (I. 113).
15. On Manu, IV. 176.
16. Cf. Megasthenes, as quoted by Strabo (McCrindle, op. cit., pp. 85–86; Majumdar, op. cit., p. 268), Diodorus (McCrindle, op. cit., p. 41; Majumdar, op. cit., p. 238) and Arrian (McCrindle, op. cit., p. 218; Majumdar, op. cit., p. 236).
17. Watters, Yuan Chwang's Travels in India, Vol. I, p. 168.
18. II.6.13. 1 and 3.
19. IV. 1.
20. I.24.
21. III. 12-13.
22. I. 55-57. Vātsyāyana also prefers marriage within the same *varna* (cf. Class. Age, ed. Majumdar, p. 564).
23. Baudhayana, 1. 8. 2, Viṣṇu, 24. 1-4. Cf. also Kane, op. cit. Vol. II, pp. 53, 448.
24. I. 57.
25. Kane, *op. cit.*, p. 449.
26. See Watters, *op. cit.* Vol. I, p. 168.
27. On Yāj., III. 283.
28. On Manu, III. 14.
29. Cf. Kane, *op. cit.*, pp. 52-53.
30. Sachau, *op. cit.*, pp. 155-56.
31. On Manth X. 11.
32. Kane, *op. cit.* pp. 449-50.

* [Act I has an interesting reference to the Chief Queen's *varṇāvara bhrātā* (brother of an inferior varna).—Ed.]

33. The offspring of a *Brahman* male and Śūdra female was called a Pārāśava or a Nisada (cf. *Ibid.*, pp. 86–88). The *Mahābhārata* (I. 109. 25) call; Vidura a *Pārāśava* and mentions (114.12) him as having married the *Pārāśava* daughter of King Devaka. [Read *Pārāśava*.—Ed.]
34. Watters, *op. cit.*, Vol. II, p. 246.

35. Cf. Class, Age, ed. Majumdar, p. 561, note 7.
36. Cf. A. Imp. Un., ed. Majumdar, pp. 183, 203.
37. Manu, X. 43-44. Manu also describes the Kambojas, Yavanas (Greeks), Pāradas, Pahlavas, Cīnas, etc., as degraded Kshatriyas.
38. On Pāṇini, II. 4. 10.
39. Ep. Ind., Vol. XV, p. 39.
40. *Arch.* Surv. West. Ind. Reports, Vol. IV, p. 140. [The Ghaṭotkaca cave inscription is a Vākāṭaka epigraph (CII, Vol. V, pp. 112ff.) and not a record of Yaśodharman alias Vtṣ́ṇuvardhana for whose Mandasor inscription, see *ibid.,* Vol. III, pp. 150ff.; Sircar, Sel. 1965, pp. 411ff.—Ed.]
41. Ep. Ind., Vol. XV, pp. 301ff.
42. *Ibid.,* Vol. XVIII, p. 87.
43. Ind. Ant., Vol. XXXIX, pp. 186ff.
44. *Op.cit.,* p. 450.
45. Ep. Ind., Vol. XV, p. 12.

* [The reign of Bukka I is now assigned to 1344-77 A.D.—Ed.]

46. Class.Age, ed. Majumdar, p. 561, note 7; Kane, *op. cit.,* Vol. II, Part I, pp. 449-50; JAIH, Vol. I, p. 93. [Cf. above, pp. 91-93.—Ed.]
47. Ep. Ind., Vol. VIII, p. 24.
48. G.S. Ojha *(Rājpūtane kā Itihās,* in Hindi, pp. 113-14), S. Chattopadhyay (E. Hist. N. Ind., 1958, p. 140). G.P. Mehta (*Candragupta Vikramāditya,* in Hindi, p. 9, note 1), V. Upadhyay (Gupta Sāmrājya kā Itihās, in Hindi, Vol. I, pp. 28-31) and others (cf. S.R. Goyal, Hist. Imp. Gup., p. 76 and notes 5-6) subscribe to the view that the Guptas were Kshatriyas.
49. Scholars including A.S. Altekar (N. Hist. Peop., pp. 342, 344), Aiyanger (Anc. Ind., etc., p. 180), V.V. Mirashi (Vākāṭaka Rājavaniśa, p. 56) and others (cf. Goyal, *op. cit.,* p. 75 and note 4) advocate the view that the Guptas were Vaiśyas.
50. Goyal, *op. cit.,* pp. 74-75, 78-81.

* [Caste practically played little part in the matrimonial alliancces of Indian rulers (above, Vol. I, p. 91).—Ed.]

51. Sachau, *op. cit.,* Vol. II, p. 156.
52. Cf. Baudhāyana, 1.8.6 and 1.9.3 Cf. also Kane, *op. cit.,* p. 56, for other authorities of this group.
53. Manu, X. 6.
54. Visṇu, 16.2 and Sankha (prose) quoted by the *Mitakśara* on Yāj., 1.91 and *Aparārka,* as cited by Kane, *op. cit.,* p. 56.
55. Sachau, *op. cit.,* Vol. II, p. 155.
56. Cf. *Gobhila Grhyasutra,* 111. 4-5; Manu, III. 5; *Vaikhanasa Smirtisutra,* III. 2; Apastamba, II. 5. 11. 16; cf. also Kane, *op. cit.,* pp. 436-37.

57. Gautama, IV. 2, Vasistha, VIII. 2; Viśṇu, 24.10; *Varaha Grhya-sutra,* 9; ŝāṇkha quoted by Haradatta on Āpastamba, 11.5. 11-16; Yaj., 1.53; cf. also Kane, loc.cit.
58. Cr. Kane, *loc. cit.*
59. Cf. Kane, *loc. cit.*
60. 1.1. 19-26. For reference in works supporting the marriage with a maternal uncle's daughter, cf. Kane, *op. cit.,* pp. 460-62. [Marriage with one's sister's daughter is also popular among South Indian Brāhmaṇas.—Ed.].
61. I.7.21.8; cf. also Kane, *op. cit.* p. 458.
62. Manu, X. 172-73. For further details on the points, see Kane, *op. cit.,* pp. 459-60; B.N. Sharma, See. L.N. Ind., p. 11 and note 5.
63. Cf. Kane, *op. cit.,* p. 452 and note 1070.
64. On Yaj., I. 53.
65. Cf. Kane, *op. cit.* p. 472.
66. Westermarek, History of Human Marriage, 1921 ed., Vol. II, pp. 71-81; Rivers, *'Marriage of Cousins in India',* JRAS, 1907, pp. 611-40; Kane op.cit., p. 477.
67. *Op. cit.* pp. 477-78.
68. *Ibid.,* p. 240.
69. X. 27. 12.
70. See Section 11 below.
71. X. 85. 26-27, 46.
72. Kane, *op. cit.,* p. 439.
73. X. 126, 6-7.
74. *Op. cit.,* p. 51.
75. *Ibid.,* p. 52.
76. Majumdar, *op. cit.* p. 240.
77. *Op. cit.* p. 55.
78. Majumdar, Class.Ac.Ind., p. xxiv.
79. *Op. cit.,* pp. 441-42.
80. *Op. cit.* p. 55.
81. XVIII. 20-23.
82. IV. I. 14.
83. XVII. 67-68.
84. IX. 90.
85. X. 89.
86. *Loc. cit.*
87. IV.1.12,
88. XVIII. 70-71.
89. I. 64; Nārada (Strīpumsa, verses 25-27) also has the same rule.
90. *Op. cit.,* p. 443.
91. *Op. cit.,* p. 56.

92. VI. 12.
93. VII. 6-9.
94. Vv. 65-66. These two verses are the same as Parāśara, VII. 6, 8.
95. Quoted in the *Smṛtieandrikā*, Vol. I, pp. 73, 81; cf. Kane, *op. cit.*, p. 444, note 1056.
96. II. 7.
97. XV. 8.
98. Cf. Kane, *op. cit.* p. 444-45 and notes; also Altekar, *op. cit.*, pp. 56-59 and notes, and Sharma, Soc. L.N. Ind., p. 15 and note 1.
99. Vaikhanasa (VI. 12, who lays down that a Brāhmaṇa should marry a Brāhmaṇa girl who is nagnika or gauri, 'defines nagnikā as a girl of over eight years but less than ten and gaurī as one who is between ten and twelve and has not had menstruation'. According to Parasara, a girl is called gaurī when she is eight, rohiṇī when nine, kanyā when ten and rajasvalā beyond ten. Kaśyapa, however, describes a girl of seven as *gauri,* a girl of ten as kanyakā and a girl of twelve as kumāri (cf. Kanc, op. cit., p. 445).
100. V. 67.
101. On Manu, IX. 4.
102. Cf. Kane, *op. cit.* p. 443 and note 1052; Altekar, *op. cit.* p. 57.
103. Kane, *op. cit.,* p. 445; cf. Altekar, *op. cit.* pp. 61-63.
104. *Op. cit.,* p. 58.
105. *Ibid.,* p. 66. For *swayaṃvara*, see below.
106. III. 47. 10-11.
107. *Op. cit.,* p. 53.
108. *Op. cit.* p. 445.
109. Rāmāyaṇa, I. 77. 16-17 (in three volumes with Govindaraja's commentary) as cited by Kane, *op. cit.,* p. 445, note 1058.
110. Ed. G. V. Bhattacharya, Calcutta, Act I, v. 20.
111. *Op. cit.* p. 53.
112. Cf. Kane, *op. cit,* p. 446.
113. Durlabhadevī and Laksmī are mentioned in the Dvyāśrayamahākāvya of Hemacandra and Kalavati's name occurs in the Pṛthvīrājavijaya of Jayāṇaka.
114. Sachau, *op. cit.* Vol. II, p. 154.
115. McCrindle, *op. cit.* p. 277; Majumdar, *op. cit.,* p. 231.
116. Sachau, *op. cit.* Vol. II, p. 154.
117. Cf. Altekar, *op. cit.,* p. 70; Sharma, *op. cit.,* p. 12. We, however, refer to only a few cases, as multiplication of instances does not seem to be necessary.
118. Raghuvaṃśa, VII. 32.
119. Chap. IV.

120. Ed. Jacbi, Calcutta, 1926, Vol. II, pp. 93-101; cf. also Sharma, *op. cit.,* p. 12 and note 7.
121. *Loc. cit.*
122. Watters, *op. cit.* Vol. II, p. 87.
123. Sachau, *op. cit.* Vol. II, p. 154.
124. Cf. Kane, *op. cit.,* pp. 526-38; Altekar, *op. cit.* pp. 79-83; Prabhu, *op. cit.* pp. 163-73. Some of rites are still observed in a Hindu marriage.
125. I. 7. 1-2.
126. 1.7.7.
127. IV.16. and V.I.
128. II.2.16.
129. 1.3.31.
130. 1.4.10.
131. III.8.
132. I.2.1.
133. I.9.
134. I.4.
135. I.8.6-9.
136. *Op. cit.,* p. 531. For different matters connected with the vivāha-samskara, see Kane, *op. cit.,* pp. 531-37.
137. The forms of marriage generally enlisted are monogamy, polygamy, polyandry and group marriage (Encyclopaedia Britannica, 14th ed., Vol. XIV, 1929, p. 949). But in discussing the *Hindu vivaha,* the expression 'form of marriage' is used 'to denote the method of consecrating a marriage union' Prabhu, op. cit., 4th ed., 1963, p. 151.
138. VI. 1.6.5 (Strī-kāmā vai Gandharvā).
139. V.I.
140. Act. III.
141. I. 94. 38.
142. Cf. Altekar, *op. cit.,* p. 43.
143. I. II. 13.
144. III. 25; cf. Nārada, Stripumsa, verse 40.
145. Madras, 1935, Act III, p. 66.
146. Cf. Kulluka's commentary on Manu, VIII. 226.
147. *Op. cit.,* p. 43.
148. Majumdar, *op. cit.* p. 279.
149. Rgveda, I. 116.17; I.119.5; X.85.14; B.S. Upadhyay, Women in the Rigveda, Benares, 1941, p. 70; E.W. Hopkins in JAOS, Vol. XIII, 1888, pp. 168ff., 357ff.; Kane, *op. cit.,* pp. 523-24; Altekar, *op. cit.,* pp. 523-24; Altekar, *op. cit.,* pp. 65-66 and notes.
150. Juridical Studies in Ancient Indian Law, Part I, Delhi, 1965, pp.

383-87; cf. H.N. Chatterji, 'A Critical Study of *Swayaṃvara* Form of Marriage', Calcutta Review, June, 1957, pp. 281-88; cf. also A.K. Chakravarti's paper 'Forms of Marriage in Ancient India', JAIH, Vol. V, pp. 226-35. Out of the usual eight forms of marriage, we have discussed gāndharva and we shall have occasion below to refer to the ārśa and āsura. The Brāhma form consists of the giving away of the daughter, after decking her with ornaments, to one who is well versed in the śrutis and of good conduct whom the bride's father himself invites, while in the daiva a girl decked with ornaments is given to a priest officiating in a sacrifice, during the course of its performance. In the prājāpatya form, the father makes a gift of the daughter, by addressing the couple with the words, "May both of you perform your religious duties together," and honours the bridegroom with Madhuparka, etc. The rākśasa form constitutes of the forcible abduction of a maiden from her home, while she cries and weeps, 'after her kinsmen have been slain or wounded and their houses broken' and the paiśāca results from the rape of a girl when she is asleep, intoxicated or unconscious. Recently D.C. Sircar (cf. 'The Ten Forms of Marriage', Indian Museum Bulletin, Vol. V, No. 1, pp. 7-9: also JAIH, Vol. IV, 1971, p. 306) has drawn our attention to the Skanda Purāṇa, Nāgara-khaṇḍa, Chapter 241, verses 33-36, which enumerates the kinds of marriages as no less than ten, the two new names being prātibha and ghātana. According to Sircar, these two forms were in vogue among the lower classes of people in Gujarat where the Nagara-khaṇḍa section of the Skanda Purāṇa appears to have been composed. As Kane (*op. cit.* p. 525) points out, 'the forms of marriage have their roots deep down in the Vedic literature', the *brahma* form being given expression in the *Rgveda,* X. 85, the āsura form (by payment of money) being referred to ibid., I. 109.2 and the Nirukta, VI. 9, the gandharva and svayamvara being indicated by the Rgveda, X. 27.12 and I. 119.5. The story of Śyavāśva narrated in the Brhaddevata (V. 50) in connection with the Rgveda, V. 61, makes an approach to the daiva form. [If *swayaṃvara* was regarded as the ninth form of marriage, the authorities would not have spoken only of its eight forms.—Ed.]

151. XVIII. 20.
152. 25.40-41.
153. Vasistha, XVII. 67-68; Manu, IX. 90; Baudhayana, IV. 1.13. The Yājṇavalkyasmṛti (1.64) allows svayaṃvara to a girl who has no parents or guardians to find out a worthy husband for her.

154. JAIH, Vol. V, p. 227.
155. Op. cit. p. 523.
156. I. 195.7.
157. Kane, *op. cit.,* p. 521. But in the case of Kālidāsa's ŝakuntalā, there was no performance of religious rites. Such rites were therefore not essential for the gāndharva marriage. They were performed at a later date only when some guardians wanted them.
158. Jaih, Vol. V, p. 227.
159. McCrindle, *op. cit.,* p, 69; Majumdar, Class. Ac. Ind., p. 270; A. Imp. Un., p. 559; Puri, Ind. E. Gr. Writ., p. 86.
160. Cf. Altekar, *op. cit.,* p. 44.
161. III. 29, 53.
162. VI. 15.
163. On the Pūrvamīmaṃsā, VI. 15.
164. Saṃskāraprakāsa, p. 850.
165. *Op. cit.,* pp. 151-52.
166. Camb. Hist. Ind., Vol. I, p. 372; Majumdar, *op. cit.,* p. 297.
167. Chattopadhyay, Soc. L. Anc. Ind., p. 63; Puri, loc. eit.
168. Cr. Kane, *op. cit.* p. 517; A. Imp. Un., ed. Majumdar, p. 559; Altekar, *op. cit.,* p. 39.
169. *Op. cit.,* p. 39.
170. Kane, *op. cit.,* pp. 503-04.
171. 1.36-37.
172. I. 10. 11.
173. VI. 9.
174. I. 109. 2.
175. Cf. Altekar, *op. cit.,* p. 40.
176. II. 6. 13. 10-11.
177. I. II 20-21. It is stated 'a woman who is purchased with wealth is not declared to be a legally wedded wife (patnī); she is not [to be associated with the husband see is a dāsi (slave girl). Those, who blinded by greed, give their daughters in marriage for a fee (śulka), are sinners, sellers of their own selves and perpetrators of great sin and they fall into hell.' In another place, Paudhayana (II.1.79) states, 'he who gives his daughter [in marriage] by sale [as a chattel] sells his merit (puṇya).
178. III. 41, 54-54; IX. 98; XI. 61.
179. III. 236.
180. Quoted in the Mahābhārata, XIII. 45, 18-19. Cf. also 93. 133 and 94.3.
181. Brahma-khanda, 24, 26.
182. Cf. Kane, *op. cit.,* p. 506.
183. McCrindle, *op. cit.,* p. 71; Majumdar, *op.cit.,* p.271.

184. Majumdar. *op. cit.,* p. xxiv. [it is probably not absurd.—Ed.]
185. Watters, *op. cit.,* Vol. I, p. 168.
186. Sachati, *op. cit.* Vol. II, p. 155.
187. V. 162.
188. XVII. 67-71.
189. *Arthasastra,* III. 4. Manu (IX. 76) also speaks of the periods that a wife should wait for her husband when he stays abroad for various reasons; but he does not state what the wife should do after these years of waiting.
190. III. 70. 24.
191. IX. 176.
192. Nārada, Strīpumsa, verse 97. Nārada lays down that 'if the husband has gone to a foreign country, a Brāhmaṇa wife should wait for eight years, but four year if she has not given birth to a child; after that period of [8 or 4 years], she may resort to another man' (ibid., verses 98-101). A lesser number of years of waiting is prescribed for Kshtriya and Vaiśya wives. If the husband is known to be living, then the periods arre double of those stated above; this is the view of Prajapati when no news can be had of persons and hence there is no sin if a woman resorts to another man 'in such cases' (cf. Kane, *op. cit.,* p. 613).
193. IV. 30.
194. 154. 5-6.
195. Vol. II, Part I, p. 53.
196. On Manu, V. 157.
197. *Op. cit.* p. 155.
198. XVII. 66.
199. II. 2. 4, 7.
200. Cf. Altekar, *op. cit.,* p. 154.
201. III. p. 75, cited by B.N. Sharma, *op. cit.,* p. 18.
202. Sachau, op. cit., Vol. II, p. 154.
203. *Arthasastra,* III. 3.
204. Cf. Viśvarūpa on Yāj., III. 253-54.
205. See discussion on Polygamy in Section 2 above; cf. also Kane, *op. cit.,* pp. 552-53.
206. *Loc. cit.*

12

Property Rights

The sociological pattern and behaviour of a society takes a long time to evolve. A civilization at a particular period exhibits relations or references to what prevailed in that society at that time. Therefore the post-Vedic civilization exhibits references or relations to what prevailed in the Vedic society. This is true in the case of all the succeeding periods of Indian society. Thus every such study has to refer to the Vedic conditions. Indian law makers were also influenced by the changes that crept in the social and political systems from time to time and influenced the pattern of women's right of inheritance in different ages.

In Vedic Saṃhitās wife was described as *ardhāṇginī* or *patnī* without whom no ceremony could be performed. Her position in the household was considered of prime importance in matters pertaining to it. However, she had no separate entity in matters of property or inheritance. Though she commanded enough respect and importance as part and parcel of the family. Exceptions to such a general pattern of life called for the formulation of rules over inheritance and thus law codes come into existence.

Wife's Property Rights

Despite the fact that the husband and wife were regarded as joint owners of the household according to Vedic texts there was no instance where wife's proprietary rights were separately recognised. There was no such necessity for this since her social security was never at stake. The wife had right to maintenance under joint-ownership, which also secured her position in case the husband was not good to her. She had no right to incur any extraordinary expenditure without the consent of her husband. The right of maintenance against her husband could never be denied to her even if she became unchaste or outcaste or persisted in immorality.

Yājṇavalkya allowed the first wife one-third share in the husband's property in case she was superseded unjustly. In cases where father himself separated his sons during his life-time, wife was entitled to a share equal to that of a son.

The position of the wife showed a marked decline after c. 650 A.D. but she continued to enjoy the right to maintenance in case she was faithful. Further, her position continued to remain secure in case the husband married for the second time.

Vijṇāneśvara showed liberality and declared that if a husband abandons a virtuous wife or wilfully misappropriates her property and refuses to restore it, she can move a court of law to get her grievances redressed. But, despite conceding such a right to her, Vijṇāneśvara declares that she can spend the family property only with the permission of her husband. He also states that giving of a share to wife in inheritance solely depended upon the will of the husband.

Extent of Wife's Right Over *Strīdhana*

The specific scope of *strīdhana* has changed from time to time due to various factors and has been subject to diverse interpretations by different law-givers. Only certain kinds of property came under the category of *strīdhana* and not all property possessed by women. From about the seventh century A.D. there was a general tendency of enlarging the scope of *strīdhana.*

Taittirīya Saṃhitā says that the wife is the mistress of her *strīdhana,* yet it does not say anything clearly about her specific powers regarding its sale or gift. Early *Smṛti* writers were not prepared to invest the woman with full powers over her *strīdhana*. According to Yājṇavalkya the husband could freely utilise his wife's property in times of dire necessity and he was not required to pay it back, whereas Kātyāyana states that if the husband had promised to return the *strīdhana* to his wife, he ought to keep his words. In course of time, landed property also began to be included in a woman's *strīdhana*.

Upto c. 650 A.D. a woman had absolute and independent ownership over *saudāyika strīdhana* (gifts from affectionate relations). The husband could use it, excepting the *saudāyika,* and could use the rest of the stridhana only in times of difficulty and distress. With regard to its repayment by the husband and the mode thereof different jurists have opined differently.

Commentators 7th and 8th say that she may have property but not ownership because she was supposed to be dependent and subservient.

The power of alienating *strīdhana* depended on two factors—first, woman's status in relation to marriage, and second, the nature of property. Vijṇānesvara allows the husband to take his wife's *strīdhana* in case of extreme necessity and ordained that he should repay the amount even if he had obtained it with the permission of his wife. But *Jīmūtavāhana* states that gifts received from strangers and those earned by mechanical arts are always subject to her husband's dominion and he could take it even if there was no distress; and it was not even necessary for him to pay it back.

Succession to *Strīdhana*

Manu and Kauṭilya stipulated that *strīdhana* should be divided equally among sons and daughters. They even allow the grand-daughters to get something out of their grand-mother's estate. They further state that the *strīdhana* of an issueless deceased woman would go to her husband. Furthermore, they state that the *strīdhana* of a sonless deceased woman would devolve upon her unmarried daughters only.

According to Yājṇa-valkya, Vishṇu and Nārada the daughters were inheritors of *strīdhana* and, in their absence, their offsprings got this right through them; on their failure the *strīdhana* would revert to the original source from where it came.

In course of time, however, gifts given by the husband during the married life came to be included in *strīdhana*. The motive of a husband in giving gifts toi his wife was no doubt to provide the wife against a rainy day, but he rarely intended to do so at the cost of his sons. His usual expectation was that the property should pass on to his sons after the death of his wife. Some jurists, therefore, felt that the most equitable course was to allow both the sons and the daughters to inherit *strīdhana*.

Daughter's Property Rights

In the ancient Hindu society and position of daughter was considered sympathetically whether she was married or not. She was always accorded some share in father's property. There was, however, a difference between the property rights of the daughters with brothers and daughters without brothers.

Daughters with Brothers

At the dawn of *Aryan* civilisation, recognition of a daughter's right in the property was out of question. The jurists of c. 300 B.C. accorded maintenance out of the father's property in case the daughter was unmarried at the time of the death of her father. It was also regarded the duty of the brother/brothers to provide for their sister's marriage even if there were no ancestral assets for the purpose.

Manu makes provisions for reasonable expenses for the marriage of the daughter and makes it a necessary charge on the paternal property in the case of the daughters who are not married in the life-time of the parents. But when both the parents died and the brothers divided the property among themselves, it was made obligatory for the brothers to set apart one-fourth of their share for meeting the expenses of the marriage of their sisters.

In the age of decline, Devala states that the money necessary for marriage should be given to unmarried daughters from the paternal estate. Asahaya and Medhatithi literally follow Manu when they observe that three-fourth of the property shall be taken by the son and one-fourth by the daughter. Visvarupa, another commentator of the period, agrees that one-fourth part should be spent by the brothers for their sister's marriage if the father had not set apart money for that purpose. Bharuchi maintained that an unmarried sister was entitled to as much money as would be necessary for her marriage and not to a definite share. the *Mitaksharda* explains that this does not mean that each brother is to give one-fourth of what she would have got had she been a male. The *Mitaksharda* his share to the sister; the unmarried sister would get one-fourth a further adds that one should take not the word 'one-fourth' literally and that the unmarried sisters gets only as much as is necessary for her marriage. On the other hand, the *Dayabhaga* school lays down that if the ancestral wealth is small, the provision for the marriage of the daughter should be made by giving her a fourth share, but if the wealth is ample, then she should get as much as is necessary for her marriage.

All the law givers felt that a brother should provide for his sister's marriage even if there were no ancestral assets for the purpose. They were, however, opposed to give her a right of inheritance in the patrimony alongwith her brother. The jurists were inclined to make adequate provision for the marriage of the girl but at the same time were opposed to the family property being transferred to the other family.

Brotherless Daughters

Among the female heirs the brotherless daughter was the first to succeed in establishing the right of inheritance. She could be appointed as a putrikā, who was considered equal to a son and, therefore, she could inherit her deceased father's property.

Till c. 400 B.C. the right of brotherless daughter to inherit her father's property continued. We come across an instance in the *Therigatha* which refers to a mother dissuading her daughter Sundari from becoming a nun because she was the only heir to her father and would inherit the whole property.

By about 200 B.C. girls began to be married at an early age and as a result their education suffered a setback and consequently their general position also deteriorated affecting proprietary rights of the daughter in general. The jurists of this period disallowed the right of inheritance even to a brotherless daughter. Manu, however, places the daughter practically at par with the sons. But the order of inheritance in his text indicates that the daughter's son stands in preference to *sapiṇḍas*. Kauṭilya also recognized the daughter to inherit the father's property through her son was in fact never disputed. The *smṛti* writers and commentators have not ignored her rights. But the practice of appointing a putrikā fell into disuse long before commentaries saw light of the day.

It appears that the right of a daughter, who was not a *putrika,* came into vogue during the first four centuries of the Christian era in order to mitigate the hardship of remaining unmarried and being brotheress. Among early authors

Apastamba allows her the right of inheritance but very reluctantly.

Yājṇavalkya says that daughter should be the next heir after the son and the widow. Bṛhaspati and Nārada are also of a similar opinion.

In the seventh century A.D. we see that the commentators tried to revive the earlier position of the *putrika*. They did not include a brotherless daughter under the category of a *putrika* and in the line of heirs placed her after the widow. It was Vijṇāneśvara accepted the daughter as an heir and strongly recommended a share to the daughter in the property of her father; but he preferred an unmarried daughter to a married one and an unprovided one to a rich one. Jīmūtavāhana and Devaṇṇabhaṭṭa, however, disallowed the barren daughter to inherit her father's property for the reason that she was incapable to confer on him the spiritual benefits through her offspring.

Thus, we see that the brotherless daughter had the right to inherit her father's property in case she had a son. From time to time jurists differed in their views on her share but most of them agree to give her a share in patrimony. Thus brotherless daughter was regarded as an heir since very early times.

Widow

Up to 300 B.C. nobody recognised the right of the widow to inherit her husband's property. Early *Dharmasutra* writers, however, were inclined to assign maintenance to the widow. Kauṭilya also concurred with them. He makes the widow's maintenance a charge upon the husband's estate. It was Gautama alone who puts forth a modest proposal of treating the widow at least as a co-heir with other *sapiṇḍas.*

Around 300 B.C. another unfavourable change took place in the widow's condition. This was the beginning of the end of *niyoga.* Ethnical and ascetic tendencies were growing in society. A school of reformers opposing *niyoga* came up. It was felt that *niyoga* was disruptive to family peace and was also against morality. *Niyoga* was also being misused by strangers to get a hold on the widow's family property. In the beginning of this change became evident only in the writings of a few *Smrtikaras* like Baudhayana, Apastamba and Manu, and crystallised around of the Christian era.

In the course of time the opinion in favour of the recognition of widow's right began to grow stronger and was first reflected in the writings of Yājṇavalkya. The change was caused probably partly by the impact of the Buddhist monastic discipline and partly by the wave favouring reform of the society from within. Yājṇavalkya definitely lays down that the widow shall inherit the whole of the estate on failure of sons. *Bṛhaspati* pointed out that the *Vedas, Smrtis* and popular usage have unanimously declared that the husband and wife are the joint owners of the family property and constitute one legal entity. Vṛddha Manu also belonged to this school. *Prajāpati* lays down that the widow had natural right to inherit all her husband's property including movables, immovables, ornaments, etc. Even if elderly relations male and female are alive, her rights are not affected.

There were, however, other *Smrti* writers who represented the orthodox view. Nārada was the chief exponent of this school. He lays down that if among several brothers, one who is childless dies or becomes an ascetic the others should divide his property except Strīdhana. They should, however, make provision for his wife till her death. Kātyayana does not allow the widow to inherit as in his list of successors of a sonless man he mentions the father, brother, mother and finally the grand-mother. However, he allows the widow to inherit her deceased husband's property in case she was chaste and was devoted to the service of her elders.

At the same time, another school came up which sought to incorporate both the reformists and conservative ideas. It recommended half-way measures like widow inheriting a definite amount of money or only the movables or being considered as the deferred heir in the absence of brothers-in-law.

A set-back to the widow's property rights came with the decline of the Gupta empire. A large number of small states came up and there was a general decline in almost every sphere. In this period Devala put the widow last in the hierarchy of heirs; Medhātithi prohibited widow from inheriting her husband's property; he allows only maintenance to her. Viśvarūpa puts forward that a sonless widow should inherit property only if she was pregnant at the time of her husband's death.

The next major change came with the Muslim invasions of India. The revival of the reformist school was led by commentators like Vijṇāeśvara in the South and Jīmūtavāhana in Bengal.

Vijṇāneśvara established that the widow, if chaste and if her husband had separated from the joint family before his death, is entitled to the whole of her sonless deceased husband's wealth. He included the inherited property of a woman in her *strīdhana*.

To Jīmūtāvahana, goes the credit of liberalising the law still further. He argues that there is no authority to hold that a woman's ownership in the husband's property, which she acquires at the time of marriage, terminates with the death of the husband. It is, therefore, fair that she should be allowed to inherit her husband's share whether he had separated from the joint-family or not.

As regards widow's right to dispose of the property, the earlier jurists had invested absolute rights to the widow over the property inherited by her. The later commentators, however, restricted the widow's right in one way or the other.

The society was clearly not willing at this time to invest the widow with the inheritance right. Most of the commentators stop short of giving her this right. Epigraphic sources show that the consent of mother-in-law and relatives was necessary before the widow could dispose of her property. However, some other inscriptions show that religious gifts of property could be made by the widows without their consent. Thus down to the twelfth century, the widow was intended to be given only a limited power over her inheritance.

Mother

Hindu culture has throughout held the mother in very high esteem. Manu conceded her right of inheritance in the property of the son dying issueless. At the same time he laid down the rule that the sons would not partition the property as long as the mother was alive.

Her claim to succeed her son is recognised by Manu. He lays down that if a son dies childless, the mother shall take the estate and if the mother is also dead, the paternal grand-mother shall take the estate. Commenting on this text Kullūka says that the mother will inherit only on failure of son's widow and her daughters.

Mother is mentioned in the text of Yājṇavalkya as the next female heir after daughter.

Viśvarūpa, the earliest commentator of Yājṇavalkya *Smrti* says that mother has priority, so does the Mitakshara. Jīmūtavāhana and Devaṇṇabhaṭṭa preferred the father to the mother because they considered a male as superior to the female, whereas Kullūka opined that both the parents should jointly inherit their deceased son's property.

However, prior to these commentators *smrti* writers like Yajnavalkya in the 2nd century A.D. favoured the mother by giving her a share equal to that of her son and thus provided her against any contingency of poverty. Some jurists of the later period suggested that a mother should be given as much money as was necessary for her maintenance.

All the commentators agree with the view that when partition takes place after the demise of the father, the mother is an equal sharer with the sons; but when she is in possession of *strīdhana*, the share should only be half of the son's share.

Thus we observe that the Hindu society, which gave a high status to mother, secured her proprietary rights in two capacities, i.e., as mother of sonless son and also an equal sharer with sons in the property of her deceased husband.

Grand Mother

The grand mother's claim to inherit her grand-son's property was also recognised very early for reasons similar to those which operated in favour of the mother. But she was a fairly distant heir and came only after the parents and brothers of the deceased.

It will be thus inferred from the survey, that proprietary rights of women were developing fairly satisfactorily. As circumstances changed they were enlarged by Indian jurists unflinchingly. Society being actuated by a genuine desire to improve their economic lot, did not hesitate to adopt these changes.

General Conclusions

From our study of women's property rights in the different periods of ancient India we can draw certain general conclusion. The organising social principle of ancient Indian society was *Dharma* where religion had acquired an architectonic role in the society. The property rights were deeply influenced by such a social order.

Ancient Indians believed in transmigration and it was considered necessary to undertake ceremonies which aimed at giving peace to the departed soul. It was belived that only a male could offer oblation and perform *śrāddha* ceremony. Hence the property should be used as far as possible for religious purposes and obviously it could be done by a male member. Inspite of their high position women remained subservient in matters pertaining to property. Her property rights remained almost nil except the privilege of maintenance and marriage expenses in the earlier periods.

All over India the position of women was not the same; while in the north *Aryan* society was patriarchal, societies in the south were matriarchal. Accordingly rights over property were different for women.

Soon after the Vedic Aryans settled down in India a cultural mixing up with the indigenous people started. It is now generally acknowledged that the resultant composite culture of India owes no less to these indigenous people than to the Vedic Aryans and that a number of its institutions and ideas should be traced to them. The institution of *putrika* seems to have been adopted from the non-Aryan society. In the *Mahabharata* we find two or three remarkable instances of *putrikas.* Chitrangada and Ulupi, whom Arjuna married, are such instances. Hidimba, the Rakshasa wife of Bhima, lived with her family after marriage. Obviously, these communities were matriarchal societies. It is likely that the institutions prevailing in the indigenous communities went to influence the Vedic society which adopted the custom with the limitatiion that sonship of the daughter's son arises only where sonless man gave his daughter in marriage with the stipulation that the son of the daughter shall be a son of the maternal grand-father.

Gradually, the Aryan beliefs and sacraments became more dominant. There was an interaction between these societies by way of conquests and marriages. There were also some other pockets of different social orders in the country, such as in Bengal. In Eastern India the enlightened were veering toward Manu, and during the period of the *Brahmanical* revival the learned men were studying the Mimamsa philosophy; Neo-

Brahmanism in Bengal was getting inspiration from the fountain source. They did not stick to medieval Yajnavalkya and Vishnu. They looked up to Vedas and Manu.

There are examples of the impact of different traditions like Brāhmanical and non Brahmanical on the woman's property rights. For example, the *Smṛtikāras* belonging to the south had softer corner for women than those who belonged to the north. Vijṇāneśvara enthusiastically advocated the widow's right of inheritance and induced even the inherited property in her *strīdhana*.

Being patriarchal in character, the society did not appreciate the idea of the family property going to another family. This adversely affected the rights of women. Marriage being a social necessity, the daughter was usually not expected to claim anything from paternal property. She was married to some outsider in a near or distant village. It was not easy for a daughter or her husband to manage her landed property situated in a distant village. To give a share to the daughter in immovable property was, not a feasible proposal. As far as movable property was concerned, she used to get a fair share as presents at the time of her marriage or as an heir to *strīdhana* estate.

Our study also shows that women's property rights were not static. In accordance with the changes in socio-political conditions due modifications used to be introduced in these rights. Inevitably, there were orthodox forces which did not want any change; and also liberal and progressive forces which wanted change. There were periods of long drawn struggle between these forces. Yet eventually women secured important property rights and, in certain cases equal to man. It is noteworthy that as the moral fibre of the society became fragile, the law-givers took steps to protect women by giving them formal property rights.

Despite absence of clear cut property rights particularly in the Ṛigvedic age and in the beginning of the later Vedic period, women enjoyed a very high position. There was no seclusion for women; they used to move freely in society, often even in the company of their lovers. Very often there were love marriages which were later blessed by parents. In social and religious gatherings they occupied a prominent position. The position of the wife was an honoured one in the family. In theory she was the joint owner of the household with her husband though in actual practice, she was the subordinate partner.

In the age of revival the impact of Muslim invasion and rule was evident in some of the changes that were introduced at this time. May be the custom of *Mehar* in Islam had some impact on Hindu women's rights. Moreover, at this time there was no central authority in India. There were a number of small states which had resulted in the emergence of local and regional customs. Moral strength of the Hindu society had also suffered a setback. The social position of women declined and she came to be confined to the four walls of the house. In such a situation it became necessary to protect her by the formal rights of property.

At this juncture it will not be out of place to briefly compare the property rights of ancient Indian woman with her counterparts in some other ancient civilizations.

In Babylonia, women were given quite high and independent legal position. The society was monogamous and the bride-price (dowry) was the property of the bride. Husband was responsible for wife's debts including those incurred before marriage. Even the property or any gift which she received, she was free to bequeath to any child. In the case of divorce, if she bore good character, she kept the custody of the children as well as the dowry. This was the position of the widow as well.

The pre-Islamic Egyptian civilization was matriarchal in which women occupied a high place and stood on an equal level with husband. All fixed property belonged to women and the house and land were inherited by the daughter through mother.

The Greek civilization offered a contrast. It was a patriarchal society and despite highly advanced culture and intellectual tradition, the position of women was very low. Throughout life their position was subject to the will and whims of man. Despite her right on dowry, she had no property rights. Indeed in ancient Greece "at no time of her life could a women be without a guardian; if her father was not alive, it would be her nearest male relation and this person remained her guardian even when she was married. After her husband's death her son was her guardian."

In ancient China woman had no property rights. She was

confined to home. Her education was restricted to spinning and embroidery. She could be divorced at the whims of her husband. Ownership of property was restricted to male only. If wife owned any, this was controlled by husband and after his death the widow was entirely dependent on her sons.

In ancient Rome a marriage with *convention in manus* was the regular form of marriage. It gave the husband right to own property which the wife had at the time of marriage and entitled him to all that she might acquire afterwards, whether by gift or by her own labour. Later on, marriage without *manus* became the ordinary marriage, which led to the result that all the wife's property was under her own control.

In England, before 1857, even a man who had abandoned his wife and left her unaided to support his family, might at any time return to appropriate her earning and sell everything she had acquired. In 1870 a law was passed securing to women the legal control of their own earnings, but all other property with some insignificant exceptions was left unprotected. And it was not until the married women's property act of 1882 was passed that full right on their own property was given to English wives.

The above brief remarks on the conditiion of women in some ancient civilisations show that the property rights of ancient Indian women can be favourably compared with their's.

Important thing to be noted in ancient India is the nature of social values within the context of which the position of woman is to be appreciated. However, at no time she was poor or unprotected. Moreover, with the passage of time she acquired formal and independent property rights. Concept of strīdhana had emerged as early as the Sūtra Period and it went on expanding and thus increasing her assets including sometimes immovable property. Widow also acquired a share in husband's property.

It may also be observed that mere acceptance of legal rights does not lead to change in women's status which largely depends on the social ethos. For instance, in the Rigvedic period women had no formal property rights but they enjoyed very high social status, while later on their property rights increased but their social status declined.

13

The Sati Ritual

This subject of sati is now of academic interest in India, since for over a hundred years,[1] (i.e. from 1829) self-immolation of widows has been prohibited by law in British India and has been declared to be a crime. The burning of widows was not peculiar to Brahmanism, as many are prone to believe, but the custom owes its origin to the oldest religious views and superstitious practices of mankind in general.

There is no Vedic passage which refers to the widow-burning as then current, nor is there any mantra which could be said to have been repeated in very ancient times[2] at such burning nor do the ancient *gṛhyasūtras* contain any direction prescribing the procedure of widow burning. It therefore appears probable that the practice arose in Brahmanical India is a few centuries before Christ. None of the *dharmasūtras* except Viśṇu contains any reference to satī. The *Manusmṛti* is entirely silent about it. The *Viśu-dharmasūtra*[3] says 'On her husband's death the widow should observe celibacy or should ascend the funeral pyre after him.' The *Mahābhārata*, though it is profuse in the descriptions of sanguinary fights, is very sparing in its references to widow burning. Mādrī, the favourite wife of Pāṇḍu, burnt herself with her husband's body.[4] The *Viśṇupurāṇa* says that eight queens of Kṛśṇa, Rukmīṇī and others, entered fire on the death of Kṛśṇā.[5] In the Strīparva the Great Epic describes the death ceremonies performed for the fallen *Kauravas,* but no mention is made of any widow immolating herself on the funeral pyre though the chariots, clothes and weapons of the warriors are said to have been consigned to fire. From the above it appears that the practice was originally confined to royal families and great warriors even in India and that cases of widow burning were rare. The authors of digests explain away these passages by saying that they only prohibit self-immolation by a brāhmaṇa widow on a funeral pyre different from that of the husband i.e. a brāhmaṇa widow can burn herself only on the funeral pyre of her husband and if his body is cremated elsewhere in a foreign land, his widow cannot, on hearing of his death, burn herself later. The *Veda-Vyāsa smṛti* says that a Brāhmana wife should enter fire, clasping the dead body of her husband; if she lives (after her husband) she should give up adorning her hair and emaciate her body by austerities.[6]

In the Ramayana,[7] (Uttarakanda 17.15) there is a reference to the self-immolation of a brahmana woman (the wife of a *brahmarsi* and mother of Vedavati, who when molested by Ravana burnt herself in fire). The Mahabharata (Striparva 23.34 ff.) on the other hand describes how Krpi, the wife of Drona, the brahmana commander-in-chief of the Kauravas, appeared with dishevelled hair on the battle-field on the death of her husband, but does not say that she burnt herself.[8] It appears therefore that the burning of brahmana widows began much later than that of Ksatriya widows.

The burning of a widow on the death of her husband is called *sahamaraṇa* or *sahagamana* or *anvārohaṇa* (when she ascends the funeral pyre of her husband and is burnt along with his corpse), but anumaraṇa occurs when, after her husband is cremated elsewhere and she learns of his death, the widow resolves upon death and is burnt with the husband's ashes or his *pādukās* (sandals) or even without any memento of his if none be available. In the Gathasaptasati (VII. 33) there is a reference to a woman being decked for anumarana (Nirn. ed.). The Kamasutra VI. 3.53 speaks of a anumarana. It has been shown (at p. 579) how Varahamihira admires women for their courage in being burnt with their husbands. The Harsacarita (Ucchvasa 5) describes how Yasomati, the chief queen of king Prabhakaravardhana and mother of Harsa, consigned herself to fire when the king was dying. But this is not a proper case of *sati,* as she burnt herself even before her husband died. In another passage of the Harsacarita (V, in the description of night) the glory of moon-lotuses is said to be laughing like a woman intent on anumarana, who is decked with ear ornaments and wears garlands on her head. Bāṇa in his *Kadambari* in a most eloquent and well-reasoned passage condemns *anumaraṇa.*[9]

In numerous epigraphic records reference is made to the practice of *satī*. Among the earliest is the one in 191 of the Gupta era (510 A.D.). In 705 A.D., Rājyavatī, widow of Dharmadeva, bids her son Mahādeva to take up the reins of government that she may follow her husband. Temara gate stone inscription of śaka 1246 speaks of Māṇikyadevī as satī on the death of her husband Āmana who was an officer of king Hariścandra. The memorial stones usually bear the figure of the upraised arm and of the sun and the moon on either side and a group of stars. Among the well-known latest historical examples of satī is that of Ramābaī, wife of the Peshwa Madhavrao I, in 1772 A.D. The Jauhar practised by the Rajput ladies of Chitor and other places for saving themselves from unspeakable atrocities at the hands of the victorious Moslems are too well-known.

In the Indian Antiquary Vol. 35 p. 129 there is a paper on *'Sati* immolation which is not *sati'*, where several examples of men who killed themselves out of devotion to their masters or for other causes are cited and it is pointed out how stone monuments (called *mastikkal* i.e. stone monument for *mahasati* a great *sati,* and *'virakkal'* for brave and devoted men) are erected in memory of *satis* and men. The Harsacarita (V. 3rd para from end) describes how many of the king's friends, ministers, servants and favourites killed themselves on the death of Prabhakaravardhana. The Rajatarangini VII. 481 narrates how when the queen of king Ananta became a *sati* on her husband's death, her litter-carrier and some other men and three of her *dasis* followed her in death. There is the example of mother burning herself on the funeral pyre of her son (vide Rajatarangini VII. 1380). Suicide at holy places like Prayaga was practised for attaining heavenly worlds and bliss. Life seems to have been deemed of small account in those ages and though the death of women or men on the funeral pyre of the husband or for their masters appears to us sophisticated people of modern days as very horrible, it did not so appear to the ancients. *Sati* was not in historic times a practice imposed by priests or men on unwilling women. It somehow grew and it is improper to say that men imposed it on women. It may be that examples of *sati* occurred because of the force of popular sentiment. It was first confined to kings and nobles, because the lot of the wives of conquered kings and warriors was most miserable in all countries as well as in India. Vengeance for the truculence of their husbands was wreaked on the poor wives by carrying them as captives and making them work as slaves. Manu (VII. 96) allows a soldier to retain women (probably 'slaves') conquered by him along with other booty. When queen Yasomati narrates to her son Harsa the great honour and glory that was hers during the reign of her husband king Prabhakaravardhana, she refers to the fact that the wives of the enemies defeated by her husband waved chowries over her. From kings the practice spread among Brāhmaṇas, though several smṛtikāras disapproved of the practice among brāhmaṇa wives. Once it took root learned commentators and digest writers were found to support it with arguments and promises of future rewards. Even in modern times we can secure learned writers to support any pet theory of a coterie or clique. When Manchester and Liverpool were prosperous, English economists preached the doctrine of free trade and *laissez faire* to all nations, but in more difficult times we have now the apotheosis of Empire Preference and discriminating preference for home-made goods. Manu IV. 178 asks people to do whatever their forefathers did. Even in modern times we can secure learned writers to support any pet theory of a coterie or clique. When Manchester and Liverpool were prosperous, English economists preached the doctrine of free trade and *laissez faire* to all nations, but in more difficult times we have now the apotheosis of Empire Preference and discriminating preference for home-made goods. Manu IV. 178 asks people to do whatever their forefathers did.

The rewards promised to a *satī* were as follows: 'she who follows her husband in death dwells in heaven for as many years as there are hair on the human body. Just as a snake-catcher draws out a snake from a hole by force, no such a woman draws her husband from (wherever he may be) and enjoys bliss together with him. In heaven she being solely devoted to her husband and praised by bevies of heavenly damsels sports with her husband for as long as fourteen Indras rule. Even if the husband be guilty of the murder of a Brāhmaṇa or a friend or be guilty of the murder of a Brāhmaṇa or of a friend or be guilty of ingratitude, the wife who dies (in fire) clasping his body, purifies him (of the sin). That woman, who ascends (the funeral pyre) when the husband dies, is equal to Arundhatī in her character and is praised in heaven. As long as a woman does not burn herself in fire on the death of her husband she is never free from being born as a woman (in successive births)'. Hārīta says 'that woman who follows her husband in death purifies three families, of her mother, of her father and of her husband'.

There were old commentators who were opposed to the practice of *satī*. Medhātithi compares this practice to śyenayāga which a man performed by way of black magic to kill his enemy. He says that though Angiras allowed 'anumarana' it is suicide and is really forbidden to women. Though Angiras speaks of it, it is really *adharma*; and that a woman who is in a hurry and extremely anxious to secure heaven quickly for herself and her husband might act according to Angiras,[10] still her action is aśāstrīya (not in accordance with the *śāstras*); besides *anvārohana*[11] is opposed to the Vedic text 'one should not leave this world before one has finished one's allotted span of life'. The Mit. on Yaj. I. 86 combats these arguments. It says that syenayaga is no doubt undesirable and therefore adharma, but that is so because the object of syenayaga is injury to another. *Anugamana* on the other hand is not so; there the result promised is heaven which is a desirable result and which is enjoined by *sruti* in such sentences as 'one should sacrifice a white goat to Vayu if one desires prosperity'. Similarly the smrti about *anugamaṇa* is not opposed to the *sruti* quoted, the meaning of which is different; that sruti means one should not waste one's life for securing heavenly bliss which is fleeting and insignificant as compared with the supreme bliss of Brahma knowledge'. As the woman in *anumarana* desires only heaven, she is not doing anything contrary to the sruti texts. This is the reasoning of the Mitaksara which looks like special pleading. Apararka p. 111, the Madana-parijata p. 199, Par. M. II. part I pp. 55–56 follow the reasoning of the Mit. and add that the Vedic text about the allotted span of life is a general rule, while the smrti about *anumarana* is a special or exceptional sastra and so there is no contradiction as the rule applies to all cases outside the excepted one. The Madanaparijata[12] (p. 200) further explains that the texts about purifying a husband guilty of brahmana murder are not to be taken literally but only as hyperbolically extolling *anvarohana.*[13] The Sm. C. also expressly says that *anvarohana* though recommended by the Visnu Dh. S. (25.14) and Angiras, is inferior to brahmacarya (leading a celibate life), since the rewards of anvarohana are inferior to those of brahmacarya. As against this may cited the extreme view of *Angiras*[14] 'for all women there is no other duty except falling into the funeral pyre, when the husband dies. The Suddhitattva remarks that this extreme or sweeping statement is made by way of belauding *sahamarana.*[13]

There were restrictions enjoined by the *smrtis* on all widows 'wives who have a child of tender years, who are pregnant, who have not attained puberty and who are in their monthly course do not mount the funeral pyre of their husbands from the *Bṛhan-Nāradīya Purāṇa*. There is a similar verse of *Bṛahspati.*[15] The wife who was in her course was allowed to burn herself after she bathed on the fourth day.

Āpastamba (verse) prescribes the Prājāpatya penance for a woman who having first resolved to burn herself on the funeral pyre turns back from it at the last moment.

The Śuddhitattva sets out the procedure of widow burning. The widow bathes and puts on two white garments, takes kuśa blades in her hands, faces the east or north, performs ācamana (sipping water); when the Brāhmaṇas say *'om, tat sat'* she remembers the God Nārāyaṇa and refers to the time (month, fortnight, *tithi*) and then makes the *saṃkalpa* (declaration of resolve). She then calls upon the eight *lokapālas*[16] (guardians of the quarters), the sun, the moon, the fire & c. to become witnesses to her act of following her husband on the funeral pyre, she then goes round the fire thrice, then the Brahmaṇa recites the Vedic verse, the woman utters *'namo namaḥ'* and ascends the kindled pyre. The long-winded preamble of the samkalps 'arundhati . . . patiputatvakama' is based upon the verses of Angiras quoted above (in *n.* 1477). The Suddhitattva as printed is corrupt but it appears that it read the last quarter of Rig. X. 18. 7 as 'arohantu jalayonim-agne' (let them ascend the watery seat or origin, O fire !) meaning probably 'may fire be to them as cool as water'. Some writers have charged the brahmana priest-hood (or Raghunandana) with having purposely changed the reading of the verse Rig. X. 18. 7[17] in order to make it suit the rite of immolating oneself in fire (i.e., 'agne' or 'agneh' was substituted for 'agre'). But this charge is not sustainable. That the verse Rig. X. 18. 7 as it actually is was held to refer to widow burning centuries before Raghunandana follows from the fact that even the Brahmapurana and Apararka (quoted above on p. 628) take it in that sense. It was therefore not necessary to alter the reading. Further even if some priests or Raghunandana had changed it that fact would have been detected in no time, as in those days there were thousands of people who knew every syllable of the Rgveda by heart. Therefore it must be admitted that either the Mss. are corrupt or Raghunandana committed an innocent slip. That mantra was not addressed to widows at all, but to ladies of the deceased man's household whose husbands were living and the grhyasutra of Asv. made use of it with that meaning. Raghunandana, a profound student of dharmasastras and smrtis (and often styled Smarta-bhattacarya), could not have been ignorant of what Asv. said. The procedure as prescribed in the Nirnayasindhu of Kamalakarabhatta, whose mother became a *sati* and who pays a very tender and touching reverence to her memory in his works, is somewhat different and it is followed by the Dharmasindhu.

It appears from all accounts of travellers and others that widow-burning prevailed more in Bengal during the centuries immediately preceding its abolition than anywhere else in India. In Bengal, wherever the Dāyabhāga prevails, the widow of a sonless member even in a joint Hindu family is entitled to practically the same rights over joint famly property which her deceased husband would have had. This must have frequently induced the surviving members to get rid of the widow by appleaing at a most distressing hour to her devotion to and love for her husband. There is a good deal of epigraphic and other evidence particularly in other parts of India that relatives tried to dissuade the widow from taking this step. Even in Bengal the number of *satīs* must never have been very large. Colebrooke, who had spent the best part of his life in Bengal and who was a profound Sanskrit scholar, observes in a paper written about 1795 A.D. 'Happily the martvrs of this superstition have never been numerous. It is certain that the instances of the widow's sacrifices are now rare'. The very fact that there was no disturbance of peace of ebullition of popular feeling or even any great verbal protest from the vast Hindu population (except a petition to the Privy Council) against Bentick's sweeping measure indicates two things, viz. that the burning of widows was a rare occurrence and that people were not very keen on observing the practice nor had they any very deep-seated convictions about its absolute religious necessity.

Modern India does not justify the practice of *sati,* but it is a warped mentality that rebukes modern Indians for expressing admiration and reverence for the cool and unfaltering courage of Indian women in becoming *satis* or performing the *jauhar* for cherishing their ideals of womanly conduct. If Englishmen can feel pride in their ancestors who grabbed one-fourth of the world's surface or if Frenchmen can feel pride in the deeds of their Emperor Napoleon who tried to enslave the whole of Europe and yet are not held up to ridicule or rebuke, there is no reason why Indians cannot express admiration for the sacrifices which their women made in the past, though they may condemn the institution itself which demanded such terrible sacrifice and suffering.

In the earliest perod, i.e., from the time of *Rgveda* down to the beginning of the Christian era, *Satī* ws practically unknown, much less practised. We have only one controversial verse in the *Rgveda,* which has sometimes been taken to refer to the existence of *Sati* during this period.

The *Atharva-veda* also refers to the lying of widow by the dead husband on funeral pyre as an ancient custom, but in the very next verse, she is asked to get up and come to this world.

The vast literature comprising the Brāhmaṇas, Āraṇyakas and *Upanishads* contains no reference to the prevalence of *satī* during this period. Even the Sūtras which provide the minute details of all the rituals, maintain complete silence to the knowledge of this custom.

Not only this, but the secular literature like the Ashtādhyāyi of Pānini and the Arthaśastra of Kautilya also do not mention it. It is not surprising that the early Buddhist literature does not show any knowledge of this custom, simply because it was not prevalent at that time. The enumeration of the duties of the widows in the *Smritis* of Manu and Yājnavalkya shows the absence of the ideas of Sati during this period. It is clear therefore that the custom was not at all prevalent till the beginning of the Christian era.

We cannot afford to ignore much quoted and much stressed references of the classical writers like strabo and Diodorus Siculus, as historical instances of Sati in India in the 4th century B.C. The latter cites the story of the younger wife of a general named Keteus, becoming Sati in 316 B.C., when her husband died fighting against the Green/strabo also refer to the custom of Sati amongst some frontier tribes like the Kathas (Cathaeans) on the authority of Onesicritus and Aristobulus who had accompanied Alexander on his Indian campaign. Here it is to be noted that the custom mentioned by these writers is said to prevalent amongst some frontier tribes and is mentioned alongwith the stories which are otherwise not corroborated in Indian history. We must not lose sight of the fact that both Diodorus and Strabo wrote around the beginning of the Christian era drawing their information from the writings of two generals who had accompanied Alexander to India for the purpose of conquest more than three centuries earlier. On the other hand the contemporary writers like Megasthenes, who spent so many years in the Mauryan court and was a keen observer of Indian life is absolutely silent on this point. Does it not stand to reason not to take the stories of Strabo and Diodorus for granted unless corroborated by some independent evidence? At best we may give them credit of noting a custom which was prevalent amongst certain tribes on the extreme north-western frontier of India.

The second phase may be counted from the beginning of the Christian era roughly up to the 9th century A.D., when we start getting references to *Satī*. The Vishṇudharmasūtra which is assigned to c.A.D.100 mentions the custom as not illogical but does not regard it as a religious duty. As pointed out by Prof. Altekar, "Vishnu does not recommend it, he merely mentions it. He is one of the earliest writers to recognise widow as an heir to her husband. He allows her to remarry also. Bṛishaspati also refers to this custom but does not make it binding. He says, "A wife is considered half the body (of her husband), equally sharing the result of his good or wicked deeds; whether she ascends the pile after him, or chooses to survive him leading a virtuous life, she promotes welfare of her husband." Thus Brihaspati not only makes it optional but also does not attach any extra merit or religious sanction to the custom of sati.

Of the two great epics, the Ramayana, which is a work of pre-Christian era, contains single reference to the immolation of Vedavati's mother, which is more legendary than historical. The Mahabharata knows of Madri becoming Sati alongwith her husband Pandu and Sairandhri being forcibly burnt alongwith Kichaka. However, these are exceptional instances as we find none of the widows of the Kaurava heroes becoming Sati. Rather they are shown as performing the last rites of their husbands. Keeping in view the fact that the Mahabharata took its final shape sometime before the Gupta period it should not be surprising if some of these references were added at a later stage. The reference to the eight wives of Krishna becoming *Sati* is conspicuously absent from the Mahabharata but finds mention in the Vishnu Purana and the Padma Purana. The Bhāgavata and the Brahma Purāṇa cite instance of Satī, thus indicating that the institution was slowly emerging in our society between A.D.400 and 600 as it is referred to by some *Smriti* writers of this period. Besides Brihaspati, whom we have already referred to, the custom is praised by Parasara and Angirasa quoted by Aprarka and Medhatithi Harita, Apastamba etc.

The only epigraphic evidence of the performance of Sati during this period comes from the Eran Pillar inscription dated 1918[18] (A.D. 510). This is the earliest epigraphic reference to Sati in Indian history. A Nepalese inscription of somewhat late period (A.D. 705) refers to queen Rajyavati the widow of Dharmadeva following her husband to the funeral pyre. In the non-religious literature of this period the poet-dramatists like Bhasa (Urubhanga), Kalidasa (Ritusmhara), Sudraka (Mrichchhakatika) and celebrated writers like Vatasyayana, Varahamihira and Banabhatta mention instances of the practice of Sati, but none of them mention any religious sanction behind this custom. On the contrary Bana dubs it as an act of suicide in the following words, "to die after one's beloved is most fruitless. It is a custom followed by the foolish. It is a mistake committed under infatuation. It is a reckless course followed only on account of hot haste. It does no good what so ever to the dēad person. It does not help him in ascending to heaven; it does not prevent him from sinking into hell. It does not at all ensure union after death; the person who has died goes to the place determined by his own karman, the person who accompanies him on the funeral pyre goes to the hell reserved for those who are guilty of the sin of suicide. On the other hand, by surviving the deceased, one can do much good both to oneself and to the departed by offering prescribed oblations for his happiness in the other world. By dying with him one can do good to neither." The most vehement, determined and rational opposition to this new inhuman practice does not come from Bāṇa alone but his views were shared by others like Medhātithi (c.A.D. 900), the commentator on Manu, who does not mince words in calling *satī* as form of suicide; Virāta, who positively prohibits it and Devanabhaṭṭa (12th century A.D.) who calls it an inferior variety of *dharma* not to be recommended at all. Medhātithi clearly says that though *anumarana* is allowed by *Angiras,* it is *adharma* like śenayāga. Thus one can clearly make out that the custom of *Satī,* though introduced and practised during this period, completely lacked the religious sanction and was vehemently opposed by a strong section of intellectuals.

The third phase which started sometime between the period of Medhātithi (A.D. 900) and Aprārka (A.D. 1125) gained full force in giving sanction to this custom and painting it in the religious colours. Now we find the commentators of the Smṛitis like Aprārka, Vijṇāneśvara and Mādhavāchārya not only praising the custom of *Satī* but also calling it as the only *dharma* for the widows. It is therefore not surprising that the *Rajatarangini* of Kalhaṇa is full of instances of *Satī*, and in the stories of the Kathāsaritasāgara it is a common feature. It is clear that it is neither an ancient custom or the Indians nor it had any religious sanction in the Vedic times through the beginning of the Christian era. However, there were many other socio-economic factors besides the foreign influence which led to the gradual introduction popularity of the practice of *satī* in India.

Like the development of the custom of *Satī*, the changing attitude of the society and the law-givers towards the proprietary rights of the widows can also be divided into three phases, which incidently also mark the significant stages of socio-economic changes through the ages. The Vedic texts declare that woman to be incapable of inheriting any property, much less a widow having any right to inherit the estate of the dead husband. No doubt, the Rgveda contains references to a brotherless less daughter seeking legal recourse to get her father's property, but such cases were exceptions. Moreover, there is not a single reference to any widow inheriting the property of her deceased husband. The Maitrayani Samhita and the Satapatha Brahmana definitely deny this right to women as also the other texts of the later Vedic age. Actually no legal writer upto C.B.C. 300 gives this right to widows. The writers of Dharmasutras, the earliest manuals of the Indian law, definitely oppose this idea. Baudhayana rejects the right of widows to inherit husband's property on the Vedic authority and Apastamba lays down that in the absence of a son the property should devolve upon the nearest male Sapinda up to the seventh degree in order and in the absence of any *Sapinda,* to the teacher and disciple respectively. The Dharmasutras were followed by the earliest Smriti writer Manu, who lays down that the property of sonless father goes to his father, brother, a Sapinda and a Sakulya in accordance with the closeness of relation. If none of these was forthcoming, then a preceptor or a disciple and finally the state could take away the property of the dead in that order.

Such views were the natural consequence of the patriarchal form of the Vedic society where joint family system prevailed. The prevalence of the custom of *Niyoga* minimised the need for any such law of inheritance for widows. The practice of the widow remarriage, which was freely allowed at that time, must have weighed heavily in the minds of the Vedic people, as no one wants the family property to go into the hands of an outsider. However, the practice of widow remarriage fell into disuse and became a taboo at a very early age and the custom of *Niyoga* also began to be discouraged at first and then became a despicable thing by c. A.D. 500.[19]

With Yājñavalkya, there arose a school of liberai thinkers who started raising their voice for the cause of widows, granting them some limited rights in the property of their husbands. There is a story that the Upanishadic sage Yajnavalkya divided his entire property between his two wives. Soon afterwards we find Gautama making a plea to recognise the widow atleast a co-heir with other male relatives of the deceased. However, the Vishnu-Dharamsutra (c. A.D.100) in the first work to recognise a widow as the sole heir. It definitely lays down that the widow shall inherit the whole estate on the failure of sons. The Yājñavalkya *Smriti* (c. A.D. 200) clearly recognises the widow as in heir to the husband's property with the first and absolute right to it in the absence of sons. The others can claim only on the failure of the widow. Here it is interesting to note that as early as the 6th century B.C., it was observed in the Nirukta that it was customary for southerners to recognise the proprietary rights of women, and may not be a mere coincidence that Yajnavalkya was a southerner.

This school of reformers was further strengthened by the Gupta period and insisted that the widow's right to inherit the full share should be recognised. Brihaspati, for instance, argues, "In the revealed texts (of the Veda), in the traditional law (of the Smritis), and in popular usage, the wife is declared to be half the body (of her husband), equally sharing the outcome of good and evil acts. Of whom whose wife is not dead, half his body survives. How should anyone else take the property, while half (his) body lives? Although kinsmen (Sakulyas), although his father and mother, although uterine brothers be living, the wife of him who dies without leaving male issues shall succeed to his share." These ideas of Brihaspati were shared and furthered by many others like Vridhamanu, Prajapati etc.

The ideas championed by these advocates of the widow's rights were not only sensational for the society of that time, they also adversely affected the vested interests of male coparceners and therefore met with a stiff resistence. The writers like Nārada, Kātyāyana and King Bhoja of the Paramāra dynasty strongly advocated the orthodox view. Narada,[20] (c. A.D. 300) repeats the old view of kautilya that the widow should only be provided with a maintenance, makes sons, daughters, Sakulyas, Bandhavas, and a member of the same caste as heirs respectively. On their failure the property was to go to the state but not to the widow. Katyayana (*c.* A.D. 500) also held the identical views. Bhoja (*c.* A.D. 1015–1055) granted the right of inheritence to only those widows who followed the practice of Niyoga. It was as good as denying her the proprietary rights because the custom had already become obnoxious. The denial of the widow's right to inheritance is echoed in the Sakuntala of Kalidasa, where king Dushyanta is advised by his minister to attach the property of the trader who had died during a sea-voyage.

The question of the widow's proprietary rights, therefore, was at crossroads during this period. There were some thinkers like Vyāsa who tried to adopt a middle path and recommended some additional money to be given to the widow in addition to her *Strīdhana.* This view is found in the Mahabharata also.

But in the third phase from about 900 A.D., the issue gained momentum and was fervently advocated by the writers of that age.

Jīmūtavāhana argues the widow's case in the most masterly fashion. There is no authority to hold that the ownership in the husband's property, which the wife acquires at the marriage terminates with the husband's death. How then can it be argued that the wife's right is destroyed the moment she is widowed? Nor can it be maintained that she is to utilise just as much of the income as may be necessary for her bare maintenance. Vishṇu says that the property of a person dying without sons will first devolve upon the widow and then upon the aughter, parents etc. Now it is admitted that in the above text the term property denotes the whole income of the estate, when construed with all other heirs like the daughter, the brothers, parents etc.

It is around this time that we start getting epigraphical references especially in the Deccan and Gujarat, to the widow's right as an inheritor of husband's property. Some inscriptions refer to her limited right where she could not gift, sell or dispossess her share, even for religious purposes, without the permission of her coparceners. However, there are instances of the widows disposing of property for religious purposes even without a reference to any coparcener. By the 18th century the proprietary rights of widows became an established law of the day, which continued to be followed as per Dāyabhaga in eastern India till the 20th century. The tenets of the Mitāksharā prevailed in the rest of the country. This development of the idea of widow's proprietary rights in three marked stages when considered alongwith the general introduction and popularity of the institution of the *Satī*, at once unfolds the cause of its zealous advocacy by the affected parties.

Our survey indicates that there must have been many centrifugal and centripetal forces working to decide the fates of the thousands of unfortunate widows in our society and it has to be admitted that many factors were simultaneously or separately responsible for each individual caste—whether it was the question of living or denying with the husband or of inheritance of his estate after his death. At any rate it cannot be denied in the light of the facts enumerated in our survey that the first was closely related to the other. When there were no proprietary rights for widows there was neither eagerness the very idea of getting rid of them, with the gradual development of the idea of the widow's right to property the emphasis on the custom of *Satī* also increased till it was given the status of the 'only *dharma*' for the widow. The role that the ulterior motives must have play in this connection hardly requires an elaboration and there is no reason for us to believe that the male relatives of the widow's husband were merely swayed by the religious sentiments of the age to become an active party to the most inhuman custom of burning the widow alive, on the funeral pyre of her husband. Nor is there any force in the idea that the widows always offered themselves, without any coercion, for the rite of *Satī*, for there is irrefutable evidence of the use of force in this connection. Kalhana, the celebrated author of the Rajatarangini records many instances of forcible burning of the widows against their desires. To quote the case of Jayamati, the queen of Uchchala, who gave her entire treasure to her minister Garga, in the vain hope to save her life. But that was not to be and she was burnt against her wishes. The instances of the use of force in such cases have been recorded by many foreign travellers during the medieval period. Manucci records that Kshatriya women were burnt even against their wishes, and he himself rescued one such woman. Nicoli conti, Bernier and others have also recorded similar instances of the use of force. The point becomes clear from the fact that in the Deccan and western India, funeral pyres were prepared in deep pits when a Sati was to be performed, thus making the escape of the victim impossible. In Bengal there was the practice of tying the feet of the widow to the posts of funeral pyre for the same purpose. To cover their crime it was advocated that the women who ran away from the pyre became an outcaste and was not acceptable either to society or to the family of her late husband. All these were the connected means adopted by the greedy coparceoners to get rid of the widow as early as possible. P.V. Kane has rightly remarked that the guide of property frequently induced the surviving members to get rid of the widow by appealing at most distressing hour to her devotion to and love for her husband, promoted *Satī*.[21] It is an irony that when woman had right to live after the death of her husband, she was denied proprietary rights and whom the latter was provided for, she was induced to die.

References

1. Raja Radhakant Deva relied upon two verses which he found in the Aukhya śākhā of the Tai. S. quoted in the 84th Anuvāka of the Nārāyaṇīya Upaniṣad as the most explicit authority for widow burning; *vide* Prof. H.H. Wilson's Works, Vol. II. pp. 293-305. The two so-called Vedic texts are: अग्ने व्रतानां व्रतपतिरसि पत्न्यानुगमव्रतं चरिष्यामि तच्छकेयं तन्मे राध्यताम् । इह त्वा अग्ने नमसा विधेमसुवर्गस्य लोकस्य समेत्यै । जुषाणो अद्य हविषा जातवेदो विशानि त्वा सरवतो नय मा पतपुरगे (pp. 295-296). These, to say the least, are of doubtful authenticity.
2. मृते भर्तरि ब्रह्चर्य तदन्वारोहणं दा । विष्णुधर्मसूत्र 25. 14 quoted by the मिताक्षरा on या. I. 86.
3. आदिपर्व 95.65 'तत्रैन चिताग्निस्थं माद्री समन्वारुरोह ।; आदि 125.29 'राज्ञः शरीरेण सह ममापीदं कलेवरम् । दग्धष्यं सुप्रतिच्छन्नमेतदार्य प्रियं कुरु ।।
4. अष्टौ महिष्यः कथिता रुक्मिणीप्रमुखास्तु याः । उपगुह्य हरेर्देहं विविशुस्ता हुताशनम् ।। विष्णुपुराण V. 38.2.
5. मृतं भर्तारमादाय ब्राह्मणी वांन्हेमाशित् । जीवन्ती (v. 1. ब्राह्मणी) चेत्यक्त-केशा तपसा शोषयेद्वपुः वेदव्यास II. 53 quoted above in note 1379.
6. अपरार्क p. 112 refers to the रामायण 'अत एव रामायणदौ ब्राह्मण्यादीनां स्वभर्तृंशीरालिंग्नपूर्वकं स्वशरीरदहनमुपाख्यायते ।'
7. तां पश्य रुदतीमार्ती मुक्तकेशीमधोमुखीम् । हतं पतिमुपासन्तीं द्रोणं शस्त्रभृतां वरम् ।। बाणैर्भिन्नतनुत्राणं धृष्टद्युम्नेन केशव । उपास्ते वै मृधे द्रोणं जटिला ब्रह्मचारिणी ।। श्रीपर्व 23.
8. देशान्तरमृते तस्मिन्साध्वी तत्पादुकाद्वयम् । निधायोरसि संशुद्धा प्रविशेज्जात-वेदसम् ।। ऋग्वेदवादात्साध्वी स्त्री न भवेदात्मघातिनि । त्रयहाच्छौचे तु निर्वृत्ते श्राद्धं प्रामोति शाश्वतम् ।। ब्रह्मपुराण quoted by अपरार्क p. 111., where अपरार्क tells us that Vedic verses like 'ima narir' (Rg. X. 18.7) quoted in note 1450.
9. यदेतदनुमरणं नाम तदतिनिष्फलम् । in paragraph 177 of my edition of the purvabhaga, which Candrapala addresses to Mahāsvetā, where

he gives instances of famous women like Rati, Pṛthā, Uttarā, Duḥśalā that did not resort to sahagamana and winds up 'अन्याश्व रक्षःसुरासुरमुनिमनुज-सिद्धगन्धर्वकन्यका भर्तृरहिताः श्रूयन्ते सहस्रशो विधृतजीविताः'.

10. आपीतौ युष्मद्विधैः पुत्रैरमित्रकलत्रबन्दीवृन्दविधूयमानचामरमरुच्चलचीनांशुकधरौ पयोधरौ । हर्षचरित V.

11. पुंवत्स्त्रीणामपि प्रतिषिद्ध आत्मत्यागो यदप्याङि.रसे पतिमनुम्रियेरन्नित्युक्तं तदपि नित्यवदवश्यं कर्तव्यम् । फलस्तुतिस्तत्रास्ति फलकामायाश्वाधिकारे श्येनतुल्यता । तथैव श्येयेन हिंस्याद्भूतानीत्यधि।कारस्यातिप्रवृद्धतरद्वेषान्धतया सत्यामपि प्रवृत्तौ न धर्मत्वम्, एवमिहापि अतिप्रवृद्धफलाभिलाषायाः सत्यपि प्रतिषेधे तदतिक्रमेण मरणे प्रवृत्त्युपपत्तेर्न शास्त्रीयत्वमतोस्त्येव पतिमनु मरणेऽपिस्त्रियाः प्रतिषेधः । किं च 'तस्मादु ह न पुरायुषः प्रेयात्' इति प्रत्यक्षश्रुतिविरोधोयम् । मेधा० on मनु V. 156. The words of शबर are 'नैब श्येनादयः कर्तव्या विज्ञायन्ते । यो हि हिंसितुमिच्छेत्तस्यायमम्युपाय इति तेषामुपदेशः । श्येयेनाभिचरन्यजेतेति हि समामनन्ति नाभिचरितव्यमिति । on जै. I. 1. 2. p. 19.

12. यत्तु विष्णुना धर्मान्तरमुक्तं मृते भर्तरि ब्रह्मचर्ये तदन्वारोहणं वा ... तदेत-द्धर्मान्तरमपि ब्रह्मचर्यध।र्माज्जयन्यम् । निकृष्टफलत्वात् । स्मृतिच० on व्यव. p. 254.

13. सर्वासामेव नारीणामग्निप्रपतनाद्यते । नान्यो धर्मो हि विज्ञेयो मृते भर्तरि कर्हिचित् ।। अगिंरस् quoted by अपरार्क p. 109, परा. मा. II. 1. p. 58, शुद्धितत्व (p. 234 reads साध्वीनामेव नारीणां). साध्वीनामिह नरीणां is also वृद्धहारीत XI. 202.

14. बालापत्याश्व गर्भिण्यो अद्यष्टऋतवस्तथा । रजस्वला राजसुते नारोहन्ति चितां शुभे ।। नारदीयपुराण quoted by परा. मा. II. part 1, p. 58, शुद्धितत्व p. 236, स्मृतिमुक्ताफल I. p. 162 (ascribes to और्ब). 'बालसंवर्धनं व्यक्त्वा बालापत्या न गच्छति । रजस्वला मृतिका च रक्षेद्गर्भे च गर्भिणी ।। वृहस्पति quoted by परा. मा. and शुद्धितत्व.

15. चितिभ्रष्टा तु या नारी मोहाद्विचालिता ततः । प्राजापत्येन शुध्येत्तु तस्माद्वै पापकर्मणः ।। आपस्तम्ब quoted by अपरार्क p. 1193 and शुद्धितत्व p. 243.

16. शुद्धितत्व (p. 235) itself quotes the ब्रह्मपुराण text 'ऋग्वेदवादात् साध्वी स्त्री'

17. Vide निर्णयसिन्धु III, उत्तरार्ध p. 623 and धर्मसिंधु pp. 483-484. The निर्णयसिंधु expressly refers to teh Gauda procedure as different form his "गौडास्तु 'इमा नारीरविधवाः' इति 'ओं इमाः पतिव्रताः ... विभावसुम्' इति च विप्रः पठेदित्याहुः ।"

18. Thomson in his book on 'Suttee' (pp. 69, 72) gives the figures for *satis* reported from the Bengal Presidency (which then included Bihar and extended up to Banares) during 1815-1828. The lowest figure was 378 in 1815 and the highest 839 in 1818. Out of the total of 2366 cases during the four years 1815-1818, the Calcutta division alone contributed 1485, the Benares division, the seat of orthodoxy, contributed only 343. Vide H.H. Wilson's 'History of India' (ed. of 1858), vol.III (for 1805-1835 A.D.), pp. 185-192. At p. 189 a table of the number of *satis* for 1815-1828 is

given, from which it appears that in 1828 there were 463 cases of *satis* out of whom 420 came from Bengal, Bihar and Orissa, out of which 287 were from the Calcutta division alone.

19. Vide दायाभाग (ed. by Jivānanda, 1893) 'अतोऽविशेषेणैव विभक्ताद्यनपेक्षयैव अपुत्रस्य भर्तुः कृत्स्नामने पत्न्यधिकारो जितेन्द्रियोक्त आदरणीयः ।' p. 46; 'पत्नी च भर्तृधनं मुखीतैव परं न तुतस्य दानाधमनविक्रयान्कर्तुमर्हति' p. 56.
20. Vide Colebrooke's Miscellaneous Essays (ed. of 1837) Vol. I. p. 122.
21. Vide Fitz-Edward Hall's paper in J.R.A.S. Vol. III New Series (1868) pp. 190-191, footnote, where he quotes extracts from the writings of Prof. Wilson, Marshman and others that show how fears of violent resistance to Bentinck's measure were singularly falsified.

Bibliography

1. Altekar, A.S, *The Position of Women in Hindu Civilization from Prehistoric Times to the Present Day.*
2. Bagchi, J., "Representing Nationalism: Ideology of Motherhood in Colonial Bengal," *Economic and Political Weekly,* Oct. 20–27, 1990, WS–65.
3. Bhattacharji, S., "Motherhood in Ancient India", *Economic and Political Weekly,* Oct. 20–27, 1990, WS–50.
4. *Boudhayana Dharamsutras.*
5. *Brahmanas.*
6. Kane, P.V., *History of Dharamsastras, Ancient and Medieval Religions and Civil Law,* Poona.
7. *Mahabharata.*
8. Horner, I.B., *Women under Primitive Buddhism,* London.
9. Woods' despatch of 1854 on education made provision for women's education.
10. *The Complete Works of Swami Vivekanand,* Calcutta, Advaita Ashram, 1969.
11. *Indian Historical Quarterly,* Vol. XIV, Dec. 1936, No. 4.
12. *RgVeda.*
13. *Atharva Veda.*
14. 'Aśtadhyāyī', *Panini*.
15. Dasgupta, *Bengal in the 16th century A.D.*
16. Altekar, A.S. *Women in Hindu Civilisation.*
17. Kangle, R.P., "Manu and Kautilya", *Indian Antiquary,* 3rd ser., 1/1 (Jan. 1964).
18. Derrett, *Critique of Modern Hindu Law,* Bombay, 1970.
19. Altekar, A.S., *Position of Wife in the Vedic Ritual.*
20. Gharpure (ed.), *Collection of Hindu Law Books.*
21. Smith, *History of Fine Arts in India and Ceylon.*
22. Sahani, E. *Catalogue of the Museum of Archeology of Sarnath.*
23. *Bhāgavatapurāna.*
24. *Vishnupurāna.*

25. Steele, *Law and Custom of Hindu Castes.*
26. Jolly, Translation of Nārada.
27. Mazumdar, B.P., *Socio-Economic History of Northern India,* Calcutta, 1960.
28. Ayyar, *Saivism.*
29. Shasti, K.A.N., *A History of South India,* Bombay, 1966.
30. Altekar, A.S. *The Rashtrakutas and their times,* Poona, 1967.
31. Devi. V. Yasoda. *History of the Andhra Country (1000–1500)* in Journal of the Andhra Historical Research Society, Rajahmundry.
32. Thomas, P., *Indian Women through the ages,* Bombay, 1964.
33. Kautilya, *Arthashastra.*

Index

M

N

O

P

R

S